Bus D ᵒᵛ

THE
THORN
IN
THE
CHRYSANTHEMUM

MAMORU IGA 伊賀

Forewords by

Edwin S. Shneidman

and

David K. Reynolds

UNIVERSITY OF CALIFORNIA PRESS

Berkeley

Los Angeles

London

THE
THORN
IN
THE
CHRYSANTHEMUM

SUICIDE AND
ECONOMIC SUCCESS
IN MODERN JAPAN

University of California Press
Berkeley and Los Angeles, California

University of California Press, Ltd.
London, England

Library of Congress Cataloging in Publication Data

Iga, Mamoru.
    Suicide and economic success in modern Japan.

    Includes index.
    1. Suicide—Japan.   2. Social structure—Japan.
3. Social values.   I. Title.
HV6548.J3I33   1986   362.2   85–24504
ISBN 0–520–05648–5 (alk. paper)

Printed in the United States of America

1 2 3 4 5 6 7 8 9

To my wife Marye Matsuura Iga

Professor Carle C. Zimmerman

Dr. Edwin S. Shneidman

CONTENTS

Foreword by Edwin S. Shneidman ———————— ix

Foreword by David K. Reynolds ———————— xii

Preface ——————————————————— xiii

I.   Introduction ————————————— 1

II.   A Psychocultural View of Suicide ——— ·—— — 5

III.   Pattern of Japanese Suicide ——————— 13

IV.   Suicide of Young Japanese Males ————— 22

V.   Female Suicides ——————————— 48

VI.   Japanese Writers' Suicides ——————— 69

       Takeo Arishima ————————— 70

       Ryuunosuke Akutagawa ——————— 76

       Osamu Dazai ————————— 85

       Yukio Mishima ————————— 92

       Yasunari Kawabata ——————— 106

VII.   Japanese Value Orientations ———————— 114

     Monism ————————————————— 117

     Groupism ——————————————— 126

     Authoritarian Familism ——————— 129

     Accommodationism ————————— 134

VIII.   Japanese Culture and Self-Destructive Adjustment —— 139

     Wide Goal-Means Discrepancy ——————— 139

     Restraint on Outwardly-Directed Aggression — 140

     Social Resources ——————————— 141

     Attitudes toward Death ———————— 144

     Attitudes toward Suicide ——————— 149

     Romanticization of Suicide ——————— 156

     Sacrificial Suicide ————————— 158

IX.   Japanese Economic Success ———————— 169

     Coordination ————————————— 171

     Motivation —————————————— 174

     Mobilization of Techniques and Funds ———— 186

X.   Summary and Discussion———————— 191

Notes ———————————————————— 205

Index ———————————————————— 219

FOREWORD

EDWIN S. SHNEIDMAN

Many people who live in civilized countries today are at least bilingual, but it is still a marvelous rarity to find an individual who is truly bicultural. A relatively new branch of neuropsychology is the study of the two hemisphere or split brain—for which a Nobel Prize was awarded recently. Professor Mamoru Iga is a bicultural man; his brain (metaphorically speaking) has Eastern and Western hemispheres; happily united in one figurative *corpus callosum* whose separate images are completely fused and come to us, synthesized, in one unique view presented in straightforward prose.

In this book Professor Iga illuminates two sides of Japanese culture, not Ruth Benedict's well-known chrysanthemum and sword but rather two aspects of the chrysanthemum itself. On the one hand, he discusses the positive aspects of the chrysanthemum side of Japan: the aesthetic qualities, the high drive and ambition, the intense cultural cohesion, and the outstanding economic success of contemporary Japan. On the other hand, he points our attention to the canker, the worm, the thorn in the chrysanthemum. In all this Professor Iga implies that there is a quid pro quo in life anywhere; and, specifically, that in Japan today there are specific aspects of the "price" of success. In this book he explicates one especially onerous aspect of that price, suicide.

In the 1960s, when I was doing a lecture tour on suicide in several cities in Japan—arranged in large part by Professor Iga—I was speaking in a great university hall. A student stood and asked me a question: Could I tell him why he should not, at his age, take his life in order to be at one with Nature? I mentally invoked Mill's Method of Difference and answered him by asking him to imagine that he was one of a set of identical twins, one of whom had committed suicide at his age and the other of whom had survived to live forty or fifty years, and whether at that future time the twin who had survived would be glad that he had done so. The student sat down, obviously totally unconvinced. Later, my host told me that my response had been a good answer, but unfortunately it had been a *Western* answer. What, I asked him, would I have to have done in order to have supplied a meaningful response? First of all, he said, I would have to have been born in Japan!

Professor Iga was born in Japan—some sixty years ago. He lived his first thirty-two years in that country, attending school and university there. He taught there. He was, in a word, Japanese. Then, through a complicated set of circumstances, he came to the United States where he completed his education, acquired a Ph.D. degree, and attended Harvard University for postdoctoral study. He married, raised a family, and had a distinguished career as a university professor. He has become an American. He tells me that he dreams and thinks in English but is also capable of thinking the Japanese way. And, even more important, he can put the two together.

There are enormous important differences in the styles of logic between Eastern and Western thinking. One cannot simply translate from Japanese (or Chinese or Korean or Vietnamese) into English as one would translate from, say, French or German (or any other standard average European language) into English. We must recognize that there are many logics other than the traditional Aristotelian logic of the Western world. The bridge from East to West has to traverse a rutted road between different mentational styles as well as between different vocabularies and different alphabets.

Professor Iga's focus on the value of suicide notes is of special importance. During one of his sojourns in Japan in 1968 to study suicide, he made an intensive study of suicide notes. Translations of many of these appear, with great force and effectiveness, in this volume. In many ways suicide notes provide a unique window into the heart and mind of the suicidal person, especially when they are put into the context of a specific life and of a specific culture.

Also noteworthy is Professor Iga's emphasis on the lives (and deaths) of certain Japanese writers. It was fascinating for me to read his insightful accounts of Yukio Mishima and Yasunari Kawabata, especially after I had read several of their novels and a series of accounts of their deaths. But in reading the explanations here, I had the feeling that I was in on the ground floor, yet reading in terms of a language that I could understand.

Professor Iga is most qualified to explain Japanese suicide to an American or Western readership. He understands suicide theory, is a close student of Durkheim's works, and knows about psychodynamic formulations. He is in a position to tell us, as perhaps no one else is, about suicide in Japan in terms that we can understand. He is reporting about a culture that he knows. He is not doing fieldwork; he is performing homework. He has an inborn understanding of his native country, of its ancient history, its recent past, its present, and its future that no American missionary or visiting scholar could ever hope to attain. And, fortunately for us, he has the wish and the gift to share it all with us in the language through which he now thinks. In my mind he is the most eminent American-Japanese suicidologist in the world. On this topic he speaks *ex templa*.

Today Japan is our giant friendly competitor, our rivalrous sibling in the economic world scene. In this sense, every sophisticated American will want to read this book in order to gain additional insights into the mind of the new "big kid on the block." And every suicidologist should read this book for two reasons: to widen one's appreciation of the cultural aspects of suicide (especially in Japan), and to deepen one's understanding of suicide as a ubiquitous phenomenon.

FOREWORD

DAVID K. REYNOLDS

Professor Iga writes with authority about the psychological cost paid by the Japanese people for their remarkable economic progress. Having lived in Japan for thirty-two years, Professor Iga has observed the chrysanthemum's thorn firsthand. His command of the English and Japanese language scholarly literature in his field is demonstrated in this careful analysis of the contributions of social structure and national character to Japan's successes and suicides. Professor Iga remains the leading expert in the West on Japanese suicide.

My research covers another personal price paid by the Japanese. Like suicide, characteristic forms of Japanese neuroses result, in part, from the overconcern with others' thoughts and evaluations—the conformism which this work outlines so sharply. Similarly, social constraints on the development of independent thinking limit solutions to the stress encountered by the Japanese.

There is a positive side to Japanese culture and society, too. Professor Iga provides us with glimpses of it now and again. But the weight of the book provides a critical balance to the excessive praise heaped upon Japan in recent years. Before the leaders of our business and educational communities leap to emulate what appears so successful an enterprise, they would do well to read this book. The Japanese people themselves can profit from the critique and the promise presented here, for "If Japan can show the way toward organic solidarity without losing social integration, it would be a great contribution to the future of mankind." Such is the possibility shining through the self-destruction vividly described and analyzed below.

The image of Japan which the author sculpts for us is somewhat stylized, I believe. But it is not inaccurate. It is an image that needs to be sculpted. Within the peaceful teahouse garden lie buried the corpses of those who did not fit within this demanding society. Professor Iga exhumes them for all to see. His book becomes their burial monument.

PREFACE

In 1944, Ruth Benedict distinguished the chrysanthemum (harmonious) and the sword (fanatic) aspects of Japanese culture. During World War II the general attitude of Western writers toward Japanese culture was negative, focusing on its sword aspects. In reaction, after the war American Japanologists have tended to emphasize only the chrysanthemum side.

Japanese people like the new trend, and it has fanned their pride to the extent of strong ethnocentrism. However, some Japanese intellectuals are not necessarily happy. They have been attempting to clarify the conception of democracy for the nation and to develop strong selfhood for individuals. For these purposes they wish to have American criticism as well as praise.

Many Japanese had to endure a police state before and during the war, and they are aware of marked daily remnants of feudalism operating in Japan—for example, sex and status prejudices. Threatened by the shadow of feudalism, some Japanese writers are serious in questioning the relationship between capitalism and democracy. Both capitalism and democracy uphold "freedom" as the primary value—but is freedom only the right to pursue self-profit, or is it "the liberty to know, to utter, and to argue freely according to conscience" (Milton, Areopagitica)? Americans may be little interested in such questions because they live in an established democracy. However, many Japanese intellectuals, who live in a society in transition from feudalism and oligarchy to democracy, cannot but be sensitive to these issues. Ultimately, democracy is a matter of educating individuals to be able to solve their own problems and to be able to evaluate leaders. However, Japanese education aims at memorization rather than problem solving. It produces conformers rather than analytical and critical minds.

Recently some Western journalists and scholars came to point to negative aspects of Japanese culture, as in the *Economist* (July 9, 1983), the *New York Times* (July 9–12, 1983), and *Time* (August 1, 1983). Robert Christopher (*The Japanese Mind: The Goliath Explained*) and Jared Taylor (*Shadows of the Rising Sun*) present prominent examples of such a critical view.

This book aims at attaining a balanced view of Japanese culture and searching for the social structural base of both aspects.

My fieldwork on the suicides of university students in Kyoto in 1968 was supported by an NIMH research grant (MH15763), for which I am greatly appreciative.

Special gratitude is due Dr. E. S. Shneidman and Dr. N. L. Farberow, for their encouragement and guidance, and Dr. David K. Reynolds, who read several versions of the manuscript and gave comments and advice. I also wish to thank the many people who contributed in various ways to the completion of this manuscript. These people include doctors Thomas T. Noguchi, Jo Yamamoto, Jushiro Koshinaga, and Kichinosuke Tatai, along with Tetsuo Okada, Katherine Yamagata, and Jane Alexander.

1

INTRODUCTION

Japan is number one among nations for her success in international economic competition, according to Professor Ezra F. Vogel. Vogel attributes Japan's success to an informed people, strong leadership, popular interest in politics and equity, quality and equality in education, and security and crime control.[1] Japan can indeed serve as a model for developing nations in these respects. Japan may also provide a lesson to Americans who are appalled by their nation's high crime rate and by the Japanese economic invasion. With their nation's economic prosperity and low rates of crime and divorce, the Japanese have become increasingly more confident of the superiority of their culture. For example, Yukio Matsuyama, a noted journalist who is highly critical of the Japanese personality type, believes that Japan is the closest of all nations to an "ideal" society, although he does not give criteria for his ideal society.[2] Despite the fact that their confidence often approaches ethnocentrism, the lesson we can learn from the Japanese feat, only forty years after the devastating defeat in World War II, is important. Their adaptability as a nation seems to be incomparable.

In contrast, the Japanese as individuals seem to be much less adaptable to difficult situations. There have been many recent reports of incidents that show weaknesses in the Japanese personality. For example, a twenty-year-old Japanese female student at a college in England committed suicide in May 1981 because she was suspected of having stolen a small amount of money from her teacher's purse. She denied the accusation vehemently and thought that her treatment by school officials and the police was excessively cold and harsh. (The British reaction was that she admitted guilt by her suicide.) In June 1981 a thirty-two-year-old Japanese male, who had acquired an M.A. degree in comparative literature at the University of Paris, killed a Dutch coed and dismembered her body. He did so because she had rejected his sexual advances. Their association had been a very brief one; she had gone to his apartment only because she was asked to help him study the German language.

In July 1981, while on a tour, a twenty-year-old Japanese male (referred to here as Y) threw rocks at cars in Athens, Greece. One rock broke a taxicab's window. The owner of a second car hit by a rock came out and started to fight with him. Y hit the driver with a brick-sized rock and killed him.

Y was a student studying French in Lance, France. He had married a French girl in July 1980, and their first son had been born in November. Since Y was unemployed, they depended upon the couple's parents for financial assistance.

The frustrations related to these circumstances (i.e., being suspected of stealing, being spurned by a woman, and being married but unemployed) are universal, but why did these people react in such extreme ways as committing suicide or murder? Apparently, such a strong emotional reaction represents intense maladjustment. Dr. Hiroshi Inamura found a strong tendency among Japanese youth to become maladjusted in foreign countries.[3] Related to the tendency toward maladjustment in a difficult situation is the trend toward an "alarming increase" in the number of cases of Japanese children who refuse to attend school and who use violence in the home.[4]

How can we explain these contradictory showings of great adaptability as a group and poor adaptability as individuals? Can we dispose of the question by saying that emotional outbursts are merely characteristic of deviants? My assumption is that the tendency toward emotionalism is common among normal Japanese. It is an essential element not only of suicide but also of economic success.

The purpose of this book is to find the common ground of this contradiction in culture. This study of Japanese culture focuses on the contrasting elements of suicide and economic success. It is a look at the thorn in the chrysanthemum.

Although the clarification of the nature of Japanese culture is the ultimate goal, the focus of the analyses in this book is on the individual rather than on the institution or the immediate situation. The ultimate explanation of any behavior is in the actor's interpretation of his life experience. From this point of view, the great adaptability of the Japanese as a group and the relatively poor adaptability of many Japanese youths as individuals are considered to be effects of Japanese culture screened through individual perception.

Suicide is eminently an individual matter, based on one's own definition of the situation—that is, one's attempt to find the best available means for attaining a certain goal under certain apparently unchangeable conditions. When one sees no other way out, suicide may take place. The conversion of motivation to action is determined by such individual traits as self-restraint, perception of social resources, and views of life, death, and suicide.

Japanese economic success has been explained mostly in terms of situational factors (such as American assistance, the Korean and Vietnam wars, and the monetary exchange rate) and organizational factors (such as governmental policy or the labor-management relationship). Questions to be answered, however, are why the Japanese people use situational factors so effectively and why their organizational factors work so well. Situational (and organizational) factors work only through the individual's perception. Although social scientists tend to place the primary focus on environmental factors because of the observability and measurability of these, Alfred North Whitehead has stated that "'Necessity [regarded as an environmental attribute, a given factor] is the mother of invention' is a silly proverb. . . . [Progress] is almost wholly the outgrowth of pleasurable intellectual curiosity."[5]

Behavior is a product of interaction between the self and the conditions given by history (and biography). These conditions include cultural conditions (technology, social structure, beliefs, etc.), geographical conditions (climate, natural resources, topography, etc.), and social conditions (war, depression, etc.). People are constrained by these conditions, but they are not passive recipients of external pressures. People fashion their world through praxis, guided by images and assumptions, by ideas about reality.[6] These images, assumptions, and ideas are functions of value orientations internalized from culture. Value orientation is the link between culture and the individual.

Therefore, the basic assumption of this book is that the real determinants of Japanese suicide and economic success are value orientations—a system of "complex but definitely patterned (rank-ordered) principles, resulting from the transactional interplay of three analytically distinguishable elements of evaluative process—the cognitive, the affective, and the directive elements—which give order and direction to the ever-flowing stream of human acts and thoughts as these relate to the solution of 'common human' problems."[7] Value orientations not only influence people's behavior but also guide their "testing" of the value orientations to determine their usefulness in adjustive adaptation.

No persons, not even social scientists and the subjects of their studies, can be mentally "value free." Every human being has ideological, moral, and political points of view. Therefore, the best understanding of behavior is offered by an understanding of the beliefs underlying behavior.[8] The social scientist's business is to show people what influences their value orientations have on their own behavior.

In the following chapter a psychocultural view of suicide, based on an interpretation of Durkheim's types of suicide, is presented. Chapter 3 contains a survey of Japanese suicides in order to show their marked characteristics. In chapters 4, 5, and 6, suicides by Japanese youths, females, and writers are discussed, with special attention given to personal documents (e.g., suicide notes, diaries, letters, etc.). These chapters provide materials for, and shed light on, later generalizations about suicidal motivation and action.

In chapter 7, Japanese value orientations are formulated as contrasted with American value orientations and are supported by statistical and other cited data. The factors in suicidal motivation and self-destructive adjustment in relation to the value orientations are discussed in chapter 8.

These discussions are followed by a study of Japanese economic success in international competition, with emphasis on social structure. In the final chapter, both suicide and economic success are explained in terms of their common denominator—Japanese value orientations. The explanation is related to some comments on the relationship between the value orientations and the new Japanese role as a world leader and also on some suggestions that are beneficial for American people.

II

A
PSYCHOCULTURAL
VIEW
OF
SUICIDE

Suicide has been studied primarily from psychological viewpoints. Psychological studies generally revolve around the following five foci:

1. Personality traits (e.g., narcissism, dependence, dependence conflict, and retaliation for real or imagined abandonment[1])
2. Emotional states (e.g., depression and rage)
3. Psychoanalytic motivation (e.g., libido and thanatos;[2] wishes to kill, to be killed and to die; [3] urge for rebirth;[4] wishes for reunion or for escape; etc.)
4. Deleterious patterns of cognition (e.g., semantic confusion[5])
5. Acquisition of ineffective adjustment mechanisms and/or patterns of inflexibility (e.g., unconstructive defense mechanism)

Elaborating on the last focus, Edwin S. Shneidman[6] explains suicide in terms of the following.

Inimicality (ineffective adjustive mechanism): an unsettled life pattern in which the individual acts against his own best interests—that is, he reduces his prospects for happiness and reacts against self by turning anger inward, leading to ruination of his own career and life.

Perturbation (emotional state): frightened, worried, depressed, agitated reactions to a stimulus.

Constriction (deleterious cognition): a narrowing of the individual's range of perception, a diminishing of opinions and options that come to mind.

Acceptance of cessation of life (motivation): death viewed as eternal sleep, with being "out of it" as a way to stop pain and distress.

Although psychological theories are important in explaining suicide, they are generally one-sided. For example, dependent and narcissistic persons do not necessarily commit suicide. Depression and rage may take other forms of reaction—for instance, mental disorder or violence. Many people have wishes to kill, to be killed, and to die or urges for rebirth, reunion, or escape, but they do not necessarily commit suicide. Similarly, ineffective mechanisms for adaptive adjustment and deleterious cognitive patterns do not necessarily lead to self-destruction. Therefore, it is necessary to combine several theories, as Shneidman has done.

The explanation of any behavior necessarily involves a multidimensional approach, since behavior is a product of personality-environment interaction. Personality, furthermore, is a product of the continual interactions among biological, psychological, and environmental factors. In actual behavior, environmental factors are inseparable from psychological determinants, which in turn are inseparable from biological variables. Thus, the importance of society in a study of suicide is evident.

A study of social structure is particularly important when we consider Japanese suicides. Akio Sugiyama died from an overdose of sleeping pills on the shore of a lake in July 1964. Although he was a good student, the financial situation of his family necessitated his working at a cotton mill after graduation from a junior high school. After six months of work, he learned that junior-high-school graduates were not treated as *"ningen to shite"* (fully human) in comparison with better educated persons. One of his superiors told him, "I feel sorry for you junior-high-school graduates. You cannot get girls, because Japanese girls would not care about those without money or a promising career." Akio wrote in his last note that "confronting many problems, like the prejudice against the less educated and the poor and the social structure based on status discrimination, ignoring humanity, I have suffered; I feel as if my own humanity is soiled. Recently I have come to think of death and suicide frequently."

While working, he saved as much money as possible. He even sent some to his parents occasionally. He attended night school and studied hard to prepare for the entrance examination for a daytime high school in order to enter college. He learned that night-school credits were not transferable to daytime high schools or acceptable to colleges. He succumbed to the poverty, pressure, and exhaustion, as shown in the last section of his note.

> However I might appear, my social life has been completely dark. Not only to myself but, I feel, to all my family members I have given agony.
>
> I could leave nothing for Father. Please give my books to my younger sister and the radio to my older brother. There are some of my clothes left. Please use whatever may be usable. I have not paid up for my radio, but please pay with the balance of my savings account. If the textbooks of the extension courses are usable for my sister, please let her use them.
>
> I feel confused. . . . My unhappiness is, I think, due to the fact that I thought too much. I realize that people are happier when they don't think.
>
> Please forgive me, accepting this as fate. I could not help it. Don't get angry at me, because I am going to be in a much better condition from now on, compared with the life of failure and a series of agonies.
>
> I am such a miserable being, but I love you all very much. Goodbye.

Sugiyama was a very normal and decent Japanese. He was a bright and mature young man. His only fault was that he was poor and undereducated. His obsession with success, the importance of formal education for happiness, prejudice against undereducated people, the necessity of accepting given roles—that is, conformance—for a comfortable life are all important causes of his suicide. They point to the necessity of studying value orientations in explaining Japanese suicide.

It was Emile Durkheim who propagated the emphasis on social factors in suicide.[7] He found a correlation between suicide rate and social integration, as indicated by such demographic variables as religious affiliation, educational achievement, marital status, and family size. The degree of social integration determines the attractiveness of a group to its members (cohesiveness) as well as the society's capability to regulate individual behavior (regulation). Social integration provides both security and pressure.

When social integration is too strong, individuality is stifled, and the individual can sacrifice himself for a group goal ("altruistic suicide"). When social integration is too weak, the individual is not identified with his group, and he has little meaningful association with his fellow members. In case of a severe frustration, such a person has nobody to count on for tension reduction and problem solving. A result may be an "egoistic suicide." When social integration drastically declines under a rapid social change, the person is extremely insecure because of the absence of clearly understood rules of behavior. The absence of rules may raise his aspiration unrealistically high, and the gap between his aspiration and reality may become frustrating. The resultant disillusion and anger may lead to an "anomic suicide."

In order to combine psychology and sociology in their explanation of suicide, A. T. Henry and J. F. Short emphasize the concepts of aggression, restraint, business cycle, and status.[8] Jack Gibbs, the most prominent elaborator of Durkheim's concept of social integration, investigates suicide rates correlated with the degree of consistency among social institutions and positions.[9] Correlation, however, does not explain causation. Therefore, many sociologists have attempted to fill the gap between correlation and explanation. For example, Jack Douglas interprets "anomic," "egoistic," and "altruistic" not as types of suicide but as terms reflecting social influences that coexist in the individual's psyche—that is, meaning given by the individual.[10] Ronald Maris also stresses the crucial role of social integration and emphasizes the concept of "constraint," which is both psychological and sociological.[11]

One sort of attempt to fill the gap between correlation and explanation is a developmental study. C. W. Mills presented a concept of "sociological imagination" that "enables us to grasp history and biography, and the relation between the two within society."[12] In light of this, we can study suicide as a point at which individual biography and society converge—life history.

This developmental aspect constitutes the focus of Jerry Jacobs's analyses.[13] Jacobs proposes that the suicidal process consists of a long-standing history of problems; the accumulation of concurrent problems; the degeneration of available adaptive techniques to solve problems and resolve conflicts; a chain reaction in which meaningful social relationships ultimately dissipate; and the internal process of rationalization through which the individual finds justification of his suicide and bridges the gap between thought and action.

Jacobs's proposal, however, does not deal with the causes of problems that might precipitate suicide, nor does it contend with the accumulation of problems, the deterioration of meaningful social relationships, or the closure of the gap between thought and action. In an effort to explicate the motives, precipitating factors, and overall process, a psychocultural viewpoint seems to be necessary.

A psychocultural perspective of suicide is exemplified by Durkheim's typology. He contends that "the private experiences thought to be the proximate causes of suicide have only the influences borrowed from the victim's moral predisposition, itself an echo of the moral state of society" (1958:300). According to Durkheim, collective representations—symbol-products that are mutually owned and mutually proclaimed—are facts. Because they are products of collective actions and not of individual actions, they are objective in nature and are accepted as objective imperative by the individual. The immediate cause of any behavior is the apperception of the situation by a personality. A personality's perception is determined by value orientations (a form of collective representations). Value orientation is not just an element of culture; it is a system of evaluative principles which includes cognitive-affective-directive aspects.

The psychocultural perspective underlying Durkheim's typology is shown through the characterization of each type by cultural, interactional, and psychological indicators (table 1). Cultural indicators show the individual's general orientation, shared with others, to institutionalized goals and means. These include (a) preferential values, which determine the selection of goals (e.g., group goal or self-oriented goal), and (b) obligatory values, which determine the selection from available means for goal-attainment (e.g., conformity to institutionalized means or innovation). A wide goal-means discrepancy is a basic cause of suicide motivation. Suicide motivation is converted to action by interactional factors, which may be divided into (c) the degree of internalized social restraint (e.g., a sense of responsibility, shame, and guilt) (d) the degree of the individual's demands for his rights (outlet for aggression), and (e) the degree to which the individual communicates with others (social resources), together with the individual's views of life, death and suicide.

Thus, Durkheim's types of suicide may be described in light of a combination of the indicators just mentioned. Altruistic suicide is viewed as the culmination of the following: (a) group goals that override individual goals; (b) a high degree of conformity; (c) a strong sense of responsibility; (d) strong group-goal oriented demands; and (e) substantial communication with other members of the group. Psychologically, this type of person is motivated to kill himself because of a strong sense of obligation, shame, and guilt. He may even experience

TABLE 1.

PSYCHOCULTURAL COMPONENTS OF DURKHEIM'S TYPES OF SUICIDE

	Egoistic	Altruistic	Fatalistic	Anomic
A. Cultural regulation				
1. Goals	Self-oriented: with some philosophical principle	Collectivistic	Accommodation of individual goals to group goals	Self-profit-oriented
2. Means	Nonconformance	Conformance	Conformance	Inconsistency between conformance and nonconformance
B. Interactional cohesion				
1. Social restraint: shame, obligation	Weak; effort to deny	Strong	Strong	Declining
2. Demands; self-expression	High for self-oriented goals	High for group goals	Low	High for self-profit
3. Meaningful communication	Low	High	Low	Declining
C. Psychological indications	Desire for meaning of life, which is obtainable only by social attachment (212);[a] nonconforming values vs. unconscious wish for sympathy (211); loss of the will to live; depression and melancholy (214)	Sense of obligation; abnegation and the state of impersonality (223); mystical joy (233); shame and guilt	Excessive physical and moral despotism, sense of "futures pitilessly blocked and passions violently choked" (276); resentment, fear, resignation	Wider goal-means discrepancy (246); sense of relative deprivation (253); inflated ego ideal and dependency; insecurity, greed, feverish imagination, disillusionment (256); jealousy (253)

[a]The numbers in the table refer to pages in Emile Durkheim's *Suicide: A Study in Sociology*, 2d ed., trans. J. A. Spaulding and G. Simpson (Glencoe, Ill.: Free Press, 1958).

a mystical joy in suicide when his death is a sacrifice for the good of the group, the most exalted of personal goals. Examples of this type of suicide are provided by elite military groups, cults, and deeply committed religious groups.

The second type, anomic suicide, results from weak social regulation. Major features of this type include (a) a compelling self-profit motive; (b) inner conflicts, involving a wish to conform to social expectations and a drive toward more effective means for self-profit; (c) a diminishing sense of shame and obligation; (d) a high degree of self-expression and of self-oriented demands; and (e) a decline in meaningful communication. This type of person grapples with feelings of relative deprivation and with conflicts involving goals. To such a person, the ends justify the means. He will never be satisfied because he compares himself with other people who have more than he does. A vicious, anxiety-producing cycle maintains an inflated "ego ideal" and dependency needs. The individual's psychological condition is characterized by greed, vanity, disillusionment, fervid imagination, and jealousy. His hostility toward others is reflected in behavior that appears accusatory, arrogant, and vengeful.

Durkheim's third type, egoistic suicide, results from a marked absence of integration of the individual into society. His behavior is characterized by (a) individualistic goals overriding social ones; (b) nonconformist means of goal attainment; (c) a weak, or weakly felt, sense of shame and obligation; (d) strong self-oriented demands and self-expression; and (e) a minimum of meaningful communications. Because of the paucity of meaningful communications, the individual will have difficulty finding life meaning in a frustrating situation, since the meaning of life is obtainable only through social attachment, which he lacks. He may unconsciously experience a painful conflict between individualistic goals and his wishes for attention and appreciation from society at large. In the case of overwhelming frustration, he may lose the courage to live.

The fourth type, fatalistic suicide, is mentioned by Durkheim only in a footnote (on p. 276 of the 1958 edition). However, although Durkheim considered it to be only of "historical interest," this type is very important in discussing Japanese suicides. It is a reaction to "the ineluctable and inflexible nature of a rule against which there is no appeal," as in the case of slaves. Fatalistic suicide may be interpreted as characterized by the individual's (a) loss of both group and personal goals, (b) strong conformity to societal norms, (c) strong sense of shame and obligation, (d) low degree of self-expression, and (e) minimal communication. Psychologically, this individual is likely to experience resentment, fear, and resignation revolving around the belief that the future will be meaningless or frightful. His passions are violently choked by oppressive discipline. He may harbor a desire to be killed, which can manifest itself in acts of submission, masochism, and self-blame, concurrent with feelings of helplessness, fatigue, and despair.

These four types—the manifestation of four "suicidal currents"—are important in explaining Japanese suicides, although in that country "fatalistic" is much more important than "egoistic" suicide.

Overall, suicide is the end result of a series of inimical, perturbed, and constricted reactions of an individual to crises, consummating in the idea of self-destruction. However, it may be divided conceptually into two phases: (1) a definition of the situation as desperate (i.e., "There is no other way out") and (2) a self-destructive adjustment to a triggering incident.

The definition of the situation may be analyzed in terms of personality and environmental conditions. A personality (ego) perceives the conditions as overwhelming and reacts to the apperception with self-destruction as a means of tension reduction. This self-destructive reaction is a function of (a) weak impulse control, (b) a tendency toward internally directed aggression (or internalized stress on self-restraint), (c) a lack of social resources useful for tension reduction or problem solving, and (d) a negative view of life and an acceptance of views of death and suicide. These characteristics may be regarded as indicators of the lethality of a person's coping mechanisms.

三

III

PATTERN
OF
JAPANESE
SUICIDE

After low suicide rates during World War II, the Japanese suicide rate hit a peak (25.2 per 100,000) in 1955 and declined until 1967, when the rate was 14.2. After that the rate rose again, to 15.3 in 1970 and 17.5 in 1974. The rate seems to be still rising. The *Japan Times* (May 6, 1984) reported that "suicides both in Tokyo and the nation hit a record high" in 1983.

The high rates of Japanese suicides are among youths, females, and writers, although recently the suicides of middle-aged males have been increasing. About 41 percent of the total suicides in 1983 were committed by persons in their forties and fifties. A large majority of this suicide group seems to have been responding to financial difficulty in combination with increased responsibility.

The Japanese suicide rate is bimodal, with two peaks, one in the twenty to twenty-four age group and the other in the sixty-five-and-over age group. The suicide rate for young Japanese males used to be the highest among modern nations, as shown by the 1960 figure for the

TABLE 2.

SUICIDE RATES AMONG MALES 15–24 IN SELECTED COUNTRIES
IN SELECTED YEARS
(per 100,000)

	1960	1965	1970	1973
Japan	41.1	15.3	14.0	19.9
United States	8.2	9.4	13.5	17.0
Austria	19.3[a]	18.7	27.0	18.7
Czechoslovakia	17.7	23.6	29.6	27.5
Denmark	12.1	10.4	11.1	12.1
England and Wales	5.7	6.3	6.0	5.7
France	6.3	6.2	9.5	11.0
West Germany	18.4	18.1	19.6	20.9
Hungary	29.8	30.3	27.8	24.8
Italy	4.0	3.3	3.5	3.4
Sweden	9.1	10.9	18.5	20.3
Switzerland	24.5	17.6	21.3	21.4

[a]for 1961
SOURCE: Japan Ministry of Welfare, *Jisatsu Shibō Tōkei* [Suicidal death statistics] (1977), pp. 228–270.

fifteen to twenty-four age group in table 2. For example, the rate was 41.1 for Japan in contrast to 17.7 for Czechoslovakia, which in 1973 shows much higher suicide rates for that age group than Japan does.

Although the peak for the younger group in Japan was declining, their suicide rate has risen again since the beginning of the 1970s. The rate for Japanese males twenty to twenty-four years old was 78.2 in 1958, 20.4 in 1967, and 25.9 in 1974 (table 3).

The seriousness of the problem of suicide among Japanese youth is indicated by the fact that in 1974–1975 about 50 percent of male college students, about 40 percent of male high-school students, and about 30 percent of male junior-high-school students in that country had "seriously wished to die" or "wished to die" (table 4).

Self-restraint (leading to internally directed aggression) has been a key factor in traditional (i.e., fatalistic and altruistic) suicides in Japan. In recent years, however, both suicide and violence (externally directed aggression) among Japanese youth have been increasing. According to the National Police Agency, social violence reached an all-time high in 1983. Suicides also are increasing. Apparently, aggressive impulses are increasing among young Japanese. Aggression may be directed

TABLE 3.

Japanese Suicide Rates by Sex and Age in Selected Years

	Total				Male				Female			
	1950	1958	1967	1974	1950	1958	1967	1974	1950	1958	1967	1974
Total	19.6	25.7	14.2	17.5	24.1	30.7	16.2	20.0	15.3	20.8	12.2	15.0
10–14	0.0	0.9	0.6	0.8	0.0	1.1	0.9	1.3	0.0	0.8	0.3	0.3
15–19	15.3	28.9	7.7	9.8	17.5	31.4	8.3	12.0	13.0	26.4	7.2	7.5
20–24	36.3	65.6	18.9	22.0	44.9	78.2	20.4	25.9	27.8	53.0	17.4	18.1
25–29	26.7	42.6	19.3	19.7	36.0	54.2	22.9	23.9	18.8	31.1	15.8	15.7
30–34	19.9	22.7	14.5	18.4	24.4	27.2	17.9	22.4	16.1	18.4	11.1	14.4
35–39	18.2	18.8	12.3	19.0	22.4	23.3	14.8	24.1	14.4	15.3	9.7	14.0
40–44	19.2	18.0	12.0	17.7	24.3	21.8	15.4	23.3	14.4	14.7	8.8	12.1
45–49	25.8	22.2	13.3	17.8	32.5	28.1	16.0	23.2	19.0	16.9	11.2	12.6
50–54	30.1	28.0	17.8	20.2	39.7	35.1	21.5	22.9	20.2	21.1	14.6	18.1
55–59	40.1	36.9	23.5	23.6	56.1	49.7	31.3	29.2	24.1	24.1	16.5	19.0
60–64	49.9	42.5	28.8	30.5	67.7	52.2	35.5	34.3	33.4	33.1	22.6	27.4
65–69	67.8	57.4	39.8	36.5	85.1	71.4	48.1	39.8	53.8	44.9	32.4	33.7
70–74	78.8	73.2	48.0	53.2	105.3	84.6	55.3	57.0	59.5	64.4	42.1	50.2
75–79	98.0	86.8	63.0	70.9	121.0	116.6	71.4	70.7	83.3	67.7	56.9	71.1
80+	116.1	89.8	80.6	94.0	136.7	119.8	88.6	103.2	105.7	74.3	76.6	88.7

SOURCE: Ministry of Welfare, *Jisatsu Shibō Tōkei* [Suicidal death statistics] (1977), p. 224; Fusa Ueda, "Tōkeiteki ni mita Nihon no Jisatsu" [Statistical View of Japanese Suicide], K. Ohara, *Jisatsugaku* [Suicidology], *Gendai no Esupuri* (Tokyo: Shibundo, 1975), p. 63.

TABLE 4.

"HAVE WISHED TO DIE" MALE STUDENTS, 1974–1975

	Jr. High School	Sr. High School	College
Total: Number	391	511	360
Percent	99.9%	100.0%	100.0%
Have seriously wished to die	6.9	5.1	8.1
Have wished to die	22.5	33.5	41.7
Have vaguely thought of dying	33.2	35.8	42.7
Have never wished to die	37.3	25.6	7.5

SOURCE: Hiroshi Inamura, *Jisatsugaku* [Suicidology] (Tokyo: University of Tokyo Press, 1977), p. 105.

TABLE 5.

SUICIDE RATES AMONG FEMALES IN COUNTRIES IN SELECTED YEARS
(per 100,000)

	Japan	United States	Austria	Denmark	West Germany	Hungary	Sweden
1920	14.7	5.7	14.1	7.5	14.6	—	6.1
1925	15.9	5.8	—	6.7	13.3	—	5.6
1930	16.0	6.9	24.4	9.9	15.7	—	6.2
1935	15.8	6.8	—	12.0	16.2	—	6.4
1940	11.0	6.8	—	11.8	—	—	7.1
1945	—	5.8	—	23.5	—	—	7.7
1950	15.3	5.1	14.7	15.0	12.0	—	6.9
1955	19.0	4.6	15.0	14.8	13.0	—	8.5
1960	18.2	4.9	14.8	13.6	12.7	14.9	8.6
1965	12.2	6.1	14.7	14.7	13.8	17.9	10.1
1970	13.3	6.5	14.2	15.7	15.0	19.8	13.2
1973	14.8	6.5	13.6	18.5	14.7	21.5	12.1

SOURCE: Ministry of Welfare, *Jisatsu Shibō Tōkei* [Suicidal death statistics] (1977), pp. 224–227.

PATTERN OF JAPANESE SUICIDE

TABLE 6.

SUICIDE RATES BY SEX AND SEX RATIO IN SELECTED COUNTRIES, 1973

	Total	Female	Male	F/M
Japan	17.3	14.7	20.1	73.1%
United States	12.0	6.5	17.7	36.7
Austria	22.1	13.6	31.6	43.0
Czechoslovakia	22.4	11.6	33.7	34.4
Denmark	23.8	18.5	29.2	63.4
Finland	23.5	10.3	37.6	27.4
France	15.5	8.7	22.6	38.5
West Germany	20.8	14.7	27.4	53.6
Hungary	36.9	21.5	53.2	40.4
Poland	11.7	4.3	19.6	21.9
Sweden	20.8	12.1	29.5	41.0
Switzerland	18.8	10.6	27.4	38.7

SOURCE: Adapted from Hiroshi Inamura, *Jisatsugaku* [Suicidology] (Tokyo: University of Tokyo Press, 1977), p. 18.

either internally or externally. It could contribute to either suicide or violence, depending on the situation. Weaker self-restraint and impulse control seems to be a product of Japan's new democracy.

The suicide rate for Japanese females has been one of the highest among modern nations (table 5). The rate declined in the 1960s and has risen slightly since then. In 1973 the suicide rate for all Japanese females was lower than the rates for such countries as Hungary and Denmark, but the sex ratio of suicide (i.e., female rate divided by male rate) (table 6) and the suicide rate for females age fifteen to twenty-four (table 7) were still the highest among industrialized nations.

If the figures on the suicide rate of Japanese writers were available, they would no doubt be extremely high. Among 100 representative writers whose works are included in the *Complete Works in Modern Japanese Literature,* six persons committed suicide: Takeo Arishima, Ryuunosuke Akutagawa, Shinichi Makino, Osamu Dazai, Yukio Mishima, and Yasunari Kawabata. If we calculate the suicide rate based on these figures, the rate would be 6,000 per 100,000. Moreover, there are other writers who also are known to have committed suicide, among them Tōkoku Kitamura, Bisan Kawakami, Shungetsu Ikuta, Eikō Tanaka, Michio Katō, and Ashihei Hino.

TABLE 7.

SUICIDE RATES AMONG FEMALES 15–24 IN SELECTED COUNTRIES
IN SELECTED YEARS
(per 100,000)

	1960	1970	1973
Japan	30.8	11.9	13.1
United States	2.2	4.2	4.3
Austria	7.2	5.7	5.2
Czechoslovakia	6.2	11.6	6.3
Denmark	4.2	5.7	5.7
West Germany	7.1	6.9	7.1
Hungary	15.0	9.6	6.1
Sweden	5.3	7.9	9.5
Switzerland	7.3	4.7	6.0
England and Wales	2.6	2.6	3.0

SOURCE: Ministry of Welfare, *Jisatsu Shibō Tōkei* [Suicidal death statistics] (1977), pp. 228–270.

In the following chapters the suicides of young males, females, and writers in Japan will be discussed. There are, however, other characteristics of Japanese suicides that are given less attention in this book. The first is *oyako shinjū* (parent-child suicides, especially the type in which the mother kills a child or children before taking her own life). This type of suicide occurred almost once every day in Japan in the 1950s, and it reveals much about Japanese culture and society. For example, *oyako shinjū* represents the beliefs that the child is not an individual human being but a family member, that the child is the parent's possession, and that it is more merciful to kill children than to leave them in the cruel world without parental protection. The mother who commits suicide without taking her child with her is blamed as an *oni no yō na hito* (demonlike person). However, *oyako shinjū* comprises only about 2 percent of all suicides in Japan; the topic is touched upon briefly in the section on male suicide.

A second characteristic suicide form is that of suicides in social and political scandals. In such cases it is usually subordinates regarded as key witnesses who commit suicide in order to cover up the wrongdoing of their superiors. In traditional Japan these suicides usually stopped any further investigation because of the covert but strong influences exerted by the coalition of bureaucracy and business leaders on the police. This type of suicide is a natural product of Japanese social structure, which is characterized by the ubiquity of governmental control, lack of objective criteria for evaluating companies for governmental subsidies and assistance, the necessity of personal connections, and the institutionalized disparity between *tatemae* and *honne*.

Tatemae (words—e.g., an emphasis on honesty) is different from *honne* (feeling and doing—e.g., accepting and expecting bribery). One has to satisfy the superior's *honne,* but it must be done in such a way that the appearance of *tatemae* can be secured. Because of such structural inevitability, political scandals are called *kōzō-oshoku* (structural corruption) in Japan. This type of suicide still occurs in present-day Japan, and it will be dealt with in the section on the attitude toward suicide in chapter 8.

The third characteristic of Japanese suicides is that, unlike in Western countries, the Japanese suicide rate is higher in rural areas than in big cities. The 1974 rate was 17.5 for Tokyo and 20.0 for Osaka, representing urban centers, in contrast to 29.3 for Akita, 28.1 for Kōchi, 27.3 for Yamagata, 27.1 for Kagoshima, and 25.5 for Niigata, all representing rural areas. The higher rate for rural areas is correlated with the concentration of older people (because of out-migrating young people), lower income, and underdeveloped welfare programs.

The direct effect of lower income upon suicide may not be as important as its indirect effects. For example, a Niigata study of the areas of high suicide rate (i.e., higher than 170 per 100,000) among old people (sixty years and over) shows the importance of children's out-migration as a cause of the old people's suicides.[1] Children's out-migration results from economic difficulty or from having little hope for a better future in the geographic area of the parents' residence. What is important is the poverty of a general area rather than that of suicide-producing families in contrast to other families in the same general area.

Children's out-migration causes a lack of meaningful communication. When the lack of meaningful communication is combined with the old parents' wishes to be supported by their children, which is traditional in Japan, suicidal motivation is aggravated. The motivation is intensified by topographical (e.g., geographic isolation) and climatological (e.g., heavy snow during much of the year) factors, which prevent social association with the outside and keep old people from participating in productive activities.

The relationship between lower income and suicide rate characterizes Japanese suicide in contrast to Western cultures, where suicide tends to be regarded as "democratic"—that is, not correlated with socioeconomic status. The inverse relationship between socioeconomic status and suicide is touched upon in chapters 4 and 5 ("Suicide of Young Japanese Males" and "Female Suicides," respectively).

Related to the rural–urban comparison is that, when comparing suicide rates among residents of big cities, those cities with stronger traditional values in Japan show higher suicide rates, especially among youths. Using the figures given by the Ministry of Welfare in *Jisatsu Shibō Tōkei* (Suicidal Death Statistics, 1977), the 1965 suicide rate for Tokyo, the most modern of Japanese cities, was 10.9 (in contrast to 15.3 for Osaka, 14.9 for Kobe, and 14.8 for Kyoto). The rates for those twenty to twenty-four years old were 15.4 for Tokyo and 23.5, 25.5, and 20.9 for Osaka, Kobe, and Kyoto, respectively. The rates for those twenty-five to twenty-nine years old were 15.0, 26.6, 20.0, and 22.2 for Tokyo, Osaka, Kobe, and Kyoto, respectively. A decade later, the suicide rates were 13.1 for Tokyo, 16.6 for Osaka, 15.6 for Kobe, and 16.5 for Kyoto. The rates for the twenty to twenty-four age group were 14.1 for Tokyo, in contrast to 18.6 for Osaka, 21.6 for Kobe, and 19.8 for Kyoto. The rates for the twenty-four to twenty-nine age group were 16.6, 23.6, 19.0 and 24.3, respectively, for the four big cities.

These figures enable us to make a few interpretations for further studies. First, the suicide rate in Japanese big cities is inversely related to average income and job availability, in which Tokyo is the highest. The Tokyo metropolis is virtually the sole center of Japanese politics, business, and education. The availability of jobs is much greater there than in other cities, and the average income is higher.

Second, the suicide rate in Japanese big cities is directly correlated with social integration and value conflict, in which the Osaka-Kobe-Kyoto area seems to be higher than Tokyo. (Social integration is assumed to be inversely related to the proportion of in-migrants.) While high social integration is regarded as a factor in a low suicide rate in Western societies, high "social integration" is a contributive factor in fatalistic and altruistic suicides in Japan because of the excessive nature of Japanese social integration. Most residents in Tokyo are in-migrants from other areas, producing a lower degree of social integration (i.e., a higher degree of anonymity) and less social pressure than in other big cities in Japan. The lesser degree of social integration, in combination with the greater job availability in Tokyo, contribute to a lower suicide rate. In the Osaka-Kobe-Kyoto area, however, where traditional values are stronger and where a larger number of residents are natives, the suicide rate is higher. This suggests that social integration in Japan stifles individuality and that strong traditional values produce more intense conflict with modern values in the rapid social change that the Osaka–Kobe–Kyoto area is undergoing. Already much more modernized than others, Tokyo's people experience less conflict with Western values than others do. The stifling of individuality contributes to fatalistic suicides and the intense value conflict contributes to anomic suicides.

Third, unlike the difference between the rural and urban areas in suicide, which has increased in recent years, the difference among big cities has declined. The decreasing difference suggests that traditional social integration and social pressure are declining in the Osaka–Kobe–Kyoto area. (The declining social integration probably is a major factor in the fact that Osaka shows the highest rate of school violence in Japan today.) However, the difference in the suicide rate between this area and Tokyo is still noticeable, particularly among youths.

IV

SUICIDE OF YOUNG JAPANESE MALES

The propensity of young Japanese males to engage in suicide wishes is analyzed in this chapter in terms of personality traits and of such environmental factors as family relations, "examination hell," financial insecurity, and ethnic prejudice.

PERSONALITY TRAITS ————————————————————

The suicides of young Japanese males are primarily motivated by despair in contrast to guilt or aggression. Suicide notes collected by the coroner's office of the Tokyo metropolis from 1948 through 1978 were classified by the Shneidman and Farberow method, based on Menninger's concepts of the "wish to kill," the "wish to be killed," and the "wish to die."[1] Sixty percent of the suicides of male Japanese youth under age twenty were primarily motivated by the "wish to die" (despair) and secondly by the "wish to be killed" (internally directed aggression; guilt), accounting for 22 percent (table 8). Only 8 percent

TABLE 8.

CLASSIFICATION OF SUICIDE NOTES WRITTEN BY MALES: JAPANESE IN TOKYO
(1948–1978) AND CAUCASIANS IN LOS ANGELES (1944–1953)
(by percent)

	Number	Wish to kill	Wish to be killed	Wish to die	Unclassified
Total					
Japanese	343	13.1	26.9	46.9	13.1
Caucasian	489	21.0	16.0	40.0	23.0
19 and under					
Japanese	37	8.1	21.6	59.5	10.8
20–39					
Japanese	175	14.9	29.1	41.1	14.9
Caucasian	99	31.3	27.3	23.2	18.2
40–59					
Japanese	82	11.0	35.4	42.6	11.0
Caucasian	215	23.0	16.0	35.0	26.0
60 and over					
Japanese	49	14.3	8.2	65.3	12.2
Caucasian	175	11.0	10.0	57.0	22.0

SOURCE: Jushiro Koshinaga, "Jisatsu to Isho" [Suicide and suicide notes], *Nihon Hōigaku Zasshi* [Japanese forensic journal] 33, 5 (1979): 476.

showed the "wish to kill" (externally directed aggression). The suicides of the age group from twenty to thirty-nine were also primarily motivated by the "wish to die" (41%), followed by the "wish to be killed" (guilt) (29%), and lastly by the "wish to kill" (aggression) (15%). In contrast, the dominant motive among age-comparable Caucasians was the "wish to kill" (31%), followed by the "wish to be killed" (27%), and the "wish to die" (23%). These figures suggest the great susceptibility of male Japanese youth to the sense of despair, together with little tendency toward externally directed aggression.

The susceptibility to the sense of despair is rooted in diffuse anxiety, which is built into Japanese personality. When young male students who had suicide wishes were asked about the reasons for them, the largest majority (41% of college, 38% of high-school, and 37% of junior-high-school students) attributed their suicide wishes to "being

TABLE 9.

REASONS FOR THE WISH TO DIE AMONG YOUNG JAPANESE MALES

	Jr. High School	Sr. High School	College
Total: Number	143	204	172
Percent	100.0%	100.0%	100.0%
"Being tired of life"	37.1	37.7	40.7
"Parents don't understand me"	24.5	18.1	26.2
"Lonely because of no friend"	4.2	7.8	5.2
"Lonely because of no parent"	0	1.0	0.6
"Cold family atmosphere"	5.6	4.9	2.3
"I hate examinations"	9.1	9.8	5.8
"Scolded by teacher"	6.3	1.0	1.7
"Suspected of wrongdoing by people"	3.5	3.9	7.0
"Betrayed by friend"	4.2	7.3	5.8
"Unrequited love"	5.6	8.3	4.7

SOURCE: Hiroshi Inamura, *Jisatsugaku* [Suicidology] (Tokyo: University of Tokyo Press, 1977), p. 106.

tired of life" (table 9). Diffuse anxiety is quite common among general Japanese youth. In 1972, the Japanese premier's office cross-culturally surveyed the opinions of young people from eighteen through twenty-four years of age.[2] In contrast to 16 percent of American youths who thought that "man is by nature evil," 33 percent of Japanese youth had that opinion (table 10). The perception may be a projection of one's own anxiety. According to the same survey, while only 10 percent of American youth stated that they had no friends whom they could trust, 23 percent of their Japanese counterparts gave the same answer. The percentage of Japanese youth who answered that "there is little hope or joy in life, only sorrow and agony" was behind only that of Indian youths among eleven countries studied. The percentage of those who said that they were proud of their nation because of the potentiality for development and of achievement in social welfare was the lowest for Japanese. In contrast to the 62 percent of the American subjects who were "satisfied with their society," only 26 percent of the Japanese felt this way. While 51 percent of the American youth believed that "their nation protects adequately their welfare and rights," only 11 percent of Japanese youth believed this.

TABLE 10.

"Do you agree with the opinion that man is by nature evil?"
Persons Age 18 to 24, 1972

	Yes	No	Other
Japan	33.0%	64.6%	2.4%
United States	16.0	80.1	3.9
Britain	16.2	79.5	4.3
West Germany	16.6	75.8	7.1
France	20.0	69.9	10.1
Switzerland	15.4	83.7	0.9
Sweden	22.3	73.3	4.4
Yugoslavia	19.5	80.5	0
India	25.6	73.3	1.1
Philippines	25.7	72.7	1.6
Brazil	19.0	78.8	2.2

SOURCE: Nihonjin Kenkyukai, *Nihonjin Kenkyu: No. 1. Nihonjin no Kokoro wa Kawatta Ka* [Has the Japanese mind changed?] (Tokyo: Shiseido, 1976), p. 113.

In addition to diffuse anxiety, which is shared with general Japanese youth, suicidal Japanese males show certain personality traits. By the use of a temperament test (*Shinjōshitsu kensa*), young Japanese males' suicide attempts were found to show a significantly higher degree of depression, asthenia, and tenacity in comparison with control groups.[3] The Thurstone test showed the suicidal subjects as consistently low in the area of "vigorous," "impulsive," "dominant," "stable," "social," and "reflective." According to the Rozenzweig *P-F* study, the subjects did not make normal efforts for dissolving frustration. The Rorschach test showed them to be characterized by a lack of social adjustability, a tendency to self-confinement, an inability to maintain normal social relations, a greater susceptibility to depression, and a lack of capability for conscious self-control and realistic cognition.[4] In short, it may be said that suicidal young Japanese males "have a considerably high degree of self-examination, regret, and disappointment. They are aware of the necessity of working hard and have the desire to do so. They are not, however, energetic or patient, and [they] lead depressed and lethargic lives. They are emotionally unstable and unsociable. They lack the capability of reality testing and are often immature in personality development."[5]

I compared four groups of male university students in Kyoto: completed suicides, which occurred during the period from 1955 through 1968; unsuccessfully attempted suicides; those who had contemplated committing, but never attempted, suicide; and nonsuicides. Information about completed suicides was acquired from the Kyoto University Counseling Office and the subjects' personal documents, supplemented by information obtained through interviews with the subjects' family members and friends. In addition to interviews, "attempted suicides" were also given the questionnaire that was administered to the last two groups. Significant differences were found in the areas of dependence, rigidity, suspiciousness, being unrealistic, and having a weak ego (table 11). Weak ego was correlated in completed and attempted suicides with unrealistically high goals and a wide gap between aspiration and available means. The subjects were competitive because of a lack of self-confidence, but they lacked in effort for goal attainment.

Three characteristics seem to be generally marked among suicidal young Japanese males: dependency, *kachiki* (literally, "unyielding"), and mental frailty. An example of an unusually strong dependency need is the case of a twenty-year-old student in chemical engineering. His parents were fairly well-to-do and were overprotective. When he was discharged from the hospital where he was treated for a minor disease, this young man was so dependent upon his *tsukisoi* that he could not leave her. (A *tsukisoi* is a subprofessional nurse who is assigned on a one-to-one basis to a patient in many hospitals in Japan. She cares for the patient continuously throughout his hospitalization. She sleeps in the same room as the patient and serves as housekeeper and companion.[6]) Yielding to their son's request, the student's parents let his *tsukisoi* care for him at home for a few weeks, thinking that during that time his dependence upon her would subside. He was so afraid of the possibility of her leaving him while he attended classes that he could not go to the university. When his parents decided to let her go, he ran away with her to her home in the countryside. She was not in love with him, but, she said to her family, he was so pathetically dependent upon her that she could not reject him. He persuaded her to die with him. They took pills. She died and he survived.

Dependence was also a key factor in the suicide of a twenty-two-year-old science student. His father had died when he was four years old, and he was suffocated by the affection and overprotection of his mother. All her hopes were concentrated upon him. She worked as a *tsukisoi*. Their financial situation was poor, and twice the boy was discovered stealing money from a friend's drawer. A counselor who had been counseling him interpreted this as a symbol of his wish for self-assertion rather than of financial pressure. The counselor's advice to this subject was, *"Kekkon sasete moratte wa dooka?"* ("How about asking your mother to let you marry?"). The son's emotional dependence upon the mother was so strong that marriage was the only hope for freeing him.

Kachiki was a characteristic of about half of the subjects. Symptoms of *kachiki* are vanity, keen sensitivity to appearance, egocentrism, temperamental instability, an underlying inferiority complex, and a high susceptibility to suggestion.[7] A *kachiki* person blames others for one's own difficulty and projects own undesirable quality onto others. An example is provided by the note left by a suicide-attempting university student:

> While there is a limit to the Japanese capability to do good there is no limit to their selfishness. It is because of their insular mentality (*shimaguni konjō*), which made them fight for a little land and a scant amount of money for several thousands of years. Especially under the present capitalistic system in Japan, if we did not become egotistic, we would be dropped out of the inhumane social machine. I cannot believe in such concepts as love or conscience in Japan.

Narcissism, another expression of *kachiki*, was especially marked among 26 percent of the suicidal subjects, as shown by an excessive concern with appearance and an unrealistically strong desire for fame and success. A twenty-four-year-old student, majoring in English, professed that "I am greater than my professors. The world is too dirty for me to live in." A nineteen-year-old freshman in law maintained that he was Christ. Three students said, "If I cannot become famous, I would rather die." A twenty-one-year-old engineering student was shocked when his report about a writer was sternly criticized by a professor. In reaction, he told the professor, "In five years I will be a famous writer." A medical student applied to Kyoto University just to show people that he was a genius, although he knew that even if he was admitted he would not be able to continue his study because of economic difficulty. A student in science became hostile toward the university because he was scolded by a professor. After the scolding he stopped attending the required lab course, which was given only by that professor. Results were his failure to graduate and a suicide attempt.

Mental frailty was indicated by oversensitivity to the reaction of others, fear and persecution delusion, an obsessive wish to be loved, and an inferiority complex—a diffuse torturing feeling of one's own

TABLE 11.

A COMPARISON OF FOUR GROUPS OF MALE UNIVERSITY STUDENTS
(COMPLETED SUICIDES, ATTEMPTED SUICIDES, THOSE WHO CONTEMPLATED
BUT NEVER ATTEMPTED SUICIDES, AND NONSUICIDES)
IN TERMS OF PERSONALITY TRAITS

		Completed suicides[a]	Attempted suicides	Contemplated suicides	Nonsuicides
Dependence	N	72	22	20	60
High		25	10	2	3
Low		42	8	9	27
Other		6	4	9	30
$X^2 = 44.33.$		$P < .001.$			
Rigidity	N	72	22	22	57
High		41	15	1	0
Low		29	6	7	45
Other		2	1	14	12
$X^2 = 99.41.$		$P < .001.$			
Suspiciousness	N	72	22	22	64
High		30	15	9	9
Low		37	6	7	32
Other		5	1	6	23
$X^2 = 36.36.$		$P < .001.$			
Unrealistic	N	73	22	22	67
High		38	15	2	3
Low		28	5	4	42
Other		7	2	16	22
$X^2 = 80.06.$		$P < .001.$			

TABLE 11. (*Continued*)

		Completed suicides[a]	Attempted suicides	Contemplated suicides	Nonsuicides
Weak Ego	N	73	22	22	67
High		20	11	0	2
Low		49	10	14	65
Other		4	1	8	0
$X^2 = 68.35.$		$P < .001.$			

[a]Completed suicides occurred during the period from 1955 through 1968. Information about them was obtained through interviews with their family members and friends, in addition to information available from the Kyoto University Counseling Office and from the subjects' personal documents. Other subjects were studied in 1968.

inadequacy. Twenty-two (23%) of the ninety-seven suicidal subjects showed a marked inferiority complex. Six had complexes about their looks. Three each had complexes about their short stature and intelligence, and two about their common backgrounds. One student was obsessed with inferiority feelings because of his athletic inability, another because of his body odor. A twenty–eight-year-old student in agriculture, a Christian, could not pass a group of girls waiting for a bus because of his painful sensitivity about his "shabby attire."

Mental health is an important factor in the subjects' suicides. There were significant differences among completed suicides, attempted suicides, those who contemplated suicides, and nonsuicidal subjects in the categories of "health failure" and on both physical and mental health (table 12:1). According to the diagnosis by a Kyoto University psychiatrist and a counselor, 28 percent of ninety-seven subjects of our study were neurotic, 13 percent were depressive, and 10 percent were schizophrenic. A majority (67%) of neurotic subjects suffered from *shinkei suijaku* and 33 percent suffered from compulsive and anxiety neuroses (table 13).

Depression was indicated by compulsiveness, melancholy, rigidity, a lack of interests, and temperamental instability, together with a wish to die, a high degree of perturbation and irritability, sleeplessness, a loss of appetite or weight, and various kinds of delusion. *Shinkei suijaku,* the most common mental disorder among Japanese students, was characterized by sleeplessness, headache, a sense of being tired, loss of efficiency and attentiveness, poor memory, a feeling of inferior-

TABLE 12.

A COMPARISON OF FOUR GROUPS OF MALE UNIVERSITY STUDENTS
(COMPLETED SUICIDES, ATTEMPTED SUICIDES, THOSE WHO CONTEMPLATED
BUT NEVER ATTEMPTED SUICIDES, AND NONSUICIDES)
IN TERMS OF SITUATIONAL FACTORS

		Completed[a]	Attempted	Contemplated	Nonsuicides
(1) Physical health	N	74	22	23	68
Good		46	11	11	57
Poor		19	3	7	4
Other		9	8	5	7
$X^2 = 24.19.$	$P < .001.$				
Mental health	N	75	22	23	68
Good		41	4	0	64
Poor		31	13	2	3
Other		3	5	21	1
$X^2 = 172.19.$	$P < .001.$				
Health failure	N	71	22	23	66
Yes		34	16	13	4
No		32	5	10	62
Other		5	1	0	0
$X^2 = 57.00.$	$P < .001.$				
(2) Family problem	N	52	21	23	68
Yes		12	10	10	4
No		36	11	13	64
Other		4	0	0	0
$X^2 = 33.77.$	$P < .001.$				

TABLE 12. (*Continued*)

		Completed[a]	Attempted	Contemplated	Nonsuicides
(3) Schoolwork problem					
	N	51	21	23	68
	Yes	41	15	9	0
	No	10	6	10	68
	$X^2 = 96.46$.	$P < .001$.			
(4) Family's economic security					
	N	72	21	23	64
	Good	11	5	3	25
	Poor	33	6	7	1
	Other	28	10	13	38
	$X^2 = 38.15$.	$P < .001$.			
Money problem as felt by the subject					
	N	51	21	23	68
	Yes	27	8	7	1
	No	21	13	15	67
	Other	3	0	1	0
	$X^2 = 50.66$.	$P < .001$.			

[a]Completed suicides occurred during the period from 1955 through 1968. Information about them was obtained through interviews with their family members and friends, in addition to information available from the Kyoto University Counseling Office and from the subjects' personal documents. Other subjects were studied in 1968.

ity, timidity, and obsessive worry. Compulsive anxiety neurosis was characterized by a diffuse fear of illness, of imperfection, and of social relations. The last category (called *taijin kyōfu*) included "fear of blushing" (*sekimen kyōfu*), "fear of other people's gaze" (*shisen kyōfu*), and "fear that one's own face is ugly" (*shūbō kyōfu*).

"Family problems" were an important factor in university students' suicides in Kyoto (table 12:2). Nationally, family problems (excluding "marital problems") caused 14 percent of the suicides of Japanese males in the age group under twenty and 22 percent among those aged twenty to twenty-nine, compared with much smaller percentages of older groups in 1974 (table 14).

A comparison of fifty-five suicide attempts (mean age being 22.2 years) in 1965 in Tokyo and Kochi Prefecture with a control (nonsuicidal) group of 917 young Japanese (416 college, 262 high-school, and 239 junior- high-school students) found a significant difference in the percentage of the presence of both biological parents.[8] Eleven percent of the suicidal subjects had lost both parents by the time they were seventeen years old, compared with 1 percent of the control group ($X^2 = 6.77$. df. 1. $P < .01$). Further support for the significant effect of the dual parental absence comes from a finding that 13 percent of the suicidal subjects came from families in which neither biological father nor mother took care of the child during the latter's grammar-school age, whereas only 3 percent of the nonsuicidal subjects had a comparable history ($X^2 = 11.1$. df. 1. $P < .001$).

TABLE 13.

COLLEGE STUDENT SUICIDES AND MENTAL DISORDERS[a]

	Number	Percent
	97	100.0
Depression	13	13.4
Schizophrenia	10	10.3
Neuroses:	27	27.8
Shinkei suijaku[b]	(18)	(18.6)
(Compulsive neuroses)	(9)	(9.3)
Taijin kyōfu[c]	(5)	(5.2)
(Anxiety neuroses)	(4)	(4.1)
Other	47	48.5

[a]Suicides occurred from 1955 through 1968.
Mental disorders were classified by a psychiatrist and a university counselor.
[b]Disorder characterized by sleeplessness, headache, a sense of being tired, loss of efficiency and attentiveness, poor memory, feeling of inferiority, timidity, and obsessive worry.
[c]Fear of social objects, including *sekimen kyōfu* (fear of blushing), *shisen kyōfu* (fear of the other's gaze), and *shūbo kyōfu* (fear of own "ugly face").

TABLE 14.

MOTIVES OF SUICIDES OF JAPANESE MALES FOR APRIL, MAY, AND JUNE 1974

(percentage of motives known)

Motives Known	Number	Total	19 and under	20–29	30–49	50–59	60 and over
		2,126	126	395	664	249	672
		100.0%	100.0%	100.0%	100.0%	100.0%	100.0%
Illness and physical defect		48.7	13.5	11.9	41.0	53.4	74.8
Marital problem		6.2	1.0	4.5	9.6	6.4	4.6
Family problem		7.6	14.3	21.6	6.8	8.4	7.1
Heterosexual affair		5.6	11.1	17.9	4.5	0.4	0.3
Financial problem		6.7	2.4	4.7	12.0	9.2	2.5
Occupational problem		11.8	9.5	22.7	15.7	12.9	1.8
Schoolwork problem		3.0	34.1	5.0	0	0	0
"Being tired of life"		3.9	9.5	6.8	2.7	2.8	2.5
Other		6.5	4.8	4.9	7.8	6.4	6.4

SOURCE: Ministry of Welfare, *Jisatsu Shibō Tōkei* [Suicidal death statistics] (1977), p. 23.

In Japan the blood relationship between parent, especially mother, and child is almost sacred and is highly glorified. The stepparent is regarded as less than a true parent—usually as *tanin* ("no relation" or "stranger"). Therefore, the existence of the stepparent-child relationship is very rare. When the stepparent-child relationship occurs, a strained relationship is taken for granted. The stepparent has been stereotyped as hostile or indifferent to the stepchild. Among the ninety-seven Kyoto subjects studied in 1968, two had stepfathers, four had stepmothers, and one had foster parents. In all but one case, the relationship between the subjects and their step- or foster parents was unsatisfactory.

The expectation of a harsh stepparent-child relationship is one of the major causes of parent-child suicides (*oyako shinjū*). In *oyako shinjū,* a parent kills the children before his or her suicide. The woman who is determined to commit suicide feels that if her children are left behind and if her husband should remarry, the children would suffer. As noted in chapter 3, the mother who kills herself without killing her children is often called *oni no yō na hito* (a person like a demon without human feelings).

An important aspect of the absence of the father in relation to Japanese suicide is that it is likely to cause financial difficulties. It is very difficult for a Japanese widow to find a job in Japan. (This factor will be discussed later, in the section on economic insecurity.)

The importance of the parent-child relationship as a cause of suicide is also shown by the subjects' attitudes toward their parents. Fewer suicidal subjects than control-group subjects provided a positive evaluation of their parents. Only 24 percent of the fifty-five who attempted suicide stated that their fathers were "satisfactory," in comparison with 29 percent of 416 nonsuicidal college students, 33 percent of 258 nonsuicidal high-school students, and 42 percent of 247 nonsuicidal junior-high-school students ($X^2 = 13.02$. df. 3. $P < .01$). Affirmative responses to the statement "Mother is satisfactory" were given by 26 percent of the suicidal subjects and 44 percent of the college, 46 percent of the high-school, and 53 percent of the junior-high-school students ($X^2 = 16.81$. df. 3. $P < .001$). The percentage of those who concurred with the statement "Father is reliable" was 20 percent for the suicidal subjects, as compared with 29 percent for college, 36 percent for high-school, and 47 percent for junior-high-school students ($X^2 = 28.49$. df. 3. $P < .001$). The percentages of those responding affirmatively to "Mother is reliable" were 18 percent for suicidal subjects and 33 percent, 37 percent, and 49 percent, respectively, for the nonsuicidal groups ($X^2 = 21.58$. df. 3. $P < .001$).

More mothers were criticized for "too strict restriction of children" (9.1%) by the suicidal group than by the three control groups (3.6, 6.6, and 8.0%, respectively). The difference is not statistically significant, but the relatively large difference between suicidal subjects and age-comparable college students, combined with the marked similarity between suicidal subjects (with an average age of 22.2) and much younger junior-high-school students, seems to show the suicidal subjects' tendency toward immaturity or maladjustment rather than parental strictness. The assumption is supported at least partly by evidence of nonrational tendencies (or emotionality) on the part of suicidal subjects. While only 18 percent of them denounced suicide on the ground that "we should look for significance of life," 56 percent of college, 48 percent of high-school, and 34 percent of junior-high-school students did so ($X^2 = 60.37$. df. 3. $P < .001$).

Suicide attempts and running away from home are closely related; their motives appear to derive from the same sources. Of fifty-five of those who attempted suicide, 66 percent had contemplated running away from home, in comparison with 31 percent of college, 34 percent of high-school, and 27 percent of junior-high-school students ($X^2 = 12.88$. df. 3. $P < .01$). Because of the correlation, the avowed reasons for "running away from home" should shed light on suicide motivation. As reasons for contemplating running away from home, 42 percent gave "rebellion against parents," 34 percent gave "desire for freedom," and 11 percent indicated "being scolded." Nineteen percent gave "family disharmony" as the reason.

These figures roughly show the nature of the family situation in which the suicidal victims were reared—that is, with lack of understanding and little intimacy between parent and child. "Rebellion against parents" and "desire for freedom" may imply not only strict authoritarian parents but also overprotective, indulgent parents. Among my Kyoto subjects there were fifty-three (55%) who had both parents living together with the subject. In nineteen (36%) of the fifty-three cases, both parents were highly indulgent. In comparison, only three subjects were living with both parents where both were regarded as highly disciplinarian. In addition, there were nineteen subjects who were living only with the mother, and in fifteen (79%) of those families, the mother was highly indulgent. Parental indulgence, together with the absence of biological parents during the subjects' childhood, probably restricted their learning of effective social techniques for social interaction and constructive adjustment mechanisms for frustration dissolution.

The suicides by Japanese males under twenty years old that occurred in April, May, and June of 1974 were, as was shown in table 14, primarily motivated by schoolwork (34%). Some sort of family problem (14%) was the second cause. If we assume that half of the family problems were caused by the child's poor school performance (which is the central concern of the typical Japanese parents), about 40 percent of the suicides of Japanese boys can be attributed at least partly to schoolwork. Since the primary purpose of Japanese education is to pass the entrance examination to a good university, "a schoolwork problem" means an expected difficulty in passing the entrance examination.

As far back as 1961, about 61 percent of the junior-high-school students in Kyoto gave "entrance examination and schoolwork" as their greatest worry (table 15). Even for females, for whom university education is not expected as much as for males, schoolwork problems were the primary concern. Today school achievement remains one of the most important qualifications for a successful marriage. Anxiety about entrance examinations and schoolwork seems to be increasing. In 1976 about 83 percent (of both sexes) of junior-high-school students in Nagoya reported that their primary concern was "schoolwork and the entrance examination" (table 16).

TABLE 15.

KINDS OF WORRIES REPORTED BY JUNIOR-HIGH-SCHOOL STUDENTS
IN KYOTO, 1961
(in percentages)

	Total	Male	Female
	997	530	467
	100.0%	100.0%	100.0%
Examination and schoolwork	60.8	59.2	62.7
Anxiety about future	9.3	10.1	8.4
Health problem	4.9	6.6	3.0
Family problem	3.4	2.8	4.1
Friend	2.7	2.8	2.6
Other	2.5	4.0	0.9
No reply	16.4	14.3	18.3

SOURCE: M. Kosaka and N. Usui, *Nihonjin no Jisatsu* [Suicide of Japanese People] (Tokyo: Sōbunsha, 1966), p. 212.

TABLE 16.

MAJOR CONCERNS AMONG JUNIOR-HIGH-SCHOOL STUDENTS IN NAGOYA, 1976
(in percentages)

Schoolwork and the entrance examination	83.4
Personality	73.8
Career; future	62.0
Health	58.5
Family problem	42.5
Friend	33.7
Other	42.0

SOURCE: Nagoya Local Government Survey, 1976, in Yoshiaki Nakano, "Some General Trends in Special Education and My Clinical Work with Autistic Children in Japan" (unpublished MS).

An eighteen-year-old boy wrote the following in his suicide note:

I feel disgusted when I see guys who make a fuss about the entrance examination all the time. Rebelling, I have not studied for about two months. I don't think I can pass. I am in bad shape. Therefore, I die, although I would like to enter a first-rate university.

I am ashamed of myself, unable to grow out of childishness. I envy others. There should be room for a stupid man like me, too. I would like to see Hell.

Why is the concern about the entrance examination so intense among Japanese youths? It is, firstly, due to their "do-or-die" attitude toward the examination. In premodern days, the basic character of Japanese government was "inescapable absolutism and sumptuary control of individuals."[9] The policy was to keep the masses dependent and uninformed (*yorashimu-beshi, shirashimu-bekarazu*). Consequently, a vast majority of the population was illiterate. At modernization, leadership was assumed by lower-rank samurai from remote provinces who were highly ethnocentric and authoritarian. Their ideology was "Might is right" and their motto was "Rich Nation, Strong Army" (*fukoku kyōhei*). In order to realize this ideal, they needed to induce bright youths to apply for higher education. Thus, emphasis on education and the entrance examination became a Japanese tradition.

Since education is the only means for raising social status and for achieving security for the masses, the desire for educational success is very strong. The desire is reinforced by the knowledge of the insecure and uncomfortable life of those who failed in education. The misery of those who failed is typical in a feudal society, which lacks the concept that the general society has a responsibility for caring for the unfortunate. In Japan, "attitudes and behavior patterns characteristic of a feudal society are still more prevalent than in the West."[10]

As *amae* (that is, depending and presuming upon another's benevolence) is a key concept for understanding Japanese personality,[11] so is status difference. *Amae* itself is possible because of the obsessive concern with status difference. For the Japanese the established ranking system, based on occupational ranking and duration of service within the group, is "overwhelmingly important in fixing the social order and measuring individual social values,"[12] and the ranking system is mostly determined by education.

The intensity of the desire for educational success among Japanese people is at least partly due to the image of limited good, or "the attitude which regards everything good as limited in quantity and which, therefore, must be fought for, and once acquired, must be carefully guarded even by force."[13] When Japan was a poor peasant society under an authoritarian government, people had to survive with what they were given. Under heavy taxation, which is suggested by the policy of "the more you squeeze, the more you can get from soybeans and peasants" (*Daizu to hyakushō wa shiboreba shiboru hodo deru*), people often starved to death. The selling of daughters to brothels was not unusual, and infanticide was commonly practiced. The imagery of limited good did not apply only to the poor. The history of warriors and feudal lords is studded with fighting and killing among siblings and between parent and child for a small piece of land.

Even now, when Japan has become a rich nation materially, the mentality of limited good persists, primarily because of the competition for educational success. Frustration due to the imagery of limited good produces aggressive impulses. When aggressive impulses are not given an outlet, they are expressed in envy, jealousy, gossiping, calumny, and mistrust. The consequent social isolation, in combination with the intense guilt, that Japanese experience in case of failure to satisfy maternal expectations,[14] is an essential element in the attitude of "success or death" among young Japanese.

The second cause of the intense concern with the entrance examination is the "one-shot" principle (*ippatsu-shugi*). The Japanese examination system is characterized by the one-shot principle culminating long, monotonous preparation. Whereas the evaluation of an individual in America is spread over many years, a Japanese person's entire career depends upon his success in a single event, the entrance examination to a university. The following suicide note written by an eighteen-year-old boy suggests that if second and third chances were given in later years, his suicide might have been avoided:

> I thank you for your taking care of me for a long time. I have been in a slump the past month and did not study. I don't know why, but I am not in the mood to study. It is impossible in this condition to pass the entrance examination, which is coming in about a month. I gave up hope of passing the examination. I give up. I have decided to die.

Preparation for the examination is long; for many Japanese it begins in early childhood. The preparation is wearisome, because it consists mostly of memorizing answers to innumerable questions on various subjects in the school's curriculum, at the sacrifice of self-expression, creativity, and physical exercise. Schoolwork tends to be monotonous. Teachers usually read from textbooks crammed with information that students may not understand. Students become passive spectators; slow learners readily become bored and "switch off."[15] Those students who lag behind can never really drop out—they are constantly pressured by parents and society and tortured by shame and guilt.

Stress is aggravated by the necessity for about 80 percent of the children to attend *juku* (neighborhood cram schools)[16] for further memorization after school hours. The extra drill lasts about three hours a day. As table 17 shows, Japanese children spend much more time in studying than do their college-age brothers and sisters (42.7 versus 29.6 hours a week, respectively). The long, arduous preparation is evaluated by the single event of the college-entrance examination.

The third cause of the intensity of the Japanese concern with the examination system is the status hierarchy of educational institutions. Japanese educational institutions are ranked by the number of graduates admitted to "better" universities. Newspapers and weekly magazines publish such rankings. The rankings correspond to the degree of expected career success of graduates, because more prestigious employers hire graduates only from the more highly ranked institutions. The employment of graduates by a company is determined by the prestige of the institution from which they have graduated, not by their individual achievement. In addition, the more highly ranked universities are mostly those sponsored by the national government, and their

TABLE 17.

STUDENTS' STUDY HOURS IN JAPAN BY LEVEL OF EDUCATION, 1975

	At school	At other places	Total	
Weekdays:				5 days Total
University students	3.0	2.0	5.0	25.0
High-school students	5.3	3.3	8.6	
Jr.-high-school students	6.0	3.5	9.5	
Elementary-school students	5.4	1.6	7.0	35.0
Saturdays:				Saturday
University students	1.5	1.5	3.0	3.0
High-school students	4.0	2.5	6.5	
Jr.-high-school students	4.5	3.0	7.5	
Elementary-school students	3.7	2.3	6.0	6.0
Sundays:				Sunday
University students	0.1	1.5	1.6	1.6
High-school students	0.3	3.7	4.0	
Jr.-high-school students	0.3	3.2	3.5	
Elementary-school students	0.2	1.5	1.7	1.7

SOURCE: NHK National lifetime survey, 1975. Quoted in Yoshiaki Nakano, "Some General Trends in Special Education" (unpublished MS).

tuitions are about one-tenth of those of private universities. Therefore, youths and parents flock to the doors of the more highly ranked national universities.

The obsessive concern with status difference produces *rōnin*. A *rōnin* (literally, "masterless samurai") is a student who is not admitted to the university of his choice upon his school graduation and is preparing for the next year's examination. He then spends one, two, or even more years cramming to retake the examination of the desired institution rather than entering an inferior one. At Tokyo University, usually about 60 percent to 70 percent of both applicants and acceptees are *rōnin*. The addition of *rōnin* to fresh high-school graduates makes the entrance examination to "better" universities more severe.

The importance of status difference in relation to suicide is exemplified by several cases. In my 1968 Kyoto study, there was a student at Kyoto Prefectural University and a student at Kyoto Teachers College who both committed suicide because they had been rejected by Kyoto University. Another example is that of a twenty-four-year-old student at one of the universities in Kyoto, who wrote the following suicide note:

> Please stay calm. Try to hide my suicide. Please don't think about causes of my suicide and don't inquire about what I have done before death. For me the present university is nothing. If we go to a university in Japan, it must be Tokyo or Kyoto. Many people attend uninteresting classes for four years and wait for employment. It is just like cows and pigs waiting in a wooden stable to be pulled out to the slaughterhouse. I cannot stand it.
>
> I believe in the fairy tale that I may be able to be reborn as a superior human being. Then I will enter Tokyo or Kyoto University, or even Sorbonne or Harvard.

Even among top-ranked universities, there is a sharp status difference that is important enough to cause suicide. One Kyoto University student who committed suicide stated:

> The only significance of life is to enter Tokyo University, which is the best in Japan. When I entered Kyoto University, students and professors here looked so inferior to those in Tokyo. The fact that I entered this university worsened my nervous condition, contrary to my mother's expectations. I could not be proud of being a student here.

Another Kyoto University student, who majored in law, entered the university after two years as a *rōnin*. One of his last letters addressed to a university counselor reads:

> During the latter half of my *rōnin* days, I fell into a slump because of overwork, I think. I studied all the time except about six hours a day, when I slept. I had no physical exercise and suffered from tension, which is expected from a person before the entrance examination. I had a sort of neurasthenia.
>
> Then I entered Kyoto University. If I had been accepted by Tokyo University, probably my neurasthenia would have been cured because of the sense of achievement and satisfaction. However, being a Kyoto University student did not give me that satisfaction, although I tried to take pride in it.

His life history shows that after he failed the examination to Tokyo University twice, he still wanted to make another try but was not really confident. Then his mother persuaded him to try Kyoto University instead. After his acceptance by that university, he apparently felt that had he applied to Tokyo he would have been accepted.

In terms of academic standards, Kyoto University is not necessarily inferior to Tokyo. In some academic disciplines, Kyoto may be evaluated as even better than Tokyo University. Most of the Nobel Prize winners from Japan are Kyoto University graduates. Probably the students described were projecting their own inferiority feelings onto the university, but status prejudice as applied to educational institutions is common in Japan.

The status hierarchy of educational institutions is observable in the United States, too, but there is a great degree of mobility among American universities; a student can transfer to a "better" institution when he proves his ability. Moreover, the consistency between the rank of a university and the prestige of available positions for its graduates is much greater in Japan. For example, the most coveted high governmental positions in the country have been virtually monopolized by Tokyo University graduates.

Stress caused by the status hierarchy of educational institutions is reinforced by costly preparation. The Japanese student does not typically work for money, and there is very little prospect of employment for high-school students. Consequently, their long preparation for the college-entrance examination is a heavy financial burden upon their parents when the parents are not well-to-do. The most typical victim of this situation is the *rōnin*, who feels "pushed to the wall." The cost is prohibitive for children from poor families, because working one's way through college, which is exceptional in Japan, is even more so for *rōnin*. If he is from a rural area, he has to leave his parents' home and live in one of the big cities, where about 130 cram schools for high-school graduates (*yobiko*) are concentrated. When a student's family scrimps for every penny for his education, the emotional cost is extremely high for all of the family members. If the student fails under such conditions, his sense of guilt may be overwhelming.

Since stress during the long, wearisome, and costly preparation for the entrance examination not only affects young people's physical and mental health adversely but also stifles their inquisitiveness into natural wonders, sensitivity to beauty, potential to create, and capability to appreciate and to love, changes in the examination system have been proposed many times, but the situation has not improved. The system appears to operate with the blessings of the nation's conservative leaders.[17] A primary value of Japanese culture is persistence (*gambaru*), which implies not only the ability to delay gratification and to endure hardship but also "the ability to practice, to repeat and repeat again without the slightest variation."[18] Therefore, an examination that tests long and arduous memorization fits well into the culture.

Another factor that intensifies the Japanese concern with the entrance examination is parental pressure. A father in Nagoya took his own life because he "lost face when his son was rejected by a prominent secondary school."[19] Concern with the entrance examination is a central issue in family plans. The Japan Broadcasting Corporation made a survey of persons who were transferred from Tokyo. The subjects were asked if they would go to the new place of work alone or take their families, and why. When Japanese workers are transferred, they usually do not know how long they will be away; it might be for two or three years or for an entire lifetime. To the question, 80 percent of the respondents with high-school children, 50 percent of those with junior-high-school children, and 20 percent with elementary-school children stated that they would go alone, because the children should stay in school in Tokyo to better prepare themselves for the entrance examinations to good universities.[20]

A mother in Sakai beat her three-year-old daughter so severely that the child died. The mother did so because the girl could not write her own name, and the mother thought that the ability to do so was a requirement for admission to a good kindergarten. A mother's pressure upon her child is intense at least partly because of her own frustration. Strong sex prejudice in Japan ascribes heavy responsibility but few rights to the mother. In many cases, her own need for satisfaction is ignored. Dr. Sho Narabayashi contends that many Japanese wives become frigid because they are neglected by their husbands, who carry on extramarital affairs. Because of the lack of legal protection and job opportunities, wives do not seek divorce. They find an outlet for their frustration in pushing their children in educational competition.[21] Sex prejudice also deprives Japanese women of the opportunity for developing their intellectual potentials or of other means for satisfying their need for self-actualization. Their desire for development is therefore channeled into pressuring the child.

The emphasis on education also makes for the overprotection of children. Typically, Japanese boys are exempt from all tasks other than studying so that they can concentrate their attention and energy in order to better prepare for entrance examinations. To the question, "Do you have a chore to perform at home?" 89 percent of male and 97 percent of female students in American junior high schools and high schools answered affirmatively. In contrast, only 30 percent of male and 69 percent of female students in Japan did so. Those who answered that they had "no chore to do at home" amounted to only 1 percent for both American male and female students, but the comparable figures for Japanese students were 47 percent and 30 percent for males and females, respectively. Overprotectiveness and consequent dependence make maternal pressure more effective.

FINANCIAL INSECURITY

It is generally the poor who commit suicide in Japan. The suicide rate per 100,000 population in Japan in April, May, and June of 1974 was 15.5 for unemployed males in contrast to 4.6 for employed men, and the comparable rates for Japanese females were 7.4 and 2.5, respectively (table 18). Among the employed, the rate is higher for occupations that require less education. The highest rates for males fifteen years old and over during the period were shown for those in mining, farming and fishing, clerical, and service work (table 19). Professionals and those in managerial positions had the lowest suicide rates.

Financial insecurity is also an important cause of Japanese youths' suicides. In a Kyoto study, 78.2 percent of the suicidal subjects without a father had financial difficulties.[22] "Economic conditions of the family" and "money problems as perceived by the subject" are important causes of our university-student subjects' suicides (table 12:4). "Money problems" includes the inability to pay tuition and fees without a scholarship or part-time work. The typical Japanese college student does not work for money, except for occasional tutoring, and the money earned by tutoring is at most a minor supplement to what the students receive from their parents or scholarships.

An example of the effect of financial difficulty upon suicide is that of a twenty-two-year-old student majoring in science. His mother worked as a cleaning woman at a university hospital. His father had

TABLE 18.

UNEMPLOYMENT AND SUICIDE RATE AMONG PERSONS 15 AND OLDER IN
APRIL, MAY, AND JUNE 1974 BY SEX
(per 100,000)

	Total	Male	Female
Total	5.9	6.8	5.1
Unemployed	9.4	15.5	7.4
Employed	3.8	4.6	2.5

SOURCE: Kōseisho (Ministry of Health and Welfare), *Jisatsu Shibō Tōkei* [Suicidal death statistics] (1977), p. 18.

died when the subject was four years old, and he and his mother lived alone. The mother worked hard just to send him to the university, placing in the son all her hopes for future security. When the son failed to live up to her expectations, his sense of guilt was unbearable, as shown in the following note to his mother:

> Not fulfilling your dream or hope, I am determined to kill myself. I cannot help dying with contempt for myself as the scum of society and an ungrateful coward. My mother's incessant but miserable efforts . . . all were beyond what I deserved. I don't know how to apologize to my mother. When I think of my hardworking mother, laboring without rest, I cannot die despite myself. I even think I should take her with me. For about two years, this kind of thought haunted my mind.

The writer of this note had failed in his schoolwork, but the failure was at least partly due to his financial worries, which not only prevented him from concentrating on his studies but also affected his confidence and social relations adversely.

ETHNIC PREJUDICE ──────────────────────────

Defiance of the established social order is an important cause of suicide in Japan. Strong ethnic prejudice, however, sometimes impels young people to defiance. In comparison with the situation in the United

TABLE 19.

SUICIDE RATES BY OCCUPATION FOR MALES, 15 AND OLDER, APRIL, MAY, AND JUNE 1974
(per 100,000)

Total employed	4.6
Professional, technical	3.1
Managerial	2.9
Clerical	6.8
Sales	3.1
Farming, fishing	8.1
Mining	12.9
Transportation, communication	4.0
Craftsman, operatives	3.8
Service workers	4.9

SOURCE: Kōseisho (Ministry of Health and Welfare), *Jisatsu Shibō Tōkei* [Suicidal death statistics] (1977), p. 18.

States, minority groups in Japan have much less opportunity to air their frustrations. A brief history of the Japanese attitude toward Koreans will shed light on the problems of Koreans in Japan.

In ancient times many Koreans came, or were brought, to Japan. Many of them were teachers of philosophy, arts, and technology; many more were laborers and slaves. In modern Japan, Koreans were people to be dominated. Through the "Incorporation of Korea" (*Nikkan Gappei*) in 1910, Korea virtually became a colony of Japan. In order to educate Koreans to be loyal so that there would be no worry about their betrayal in case of emergency, Koreans were taught to memorize and recite constantly·

> I am a subject of the Great Japanese Empire.
> We shall cooperate and be loyal to the Empire of Japan.
> We shall endure difficulties and discipline ourselves, so that we shall be model subjects of Japan.[23]

Koreans were forced to wear only Japanese clothes, and their names were changed to Japanese names, although—with a few exceptions—they were never given Japanese citizenship. Koreans were stereotyped as violent, untrustworthy outlaws, and during the period following the Great Kanto earthquake in 1923, thousands of Koreans were murdered by Japanese who were afraid of Korean uprisings. In World War II, over 35,000 Koreans were conscripted into the Japanese armed forces. Additional tens of thousands were forced to serve as laborers, and thousands of Korean women were forced to serve as prostitutes for Japanese soldiers. These prostitutes were euphemistically called *ianfu* ("comfort girls") and served even in the front lines of battlefields. When they were wounded, they were abandoned or shot.[24] More than 200,000 Koreans were among the 2 million Japanese who were killed or who were missing in action during the war. There were 50,000 Koreans among the casualties of atomic bombs at Hiroshima and Nagasaki. About one of every four civilians who died in Hiroshima on August 6, 1945, was a Korean.

Today there are about 600,000 Koreans in Japan, about three-quarters of whom were born, reared, and educated in that country. They speak only Japanese, but most of them are still not allowed citizenship. They are ineligible to vote; they must carry registration cards at all times and are required by law to show the card upon request. When such a person studies abroad, he must return to Japan every year in order to renew his registration (Japanese citizens do not have to do so). Any violation of the law is severely punished.

Even against some Koreans who are allowed to be naturalized, prejudice is both intensive and extensive. "Koreans have difficulty gaining entrance into Japanese schools. Their ethnic schools are not recognized by Japanese universities. There is no possibility of public employment, but in private industry they face hiring discrimination as undesirable foreigners. Unemployment is a major phenomenon."[25] Occasionally, because of the Japanese names Koreans assume, they may be hired by Japanese companies, but when their Korean backgrounds are revealed they are likely to be dismissed. Despite their being Japanese in all respects except that of their parents' alien-registration cards, second- and third-generation Koreans in Japan are barraged by insults and slurs. One twelve-year-old Korean in Kamifukuoka, north of Tokyo, could no longer take the taunts of his schoolmates and committed suicide.

Another example of the prejudice against naturalized Koreans is the case of Masaaki Tamura, a student at Second (evening) Waseda University. Because of his resentment of anti-Korean prejudice, Tamura joined a radical student group. Many such groups fight against one another; they often resort to violence and harass members of competing groups rather than cooperating with each other for a better future. Tamura was a victim of violence and harassment, which prevented him from attending classes. The result was his failure in schoolwork. His suicide note, addressed to his university, expresses frustration anger, and despair:

> This is a demonstration of resistance to present-day Japan by a person who has wriggled for twenty-five years at the bottom of this society, because of his Korean ancestry.
>
> I was born in Japan, the second generation from Korea. Koreans here still live under the colonialistic control of Japanese people. Even if it was not my intention, I was naturalized as a Japanese by my parents. The naturalization has simply aggravated my suffering, because while I cannot be treated as a Japanese, I am a betrayer to the Korean people and the land of my fathers.
>
> I entered Waseda University in order to learn and to pursue truth, but . . . I was deprived of my freedom to attend the university; my life was disrupted, and my aspirations were broken.
>
> Facing death, what I want is for the university to provide assistance to those students who struggle to continue their studies. . . . Decent students should be protected from physical danger and economic bankruptcy caused by violent students who threaten them, and they should regain their legitimate rights as university students.

五

V

FEMALE
SUICIDES

PERSONALITY ─────────────────────────────

Unlike young Japanese males, whose suicide is primarily motivated by despair (or the "wish to die") (see table 8), young Japanese female suicides are primarily motivated by "externally directed aggression" (or the "wish to kill"). The "wish to kill" is the primary motive in about half of the suicides of Japanese females twenty to thirty-nine years old (table 20). The proportion (47%) is higher than that of age-comparable Japanese males (15%) or of age-comparable American males and females (31% and 32%, respectively). Although suicides of Japanese females under twenty years old were primarily motivated by despair (45%), like those of their male counterparts, their second motive was the "wish to kill" (30%), in contrast with their male counterparts, whose second motive was the "wish to be killed." Only 8 percent of suicides of Japanese males of this age group were motivated by the "wish to kill." The "wish to kill" is the primary motive for suicides

TABLE 20.

CLASSIFICATION OF SUICIDE NOTES WRITTEN BY FEMALES:
JAPANESE IN TOKYO (1948–1978)
AND CAUCASIANS IN LOS ANGELES (1944–1953)
(by percent)

	Number	Wish to kill	Wish to be killed	Wish to die	Unclassified
Total					
Japanese	243	34.6	14.4	41.1	9.9
Caucasian	130	25.0	15.0	41.0	19.0
19 and under					
Japanese	27	29.6	22.2	44.5	3.7
20–39					
Japanese	135	46.6	16.3	30.4	6.7
Caucasian	38	32.0	21.0	21.0	26.0
40–59					
Japanese	46	15.2	15.2	56.6	13.0
Caucasian	52	29.0	17.0	29.0	25.0
60 and over					
Japanese	35	17.1	0	60.0	22.9
Caucasian	40	15.0	5.0	75.0	5.0

SOURCE: Jushiro Koshinaga, "Jisatsu to Isho" [Suicide and suicide notes], *Nihon Hōigaku Zasshi* [Japanese forensic journal] 33, 5 (1979): 476.

of both Japanese and Caucasian females in the age category of twenty to thirty-nine years (47% and 32%, respectively). Apparently, young female suicides both in Japan and the United States are primarily motivated by externally directed aggression—more than is true of their male counterparts—but the degree of aggression is higher among Japanese than among American females.

The importance of externally directed aggression in Japanese female suicides is also indicated by psychological tests. Those Japanese females who are self-assertive and who direct aggression externally are overrepresented in suicide statistics. In comparison with a control group matched for age and class status, Japanese female suicide attempts showed a significantly higher degree of impetuosity (*sokukō-sei*), unstable temperament (*kibun ihen-sei*), ostentation (*jiko kenjisei*), explo-

TABLE 21.

MOTIVES OF SUICIDES OF JAPANESE FEMALES FOR APRIL, MAY, AND JUNE 1974
(PERCENTAGE OF MOTIVES KNOWN)

Motives Known	Total	19 and under	20–29	30–49	50–59	60 and over
Number	1,753	44	303	396	219	841
	99.9%	100.0%	100.0%	100.0%	100.0%	100.0%
Illness and physical defect	54.4	16.0	19.1	38.0	59.4	76.2
Marital problem	10.6	2.3	19.8	19.2	9.6	3.9
Family problem	14.3	16.0	14.8	17.4	17.8	11.4
Heterosexual affair	8.8	36.3	30.1	11.6	0.5	0.1
Financial problem	1.6	0	1.0	4.4	2.8	0.3
Occupational problem	2.4	2.3	6.2	2.9	3.7	0.2
Schoolwork problem	0.6	13.6	1.9	0	0	0
"Being tired of life"	1.6	2.3	1.4	1.3	1.8	1.9
Other	5.6	11.4	5.7	5.2	4.5	6.0

SOURCE: Ministry of Welfare, *Jisatsu Shibō Tōkei* [Suicidal death statistics] (1977), p. 23.

siveness (*bakuhatsu-sei*), compulsiveness (*kyōhaku-sei*), high susceptibility to environmental pressure (*ishi-ketsujo-sei*), depression (*yokuutsu-sei*), aesthenia (*muryoku-sei*), and oversensitiveness (*kakan-sei*).[1] The Thurstone test showed that suicide attempters were significantly lower than control-group subjects on vigor or vitality, stability, and impulsiveness. (High scores on impulsiveness indicate a happy-go-lucky and carefree person who makes decisions quickly, enjoys competition, and changes easily from one task to another.)

These characteristics point to a hysterical personality, characterized by egotism, vanity, ostentation, emotional instability, and extreme susceptibility to suggestion. The female with such traits has great difficulty in both reality testing and impulse control, and in Japan these traits are incompatible with the traditional female role, which requires a woman to be dependent, conforming, deferential, reserved, self-abasing, self-sacrificing, and yet hardworking. A twenty-five-year-old female poisoned herself and left a note to her unfaithful husband: "You have tortured me until the very end. Wait and see how I will take revenge on you." This woman is not Japanese-like. The Japanese wife is expected to blame herself rather than her husband and to endure the husband's misdeed. An extramarital affair is often regarded as a privilege of a worthy man.

PRECIPITATING CAUSES

The Japanese Ministry of Welfare found in 1977 that the most important cause of Japanese female suicides overall was illness and physical defects (54%), followed by family problems (14%), marital problems (11%), and heterosexual affairs (9%) (table 21). Table 22 shows similar findings in Tokyo, except that "being tired of life" and "unrequited love," especially for youth, are more important in big cities than in rural areas.

In order to shed light on the nature of "family problems," "marital problems" and "heterosexual affairs," the motives underlying suicides of unmarried and married females are considered. According to Professor Hisao Naka's study in 1955–1959, 56 percent of unmarried females' suicides in Kyoto were caused by love affairs, including 25 percent due to "unrequited love," 16 percent to "no parental permission for marriage," 10 percent to "pregnancy without a promise of marriage," and 6 percent to an "affair with a married man" (table 23). These data show traditional causes of unmarried Japanese female suicides. Naka states that suicides because of love affairs have increased in recent

TABLE 22.

Motives of Suicides of Japanese Females in Tokyo, 1974

	Total		Under 25	
	Number	*Percent*	*Number*	*Percent*
Total	1,683	100.0%	525	100.0%
Mental illness	341	20.3	76	14.5
Physical illness	304	18.1	25	4.8
Family problem	217	12.9	48	9.1
Financial problem	20	1.2	3	.6
Marital problem	117	7.0	43	8.2
Extramarital affair	107	6.4	38	7.2
Unrequited love	239	14.2	158	30.1
School problem	12	.7	11	2.1
"Being tired of life"	228	13.5	77	14.7
Other	98	5.8	46	8.8

SOURCE: Hiroshi Inamura, *Jisatsugaku* [Suicidology] (Tokyo: University of Tokyo Press, 1977), p. 60.

years,[2] although "parental permission for marriage" has lost its strength somewhat.

About half of the suicides of married women were caused by marital problems, including "marital disharmony" (20%), "the husband having extramarital affairs" (15%), and "breakups" (including the husband's desertion) (13%). (These are percentages of those whose suicidal motives were known, and the figures may be larger if suicide motives of all subjects were known.) Females in the twenty-five-to-twenty-nine age group are especially vulnerable to suicide when their husbands have extramarital affairs; this was the motive behind 27 percent of the suicides committed by Japanese females within this age group (table 24).

Such motives as "pregnancy without a promise of marriage," "husband's extramarital affair," and "breakups," not to mention "no parental permission for marriage," suggest strong sexism as the primary cause of the traditional Japanese female suicides. Without severe prejudice these situations probably would not result in suicides. It is to be noted that these findings were obtained about ten years after the enactment of the new Constitution in 1947, which specifically forbade discrimination in political, economic, or social relations because of sex as well as because of race, creed, social status, or family origin.

TABLE 23.

KINDS OF LOVE AFFAIR AS CAUSES OF SUICIDES AMONG UNMARRIED FEMALES 29 OR UNDER IN KYOTO, 1956–1959

(by occupation)

	Total		Love affair total	Affair with a married man	Pregnancy without promise of marriage	Unrequited love	No parental permission for marriage	Other
Total Number	183		103	10	18	45	30	80
Percent	100.0%		(56.3%)	(5.5%)	(9.8%)	(24.6%)	(16.4%)	(43.7%)
Nurse		3.3	3	—	—	2	1	3
Clerk		9.8	8	—	—	5	3	10
Sales		4.9	1	1	—	—	—	8
Helping family farm		0.5	1	—	1	—	—	—
Factory worker		18.6	17	1	2	8	6	17
Domestic service		7.7	9	3	3	3	—	5
Waitress		15.3	19	4	4	9	2	9
Beautician		6.0	8	—	1	2	5	3
Student		5.5	4	—	2	2	—	6
Unemployed		28.4	33	1	5	14	13	16

SOURCE: M. Kosaka and N. Usui, *Nihonjin no Jisatsu* [Suicide of Japanese People] (Tokyo: Sōbunsha, 1966), p. 78.

TABLE 24.

Family Relationship of Married Women Who Committed Suicide in Kyoto, 1956–1959
(by age)

Age	Total		Marital problems						Other problems			
			Husband's extramarital affair		Disharmony between spouses		Breakup		Family disharmony		Other	
	N	%	N	%	N	%	N	%	N	%	N	%
Total:	201	100.0%	31	15.2	40	19.9	27	13.4	22	10.9	81	40.6
24 and under	44	100.0%	8	18.2	10	22.7	8	18.2	8	18.2	10	22.7
25–29	41	100.0%	11	26.8	7	17.1	7	17.1	5	12.2	11	26.8
30–39	44	100.0%	7	15.9	13	29.5	6	13.6	3	6.8	15	34.1
40–49	40	100.0%	2	5.0	7	17.5	5	12.5	3	7.5	23	57.5
50–59	32	100.0%	3	9.4	3	9.4	1	3.1	3	9.4	22	68.8

SOURCE: M. Kosaka and N. Usui, *Nihonjin no Jisatsu* [Suicide of Japanese People] (Tokyo: Sōbunsha, 1966), p. 78.

TABLE 25.

"IF YOU COULD BE BORN AGAIN, WOULD YOU RATHER BE A MAN OR A WOMAN?"
JAPANESE IN JAPAN AND PERSONS OF JAPANESE ANCESTRY IN HAWAII

Female Respondents	Total		Would rather be:		Other
	Number	%	Man	Woman	
			%		%
1958	765	100	64	27	9
1963	1,446	100	55	36	9
1968	1,606	100	43	48	9
1973	2,534	100	42	51	12
Hawaii (1971)	205	100	15	73	12

Male Respondents	Total		Would rather be:		Other
	Number	%	Man	Woman	
			%		%
1958	684	100	90	5	5
1963	1,252	100	88	7	5
1968	1,427	100	89	5	6
1973	2,063	100	89	5	6
Hawaii (1971)	229	100	92	3	5

SOURCES: *Dai-san Nihonjin no Kokuminsei* [Social character of Japanese people], no. 3 (Tokyo: Shiseido, 1975), p. 52. Institute of Statistical Mathematics, *A Study of Japanese Americans in Honolulu, Hawaii* (research report) (1973), p. 26.

SEX PREJUDICE ——————————————————————

Since the enactment of the new Constitution, the status of Japanese women has risen considerably, as shown by the response to the question: "If you could be born again, would you rather be a man or a woman?" The percentage of Japanese women who wished to be reborn as women rose from 27 percent in 1958 to 51 percent in 1973 and 52 percent in 1978. However, the figure is still very low in comparison with a 1971 study in which 73 percent of women of Japanese ancestry residing in Hawaii wished to be reborn as women (table 25).

As Robert Christopher observed, "Japan moved directly from feudalism into the industrial age. As a consequence, attitudes and behavior patterns characteristic of a feudal society are still more prevalent in Japan than in the West."[3] One of the most marked feudalistic remnants

TABLE 26.

"WHAT DO YOU THINK ABOUT THE IDEA THAT WOMAN IS INFERIOR TO MAN?"
1975
(by percent)

	It is natural	Cannot help it	Not good	Don't know
Total	20%	52%	18%	10%
Male	23	54	14	9
Female	18	51	20	11

SOURCE: Japanese Government Premier's Office, reproduced in *Jurist: Gendai no Jyosei* [Modern women], no. 6 (June 1976), p. 304.

is sex prejudice. The Japanese Government Premier's Office reported in 1975 that when Japanese people were asked whether they would or would not endorse the idea that woman is inferior to man, 77 percent of males and 69 percent of females answered, "It is natural" or "Cannot help it," while only 14 percent of males and 20 percent of females disapproved (table 26). Japanese mores also dictate that a woman should quit her employment upon marrying or giving birth. This idea was accepted by nearly 80 percent of both Japanese men and women, including "It is natural" and "Cannot help it." The idea was rejected by only 12 percent of the males and 13 percent of the females (table 27).

TABLE 27.

"WHAT DO YOU THINK ABOUT THE INFORMAL RULE THAT WOMEN QUIT
WORK IN BUSINESS WORLD AT MARRIAGE OR CHILDBIRTH?"
(by percent)

	It is natural	Cannot help it	Not good	Don't know
Total	19%	60%	13%	8%
Male	22	58	12	8
Female	17	61	13	9

SOURCE: Japanese Government Premier's Office, reproduced in *Jurist: Gendai no Jyosei* [Modern women], no. 6 (June 1976), p. 304.

TABLE 28.

"WHAT DO YOU THINK ABOUT THE PRACTICE THAT WOMEN GET LESS
WAGES OR ARE PROMOTED MORE SLOWLY THAN MEN WHO DO THE
SAME WORK?" RESPONDENTS IN SELECTED COUNTRIES, 1975
(by percent)

	Total	It is natural	Cannot help it	Not good	Don't know
Japan	190	11.5%	47.9%	28.4%	12.2%
United States	228	0.4	5.3	90.8	3.5
Britain	90	3.3	3.3	77.8	5.6
France	93	2.2	1.1	88.2	8.6
West Germany	125	0	6.4	90.4	3.2
Sweden	110	0	5.5	92.7	1.8
Thailand	99	3.0	3.0	82.8	11.1
Hong Kong	74	2.7	5.4	85.1	6.8

SOURCE: Japanese Government Premier's Office, cross-cultural survey, October 1975, quoted in *Jurist: Gendai no Jyosei* [Modern women], no. 3 (June 1976), p. 306.

The practice by which women receive smaller wages and/or fewer promotions than do men in the same employment was disturbing to only 28 percent of Japanese respondents, in comparison with 91 percent of the Americans, 78 percent of the British, 88 percent of the French, and more than 90 percent of the West Germans and of the Swedes. Japan is apparently even more sexist than other modernized Asian nations, such as Thailand and Hong Kong, based on the frequency of responses (83% and 85%, respectively) to the question in table 28.

The combination of the nature of family life, educational attitudes, and informal policies and practices in the employment world makes it difficult to convert the traditional reality of sexual inequality to that of sexual equality. The difficulty is enhanced by the Japanese propensity toward the juxtaposition of contradictory ideas[4] without an attempt at logical and ideological integration. Moreover, the equality ideal itself was imposed upon the Japanese by the American occupation forces, and it therefore tends to erode with the resurgence of Japanese traditionalism since the 1950s. With the relative decline of American prestige, Japanese people appear to be on a "restorationism" swing.

Sex discrimination in Japan assigns heavy responsibilities but few rights to women. A woman is supposed to follow men throughout her life. If a husband is profligate, his wife is blamed for providing a poor home atmosphere. If a child fails in school, it is due to his mother's lack of supervision and guidance. A thirty-one-year-old mother's son became ill, and she feared that this would cause family disharmony. She blamed herself for the entire situation, saying:

> I do not understand why my life has become so unhappy. I have given trouble to my ill mother. Because I put Kazuyoshi [the son] in the day-care center, he got ill, and I don't know what his illness is. I am sorry. This way, I shall ruin everybody's life.
> I regret that I have given much trouble to everybody. Papa [husband], please take care of Kazuyoshi. I have wished to commit *shinju* [multiple suicides], but I could not persuade you. Please forgive this willful me.

Even when a wife is neglected by a husband who engages in extra-marital affairs, she is not expected to rebel. She does not usually seek divorce, because legal protection and job opportunities are lacking. The Japanese divorce rate was 1.09 per 1,000 population in 1975, and divorce is traditionally an alternative available only to educated female professionals earning a stable income.[5] Considering the difficulties after divorce, the more likely alternative for ordinary Japanese women who believe they have failed in building a happy family is to resign themselves to the situation.

Therefore, for a majority of Japanese women it is imperative to hold onto one's husband. In order to do so, the wife is required to be tolerant of her husband's defects, including unfaithfulness. When she is not tolerant, she may be pushed to suicide. When the forty-four-year-old wife of an official of a construction company found out that her husband went on a trip with his lover, she killed herself, leaving the note: "I cannot believe in anything. Even if I live on, I can expect nothing good."

The problem of Japanese women which can lead to suicide is typically exemplified by the *naien* relationship, meaning "marriage without legal certification." There are many reasons for not applying for marriage licenses, such as not having parental permission, the "husband's" having a legal wife, or the desire to wait until the first birth. However, frequently the real reason involves irresponsibility on the part of the man. Women are often willing to become "kept women," mostly for economic reasons, although they may later find the situation intolerable for various reasons. At that point such women find that the laws and society as a whole are full of condemnation, regarding them as "loose" women.

Naka found in Kyoto that 18.3 percent of suicidal females were involved in *naien* relationships, in contrast to only 2.7 percent of women in the general population.[6] Of suicides involving females between twenty and twenty-four years of age, 29.3 percent were in *naien* relationships. The women were mostly waitresses, geishas, and domestic servants. Reasons for these suicides were "the husband's parents not permitting the marriage" (32%) and "the husband having a legal wife" (24%). Because of the Japanese modernization in the past decade or so, the *naien* relationship appears to have lost much of its significance in relation to suicide. However, its significance is still considerable in rural areas, and the practice of becoming "kept women" for financial reasons is still frequently observable among those women engaged in "entertainment" businesses. The prejudice against these "entertainment" (*sekkyakugyō*) women as possible legal spouses is still strong.

Two consequences of sex prejudice are especially important factors in Japanese female suicides: financial insecurity, which contributes importantly to fatalistic suicides, and role conflict, which contributes to anomic suicides.

FINANCIAL INSECURITY

The financial insecurity of Japanese females is suggested by the figures in table 29. Of all modern nations, Japan has the lowest ratio of the average female wage to the average male wage. Japan is the only country where the average wage for women in 1972 was less than half that of men. Japan also has one of the highest ratios of female suicides as compared to male suicides, which seems to show the close relationship between financial insecurity and suicide in that country (table 30).

According to Naka's Kyoto study, of 288 employed females who committed suicide, 29 percent were waitresses and beauticians, 28 percent were factory workers, and 15 percent were clerks (table 31). The highest suicide rate per 100,000 population in the fifteen-to-nineteen age group was shown by nurses (290.7), followed by waitresses (75.7) and domestic servants (51.8). The highest rate within the age group from twenty to twenty-four involved farm women (234.8), followed by waitresses (169.2) and domestic servants (107.4). Waitresses and domestic servants also showed higher rates among older females. These are all low-prestige occupations with small or unstable incomes.

Americans may wonder why nursing is a low-prestige occupation in Japan. Nursing is traditionally regarded as a "dirty" occupation, and, therefore, ordinary Japanese girls tend to despise and avoid it.

TABLE 29.

RATIO OF FEMALE WORKERS' AVERAGE WAGES TO THOSE OF MALES,
1963 AND 1972

	1963 %	Rank order	1972 %	Rank order	Difference %
Japan	44.2	10	47.5	10	+ 3.3
Sweden	72.1	1	83.2	1	+11.1
Australia	69.8	2	76.1	3	+ 6.3
West Germany	68.7	3	70.7	5	+ 2.0
Denmark	68.6	4	77.9	2	+ 9.3
Finland	66.7	5	71.3	4	+ 4.7
Switzerland	62.7	6	64.7	6	+ 2.0
Belgium	60.3	7	64.4	7	+ 4.1
England	57.2	8	59.3	8	+ 2.1
Ireland	57.2	9	57.2	9	0

SOURCE: Yasusaburo Hoshino, "Jyosei to Jinken" [Female and human rights], *Jurist: Gendai no Jyosei* (June 5, 1976), p. 35.

This attitude is rooted in the Shinto abhorrence of pollution as evil and in the Confucian contempt for menial and manual work, together with the samurai emphasis on "appearance" (that is, obsessive concern with how one appears in the eyes of others). In 1973 the qualification for applying for nursing was a junior-high-school level of education. Nobuhiko Matsugi counts nursing as one of the few occupations in which *burakumin* (formerly *eta,* "outcastes") are concentrated.[7] Because of the shortage of applicants for nursing jobs, hospitals recruit nurses from poor families in Korea. It is said that about 7,000 Korean nurses are working in Japan and that their status is not much better than that of indentured servants.[8]

For the most part, class consciousness, based on economic status difference, has declined in Japan. However, consciousness of status difference—that is, difference in an individual's prestige relative to others'—still strongly prevails, leaving lower-status females vulnerable to exploitation. Since poor women have almost no choice in the selection of jobs and since social welfare programs are underdeveloped, these women, like divorcees, tend to enter *sekkyakugyō* ("entertainment" work, with emphasis on sex appeal). *Sekkyakugyō* is a big industry in the present-day Japanese economy; its earnings total more than 1 *chō* (trillion) yen per year. Despite the industry's prosperity,

TABLE 30.

SEX RATIO OF SUICIDES (1973) AND OF AVERGE WAGES (1972)

	Sex ratio of:	
	Suicide rate[a]	Average wages[b]
Japan	73	48
England	66	59
Denmark	63	78
West Germany	54	71
Australia	48	76
Belgium	47	64
Sweden	41	83
Switzerland	39	65
United States (1975)	37	62
Ireland	36	57
Finland	27	71

[a]Female suicide rate/male suicide rate × 100
[b]Average female wages/average male wages × 100

SOURCE: *Jurist* (June 1976), p. 35; Stuart Picken, *Nihonjin no Jisatsu* [Suicide of Japanese people] (Tokyo: Simul Press, 1979), p. 272.

its employees generally are not affluent, and they often have to supplement their incomes by selling sexual favors. Ever since Monzaemon Chikamatsu's glorification in his seventeenth-century plays of *shinjū* (love-pact suicides), most of which involved *sekkyakugyō* girls, the correlation between high suicide rates and *sekkyakugyō* girls has been a strong one.

Despite the importance of financial insecurity in female suicides, women's suicide notes seldom specify economic difficulty as a cause. A fourteen-year-old girl who drowned herself in 1970 presents an exception. Her suicide note shows despair due to poverty, in addition to altruism:

> My family is so poor that my ill mother cannot go to a doctor. My medical treatment is expensive. Mother, please use the money in my place. I regret that I could not repay the *on* [favor, or obligation to repay] from Father, Mother, Older Brother and Sister. Recalling the various sufferings which I have endured, I am tired of living on this earth. Forgive me, Mother.
>
> From an undutiful daughter.

TABLE 31.

SUICIDE RATES OF EMPLOYED FEMALES IN KYOTO, 1955–1969, BY AGE AND OCCUPATION
(per 100,000)

	Total		15–19	20–24	25–29	30–39	40–49	50–59
	Number	%						
	576		84	189	87	84	72	60
Unemployed	288		22.1	67.5	29.6	23.5	20.5	28.4
Employed	288	100.2	52.8	80.1	59.5	25.4	28.4	26.4
Nurse	15	5.2	290.7	90.7	72.7	0	37.8	39.9
Other semiprofessional technical	2	1.0	—	50.4	—	—	—	—
Clerk	43	14.9	48.4	49.9	41.9	43.2	15.7	58.4
Sales	37	12.8	36.4	75.5	51.0	19.7	15.9	35.6
Farm	4	1.4	—	234.8	—	12.5	—	—
Factory work	81	28.1	39.7	70.4	72.9	33.7	36.2	32.7
Domestic service	23	8.0	51.8	107.4	113.3	74.4	69.1	—
Waitress, hostess, beautician	83	28.8	75.7	169.2	120.9	43.8	54.0	45.1

SOURCE: M. Kosaka and N. Usui, *Nihonjin no Jisatsu* [Suicide of Japanese people] (Tokyo: Sōbunsha, 1966), p. 80.

In addition to financial difficulties, sexism also produces role conflict. An example of role conflict leading to the suicide of a Japanese female is the case of Etsuko Takano. She committed suicide by jumping in front of a railway train at the age of twenty in June 1969. Etsuko was born in Tochigi Prefecture, about 100 miles north of Tokyo. She was a sensitive child, honest and straightforward. Although she was short in stature, even for a Japanese girl (the smallest in her classes), she was a good athlete; she excelled in swimming and was fond of playing table tennis in junior high school. She was a good student, with an interest in journalism. When she developed a mild heart ailment in high school, she had to drop all sports activities. She entered Ritsumeikan University in Kyoto. Her choice of Ritsumeikan was primarily motivated, it is said, by her interest in Professor Tatsuya Naramoto, the authority on the *buraku* (or *eta,* "outcaste") problem. Etsuko's interest in the *buraku* problem shows her critical attitude toward the Japanese tradition of caste prejudice. This critical attitude toward Japanese tradition operates as an inimical force in Japanese women. She participated in radical student movements, and she experienced the futility of their fight against the conservative government. She embraced Communism, attracted by the Communist Party's slogan "A better life for everybody." (It is noted that Japanese intellectuals who are critical of the feudalistic remnants of Japanese culture tend to be attracted to either Communism or Christianity, or more often to both. Both are regarded as representing universal and humanistic values, emphasizing selfhood and social conscience.)

In addition to her ideological frustration, Etsuko experienced a dependency conflict. Her decision to enter Ritsumeikan University, which was further away from her home than was Rikkyo University in Tokyo, which had also admitted her, reflected her wish to be independent of her parents. Since Etsuko's parents were well-to-do, she did not have to work (as is typical with female college students in Japan). However, she wanted to be as economically independent as possible, and she took a job as a waitress at a hotel restaurant. She found herself increasingly lonely and became attracted to a man at work, who was her superior. (He was most likely a man whom her parents would have not wanted her to marry, because of the class–status difference.)

Her seemingly unrequited love intensified her feeling of inferiority about her small size and about the heart condition that prevented her from participating in sports. Unable to endure the conflict and her feelings of inferiority, she chose to escape through suicide, leaving this note:

I go on a trip
With a sack on my back,
With a pack of cigarettes,
And a flute in my pocket.

I go on a trip.
I am pleased that it is raining as I leave,
Raining gently like mist.
A rainy day in the Spring,
Buds sprouting
Wet and soft.

I go into the virgin forest,
Said to be in Mount Fuji
Leisurely without haste.
When I come to a big old cedar
I rest in the dark shadow under the tree.
Then I smoke a cigarette
Made by a monopolistic capitalist.
To the smoke, smelling of modern society,
How do you react, Old Tree?

I search for a lake,
Supposed to be in the virgin forest.
Lingering on the shore
I smoke a cigarette,
Exhaling all smoke,
I will rest by my pack.

When the forest is enveloped by darkness
I will float a little boat.

Taking off all my clothes,
Having my smooth skin wrapped with darkness,
With the flute in my left hand,
Drifting on the dark lake,
I play on the flute.

In the faint rippling murmur surrounding me,
Letting the heavenly breeze flow around my body,

I will quietly sleep,
Only to let the flute sink
To the deep bottom of the lake.

The note shows that Etsuko shared the Japanese tendencies to beautify the saddest experience and to identify closely with Nature.

ETHNIC PREJUDICE

Frustration from role conflict between the expectations of the submissive female and the modern conception of the individual human being is keenest among those who suffer from double prejudice against the female and the outcaste. The most typical caste group in Japan is called *burakumin* (formerly called *eta,* literally, "full of dirt"). *Burakumin* means "people of a *buraku* or hamlet," but in present-day Japan it specifically means "people of an *eta* settlement." The *burakumin* status is inherited and immutable. There were approximately 1,860,000 *burakumin* in 1963, residing in about 500 segregated communities. (Some say that there are nearly 3 million *burakumin,* in about 5,000 communities.)

In the beginning of the Tokugawa Period (1600–1868), in order to solidify its control the government imposed a strict caste stratification on the populace: warriors, farmers, artisans, and merchants. All those whose family backgrounds were ambiguous were categorized as outcastes. The establishment of an outcaste group provided scapegoats for commoners, especially farmers. Despite their formal status, which was second only to samurai, farmers suffered most from severe taxations. Their sufferings were aggravated by frequent natural calamities. Samurai and their lords, whose income was measured by the amount of rice due them from their fiefs, were completely dependent on farmers. The more dependent they were, the more necessary it was for them to control the farmers. Their motto was *"Hyakushō wa ikasazu korosazu osamubeshi"* ("Control farmers in the condition between life and death"), so that peasants could not rebel. Because of heavy taxation by lords, farmers often could not eat the rice that they produced. Frustrated farmers used *eta* as scapegoats; they looked down on the *eta,* whose life was regarded as worth only one-seventh the lives of ordinary persons.

Today, *burakumin* are still largely segregated in residence, and they remain the target of severe prejudice. A few years ago at a PTA committee meeting, a *buraku* member found that her teacup was marked with a cross, so that other members would not make the mistake of touching the allegedly polluted cup. The primary method of maintaining anti-*burakumin* sentiment is through the census register. When Japanese people want to apply for employment, they have to present their family register. On the register, the place of birth and the permanent residence of each applicant is recorded. Thus, the register will indicate a possible *burakumin* background.

There is some statistical evidence of *burakumin* prejudice and its effects. According to a Kyoto study in 1960, the percentage of *burakumin* children who were not attending junior high school was 11.2 percent, which was about ten times greater than for non-*burakumin* children.[9] The percentage of nonattendance on the elementary school level was 3 percent for *burakumin*, seven times higher than the percentage for ordinary children. The primary reason for nonattendance by junior-high-school children in the *buraku* was "the necessity of helping the family" (56%), followed by illness (14%), "own indifference to, or dislike of, school" (14%), and "indifferent parents" (8%). The primary reason for nonattendance by elementary-school children from *buraku* families was illness (38%), followed by "own indifference to, or dislike of, school" (16%), parental indifference (11%), and "the necessity of helping the family" (6%).

Burakumin parents had greater financial difficulties. Thirty-two percent of *buraku* parents were employed as day laborers, in contrast to 5 percent of non-*buraku* parents. In the area studied, only 7 percent of *buraku* but 26 percent of non-*buraku* parents were "company employees," which meant economic security. Virtually all *buraku* parents were restricted to the production and selling of footware or to work dealing with dead bodies.

While there was not a significant IQ score difference between *burakumin* and non-*burakumin* at a Kyoto junior high school, the *burakumin* students, who comprised about half the student body, averaged lower grades than did non-*buraku* students by sixteen points in social studies, thirteen points in mathematics, ten points in science, and nine points in the Japanese language.[10] While 72 percent of non-*burakumin* junior-high-school students wanted to go to high school, with 28 percent intending to seek immediate employment, the numbers for *buraku* children were reversed: 23 percent aspired to enter high school, and 77 percent planned to apply for a job.

The prejudice against *burakumin* is severest when heterosexual relationships are involved. Often *buraku* girls fall in love with non-*buraku* youths, and when a premarriage investigation is conducted—an informal requirement for many marriages in Japan—and the girl's outcaste status is revealed, the possibility of marriage is usually terminated. It is said that about twenty cases of suicides by *buraku* girls occur annually because of the effects of caste prejudice on their romantic affairs. An example is the case of Mariko Fukumoto, a nurse who committed suicide in 1963 at the age of nineteen.

When Mariko received a marriage proposal from one of her former patients, she sought her father's permission, whereupon he told her that she was a *burakumin*. She reported the fact in a letter to her suitor, who reacted to the news with a change of heart. He probably had to consider not only his own future but also that of other members of his family; if he married a *burakumin,* it would have ruined his sisters' marital lives and all family members' future fortunes. After that, Mariko began to show intermittent signs of depression. Once a cheerful and sociable girl, she began to avoid social contact. She grieved in her diary:

> It is painful to meet people. I put up a fence lest they should read my mind, partly because of pride and partly because of my wish to let people see me as an ordinary person.
>
> Whenever I attempt to behave like an ordinary person, I am overwhelmed by the miserable and irritating feeling that I cannot really communicate with ordinary people. I want to talk just like others do. But something stops me. Something different from ordinary people makes me isolated.

Mariko's diary entry, which was written the day before her suicide, demonstrates her affection for her lover and for everyone around her, with a strong wish for belonging. She tried to convince herself that her lover had rejected her because he grew to dislike her rather than because of her *burakumin* status. Even on the verge of death she appears to have repressed what she was most fearful of—her outcaste status—emphasizing her own unworthiness in her first note.

> Father, forgive me for forsaking this precious life for my own selfish reasons. You have always supported me, but I cannot go on. You think that I am a nice daughter but in my real self I am a liar and a mean, stubborn egotist.
>
> I would prefer death to giving trouble to everybody and driving myself into an awful mess. The more I want to go straight, the more I am warped by my defiant character. I am afraid that I would cause trouble to other people, too. . . .
>
> I don't have the courage to live alone. I don't know how to express my feelings.

At any rate, I cannot do as other people do. Although I have not recognized it until now, I have something which I cannot correct. Weak-spirited, awkward, inconsiderate, careless, ignorant—I would like to correct these traits. My weak will makes me shrink in the presence of other people, and ruins all my hopes.

Please forgive this most undutiful action of mine. I have been possessed by the death spirit, and I am helpless. . . . Everything is lacking.

Mariko made her effort to avoid pain and perturbation by isolation, which aggravated her suffering. For the suffering she blamed herself. A result was further constriction. She wanted to correct what was lacking in her, but she knew that she could never do so. She gave up, saying "I have no will of my own." Caste prejudice was beyond her comprehension, but she felt its effects desperately, as evidenced by the second note.

Something is lacking in me.

I cannot think about other people's interests. I am an egoist, only concerned with myself. The more I try to correct this fault, the more I feel other people turning away from me, one after another.

I have no will of my own. From now on, I cannot escape from the agony. Since I began feeling other people's minds, I have come to feel even more miserable.

I may look human from the outside, but my inside is empty, stupid, dull-witted and self-isolating. What on earth is in me? I may be breathing, thanks to the support of parents and other people around me, but my real self is like a lifeless doll.

I should be more positive. But my mind shrinks in front of others. A narrow-minded, lifeless doll, unable to understand humor.

I wish to live. But something in me, like an abyss, leads me to death. Laugh at this egoistic me, call me by any foul name. But it is my decision. Nobody else has anything to do with this.

I am going to be twenty years old soon, but how weak my willpower is—weaker than that of a little child. No more can I escape from death.

Mariko says, "I may look human from the outside," but she implies that she is not treated as human. In the society where individuals are only status carriers, there is little recognition of the dignity of humanity in this thoughtful and affectionate individual.

VI

JAPANESE WRITERS' SUICIDES

In addition to the high frequency of suicides among Japanese writers, as mentioned in chapter 3, the strong concern with suicide among them is indicated by a large number of works with suicide as the primary theme.[1] The number of "suicide" novels or stories are as follows (writers who wrote fewer than five suicide novels or stories are not included):[2]

Writer	Number of "suicide" novels or stories
Yukio Mishima (committed suicide)	26
Yoshio Toshima	19
Yasunari Kawabata (committed suicide)	18
Torahiko Tamiya	13
Takehiko Fukunaga	13
Tsutomu Mizukami	13

Kyōka Izumi	10
Mokuami Kawatake	10
Katai Tayama	10
Ogai Mori	8
Kan Kikuchi	7
Masao Kume	7
Ryuunosuke Akutagawa (committed suicide)	6
Osamu Dazai (committed suicide)	6
Kafu Nagai	6
Yasushi Inoue	5

Considering that writers are more capable than ordinary people of analyzing their own thought processes, their suicide notes, other personal documents, and literary works should shed much light upon suicidal motives. On the following pages, the suicides of Takeo Arishima, Ryuunosuke Akutagawa, Osamu Dazai, Yukio Mishima, and Yasunari Kawabata—all highly representative of Japanese culture—will be discussed.

TAKEO ARISHIMA

Takeo Arishima was born in Tokyo in 1878, the eldest son of Takeshi and Kō Arishima. Takeshi was a bureaucrat in the Finance Ministry and was later an executive of a business corporation. He was rigidly authoritarian, emphasizing self-control in accordance with the samurai code of behavior. Plays and literature were immoral in his eyes, and he did not allow his family members to go to the theater. He insisted that a man was not to speak or laugh unless it was absolutely necessary. Takeo's mother was an intelligent idealist, but she had to stifle her intellectual inclination in order to adjust to the traditional woman's role in Japan, which called for conformance, submissiveness, self-restraint, and hard work. Occasional hysterical fits were probably a consequence of her internal conflict.

Arishima's parents loved him dearly, but their love contributed to his susceptibility to a suicidal wish. The father's love made his teaching of self-control most effective and produced a highly inhibited personality in his son. The suppressed individuality reinforced the traditional Japanese tendency to romantic love. Arishima's romanticism was strengthened by his education, which was strongly colored by Christian ethics. In addition to traditional training, Arishima's bureaucrat father saw the need for learning foreign languages and sent his son to a (Christian) mission school. He probably thought that foreign languages were necessary tools for Takeo's success. This was the time when Japanese leaders tried to absorb every aspect of Western civilization which might contribute to their ultimate goal: *fukoku kyohei* ("Rich Nation, Strong Army"). The exposure to Western influences contributed to Arishima's feminism—an important factor in his love-pact suicide later. His mother's love produced a strong mother identification, probably another factor in his feminism.

Arishima's self-control was reinforced by his being the eldest son. The eldest son in the traditional Japanese family is the heir to the family name and property. He is expected to be conservative, because his primary functions are to maintain family property, to supervise the family members' behavior so that they do not soil the family name, and to care for the parents when they are old. Takeo's traits of *uchiki* (social introversion), *donjū* (phlegmaticism), fastidiousness, and a certain degree of gloominess seem to be at least partly attributable to the ambivalence between self-control and the yearning for freedom.

When he was graduated at the age of eighteen from the Peers School, where students were mostly from aristocratic or extremely wealthy families, he entered Sapporo Agricultural College. Under the direction of W. S. Clark of Amherst College of Massachusetts, the college (which later became Hokkaido University) was one of the most progressive institutions of higher education in the nation at that time. On the campus, Arishima was strongly influenced by Kanzo Uchimura, at that time the central figure of Japanese Christianity. He also became intimate with Atsukichi Morimoto, a male Christian student. They once contemplated committing suicide together, primarily motivated by despair due to their sense of sin, which had been aroused by Christian teachings about sex. It is said that Arishima and Morimoto had a homosexual relationship.

Ironically, Christianity, with its negative attitude toward suicide, promotes a suicidal tendency in Japan, especially among intellectuals. This is primarily because self-awareness and the sense of guilt are emphasized in Christianity. Self-awareness produces internal conflict in that country, where "selflessness" (or merging into society) is the basic value.

From 1903 to 1907, Arishima studied at Haverford College and Harvard University. During this period he became increasingly more skeptical of the spirit-body dualism of Christianity. To him the inhibition of sex was "unnatural." Arishima rebelled against this strict attitude toward sex, despite the fact that he himself was highly moralistic according to Japanese standards. It is said that he never indulged in a geisha party or patronized prostitutes, as Japanese writers and artists generally do. When Arishima died for his love of Akiko, one of his younger brothers explained his suicide with the statement "My brother did not know women." This statement implied that if Arishima had been a veteran of love affairs, he probably would not have become so emotionally involved with Akiko as to commit double suicide, and that a woman or the relationship with a woman is not so important as to place a man's life in jeopardy.

With skepticism about the spirit-body dualism of Christianity, Arishima was more attracted by socialism which emphasized social conscience. It is ironic that in contrast to the traditionally accepting attitude toward sex among Japanese intellectuals, including socialists, the socialism of Marx, Engels, and Lenin has a strong undertone of Judeo-Christian moralism.[3]

Returning to Japan, Arishima taught at his alma mater in Sapporo. He married in 1908. The next year, he participated in the Shirakaba Group, a utopian movement under Saneatsu Mushakoji. The movement aimed to give creative thinkers the opportunity to work together on a farm, *Atarashii Mura* ("New Village"). The participants were to establish an identity with Nature (the transcendental universal spirit), to minimize work time through cooperation in order to enable themselves to be engaged more in creative works, and to cross-fertilize and mobilize their knowledge, talents, and perspectives. The participants in the movement were aristocrats and prominent artists, mostly graduates of the Peers School. They were far above the difficulties experienced by commoners. Despite the fact that his brothers were among the movement's most prominent members, Arishima could not endure the elitist complacency and uncritical acceptance of the established social order. (Their attitude toward the established social order was represented by their leader, Mushakoji, who once called Stalin, Churchill, and Roosevelt "three big idiots" because they were enemies of the established Japanese social order.)

Arishima's criticism of Shirakaba elitism and its romantic conception of man was partly based on his guilt and inferiority complex, which were rooted in his personal experience. Once, when he and his sister had been near drowning, he had attempted to save himself rather than trying to help her. This experience convinced Arishima of the wickedness not only of himself but also of all human beings (original sin).

Arishima's wife died in 1916, leaving three children. The same year brought the death of the father who had prevented Arishima from becoming a professional writer. The father's death liberated him and allowed him to concentrate on writing. His writing career reached its peak in 1920, when *Aru Onna* [A certain woman] was published. After that work, he felt his creativity draining and suffered a spell of depression. He wrote:

> You cannot feel life firmly.
> Vacuum-Vacuum, deadlier than death, began to gnaw on me.
> Die without reluctance.
> When I can muster strength I don't need your direction.
> Come a beautiful power, which pulls my strength together like a magnet.

In one of his letters to Motoichi Asuke, he described his feeling of meaninglessness: "From now on, I don't know what kind of fate will come upon me. Nowadays I feel it would be best if I could get a lover on whom I can focus my life, and die in passionate pleasure. I feel I am getting rather crazy."

For the decline of his creative energy Arishima blamed his bourgeois life. He was under the influence of the socialism that swept Japanese society after World War I. Then, the mainstream of literary activities centered on proletarian novels and naturalistic writings. Both placed focus on everyday life and human impulses, but naturalistic writing focused especially on sex. In a speech (entitled *Sokujitsu,* or "Being true to fact"), Arishima said:

> If I could get into the mind of the proletariat, I would be able to write terrific things. I think I could. However, I am a bourgeois. Therefore, I can write nothing but what appeals to bourgeoisie. Considering thus, there is no other way for me than to delve into my inner self . . . and death. I just gaze at death.

Wishing to understand the life of the masses, Arishima attempted to give away his family property. He gave his ranch in Hokkaido to his tenants and directed them to form a commune. However, he had to discontinue further attempts to share his property with tenants because of his sympathy for his old mother, who would have suffered most from the change. He hated himself for not being able to become one of the simple folk and write about them.

Americans may find it difficult to understand why, in Japan, a bourgeois cannot understand the "humanity" of the masses. In the Western world, concern for the individual was the major factor in the opposition to feudalism. However, the Japanese revolution against feudalism resulted in the Meiji Restoration. It simply replaced Tokugawa elites with anti-Tokugawa elites. Strong sensitivity to status difference remained intact, as symbolized by class stratification under the emperor. When the bourgeoisie came to participate in government, the gap between the aristocrat/bourgeois coalition and the masses was as deep as the one between the lords/samurai and the peasants. Japanese life was highly segmented, and the life-styles of classes were distinct from one another, preventing common understanding.

In 1922, Arishima became involved in a love affair with Akiko Hatano, a member of the staff of a publisher and the wife of another man. Arishima attempted to dissuade her from seeing him because of his fear of adultery, but the attempt backfired. In the following letter to Akiko, written on May 17, 1922, he equates love with Nature, in conflict with the common Japanese attitude that regards sex, not love, as natural:

> I want to write to Mr. Hatano [Akiko's husband] and tell him about our relationship in order to beg for his pardon. However, I cannot dissolve my love for you and your love for me. I cannot do that as long as Nature cannot be destroyed. Don't laugh at my uncontrollably sensitive heart. I cannot but have compassion for this weakness of mine.

When the affair was revealed to Akiko's husband, the husband demanded monetary compensation and threatened to sue Arishima for adultery. At first Arishima wished to fight for his love, as he told Motoichi Asuke on June 7:

> It is strange to say something like this, but we entered upon this love affair with the purpose of dying. We wished to die. Akiko suggested it in Funahashi, but I told her, "I don't care about people, but I feel it regrettable to tear myself away from Nature." So we postponed our death until October. Having been insulted by Hatano like this, however, I feel we cannot die under such conditions. . . . We would feel vexed. We should't die, because if we do, people would think that we died because we were beaten. We have to survive even just for our prides' sake.

Despite this resolution, why did he commit a love-pact suicide? It is possible that Arishima was swayed by Akiko or that he reacted impulsively with his idealistic resentment against her husband's attempt to use their love for monetary gain. To Arishima, love must have been so pure and passionate that it glorified even death. He also might have reacted to his own sense of cowardliness and guilt, from which he had suffered ever since his sister's near drowning. At any rate there was little resistance to death in him, as is expressed in his suicide note to his brothers and sisters:

> I have now only warm memories. My life, which had been getting increasingly darker, suddenly became brightened when I came to love Akiko.
> The joy I can tell you is that my death is not even a little bit pressured by external influences. We are welcoming death most freely and joyfully.

Arishima's suicide resulted from an ideological conflict between the emphasis on selfhood (i.e., love) and social expectations and probably more important from the decline of his creativity. His self-destructive reaction to the conflict and to the decline was promoted by his attitude toward death, which is characterized by fatalism and justification. His fatalism is clear in the following note to Akiko's husband:

> I cannot say who is good and who is bad. Whether we are good or bad seems to be due to our fate. We have just followed our fate. . . . We were finally trapped by the great force of Nature.

To Arishima, death was justifiable if it was done for love, because love is the culmination of self-fulfillment:

> What is timely death other than to die when love is consummated, or to destroy one's body when selfhood is matured? No death is more peaceful or purer than the one by lovers. All other deaths are suffering. Lover's suicide is not self-destruction by external pressure. The selfhood of the suicidal person is at the peak of its maturity at the moment of death.
> Love fertilizes selfhood by taking unhesitatingly from others; it is an expanding creative force. As cases of love operating to an utmost extent, *junshi* [suicide to follow the deceased master] and *jōshi* [love-pact suicide] are to be praised.

To Arishima, "fulfilling selfhood" meant to liberate the nature which is within oneself and to expand one's individual world. Nature within us is instinct. In his diary entry on May 25, 1903, Arishima defined "instinct" as "the willpower which Great Nature possesses" and said that this instinct is expressed only in love. He wrote:

In our life in this world, which is surrounded only by arrogant and retrospective lives, I find the purest life in the embrace between wholesome lovers at the apex of their love. When they approach the bed, they are above worldly morality and knowledge. The two become the embodiment of the instinct of love. The purest phenomenon of man's creative force, which is rooted in instinct, is ultimately found in love and the embrace between healthy lovers.

Because love is the only creative force, love makes even death creative.

Arishima's idea was (1) to dissolve the spirit-body dualism by living an instinctive life and (2) to establish an absolute inner world by transcending the world of relativity. This is the way in which he sought to defy an oppressive society.

Arishima's glorification of love is humanistic. Love is an endowed human potential that should be developed for human fulfillment. This idea is inimical in Japan, where the established social order, not the individual self, is the ultimate value, and where sex, not love, is regarded as natural. Heterosexual (or romantic) love, in contrast with sex, presupposes the ideal of love between two humans. In traditional Japan, however, individuals were role carriers rather than humans, and love meant a maternal rather than a heterosexual love. Therefore, heterosexual love is a disturbing force in that highly status-conscious society and must be suppressed.

However, romantic love thrives on obstacles. Because of the obstacles that love faces in Japan, it is even more romanticized. This explains why love is generally associated with tragedy and death among Japanese people, as represented by Arishima's death. The influence of the love-tragedy association is expressed in the fact that a common theme of postwar popular songs was generally that of loneliness, helplessness, parting, and "giving up."[4]

RYUUNOSUKE AKUTAGAWA ————————————————

Ryuunosuke Akutagawa was born in 1892 and died in 1927. In contrast to Takeo Arishima, who died to rebel against the Japanese tradition in the Meiji era (1868–1911), Akutagawa represented the Taisho Period (1911–1926) and could not rebel; he yielded to tradition. The period was a time of intense conflict between traditional values and Western influences. It was a period of instability. Many banks went bankrupt in the great financial panic that swept the world. At that time, the revolutionary movement hit its peak in Japanese history, and social change swept the nation.

The conflict with traditional powers because of the rise of democratic ideology was manifested in the revelation of repeated political scandals: the Siemens-Bickers case (1914);[5] Oura, the Minister of Domestic Affairs case (1915);[6] the Kyoto City Assembly case (1916); the Yawata Steel case (1918); the Tokyo City Assembly case (1920); the Southern Manchuria Railroad case (1921); the Army Secret-Fund case;[7] and the Matsushima Brothel case, the Gold Ore case, and the Fukkōin (Office of Metropolitan Restoration) case, all of which occurred in 1926.

These cases have a number of characteristics in common. First, the higher officials involved in scandals were seldom punished. In most cases they were not prosecuted, although their subordinates were often victimized as scapegoats. The subordinates often committed suicide, sometimes willingly and sometimes not. Some also might have been killed by professional killers, although public records indicated accidental deaths. Second, in some cases the prosecutors were killed, but the killers were seldom arrested. There was little effort at investigation into the agents behind the killers. This is not surprising in Japan, where the coalition of politicians, police, and gangsters was traditional. Third, an elaborate bureaucratic system made the detection of illegality and the punishment of culprits more difficult than in traditional simple bribery cases. Fourth, the Japanese public was seldom stirred up by the illegal use of tax money by the armed forces, industrialists, and politicians. Fifth, many scandals were revealed not by Japanese themselves but instead by foreign sources.

In the period of newly acquired democracy, the awareness of the undesirable aspects of Japanese tradition, which had been accepted as more or less sacred, produced strong mistrust and insecurity among Japanese intellectuals. They were dissatisfied with stifled individuality of traditional culture, and many of them reacted to the dissatisfaction by embracing Marxism or Christianity. Akutagawa, however, was closely bound to his family tradition; he could not give outlet to his anxiety and mistrust.

Since no social problems were directly dealt with in his works, Akutagawa appeared to be unconcerned with social problems. However, he read socialistic literature and the Bible. His social conscience was apparently stronger than that of many of his contemporaries. He criticized the elitist complacency of the Japanese intellectuals—especially Naoya Shiga and Ton Satomi—and their indifference to social problems.[8]

Akutagawa's father was a cantankerous dairy businessman. Because his mother became mentally ill when he was seven months old, Akutagawa was reared by his maternal uncle. His mother died when he was eleven. His father then married the deceased wife's younger sister, who gave birth to a boy. This boy died while very young. The only person with whom Akutagawa had a warm relationship was his mother's older sister, who was never married and who was forty years older than he.

Thus, Akutagawa's childhood was dotted with deaths, illnesses, and social isolation. He himself was in poor health, and at the age of nineteen he thought he would not live to be twenty-five. He was always lonely and fearful. He feared mental illness especially. He was afraid of strangers walking near him. He felt choked with fear when he passed a tall building.

Akutagawa reacted to his loneliness and fear with a craving for love, both homosexual and heterosexual. His homosexual love is expressed in a letter written in 1910, addressed to Kiyoshi Yamamoto, a classmate at a middle school (comparable to a high school today):

> I began this letter only to inform you of the situation at the Ichi-Kō [Dai Ichi Kōtō Gakko—First Higher School]. While writing, however, my yearning for you has become unbearable. Frankly, I feel jealous of the people who are around you. When I think that there are many among us who feel the same as I do toward you, I am tormented by worry that you might leave me sooner or later; the anxiety intensifies my jealousy. . . . My loneliness is really bad these days. In loneliness, however, my mad love is constantly burning. Ah! I love you. I don't even mind if I discard every other thing for you.

In 1914, when he was a freshman at Tokyo Imperial University, Akutagawa wrote Rōjin [Old man], and in the next year, Seinen to Shi [Youth and death], Hyottoko [A man with a distorted mask], and Sennin [Hermit]. His concerns were old age, loneliness, distorted ego, and death. Even though he was young, his perception of human beings was dark, pessimistic, skeptical, and cynical. This attitude is manifested in another letter addressed to Yamamoto in 1915:

> I am an egoist toward society. . . . This maintenance includes both strength and weakness. Its weakness is the individual's isolation, and its strength is his freedom. I think that the only thing which counter-balances the weakness is love. Only love cares for a soul which is separated from all other attributes, e.g., title, income, education and all other things like that. Only passing through the flame of love may

two souls attain complete unity. . . . It is this love that I am starved and thirsty for.

However, can there really be such a love in this world? Perfect mutual understanding, mysterious above reasoning—can we expect this kind of love from a woman? No! I cannot expect understanding from a woman.

Do you understand the loneliness of a person who seeks after this kind of love?—the loneliness of pursuing selfhood (and art) in a society where individuality has no place?

Nowadays I don't like most people (myself either). Street cars are full of hateful people. I feel Japan is crowded with stupid men and women. College students are all idiots. . . .

All great arts have some unspeakable power—power which strikes everybody with awe. That power is universal to all art regardless of time and space. Are there any Japanese artists who devote themselves to the pursuit of this power? Most Japanese artists are "bourgeois" and not qualified to be artists.

In 1914, Akutagawa was in love with Yayoi Yoshida, but this love was not consummated by marriage because of his parents' disapproval. The reason for their rejection was that she was not from a *shizoku* (former samurai) family. (Akutagawa's father was not from a *shizoku* family either, although his mother was.) Frustrated, Akutagawa reacted by blaming the ugliness, selfishness, and hypocrisy of people.

Family pressure was probably one of the basic causes of his suicide. Most writers in Japan leave their homes for Tokyo, where the soil is more fertile for cultivating and developing creative ability. By leaving home they establish their ego identities and accumulate experiences from which they can draw materials for their writings. Akutagawa, however, could never leave his home; he was born in a most traditional part of Tokyo and trapped by stifling family relations among ancestors and relatives. He compared himself to a clown doll, which had no individuality but tried to please others. Akutagawa's identification with his family was so intense that he became emotionally dependent upon it. It appears that when he moved away from home, even within a restricted area, he felt lost.

In 1916, he became engaged to Fumi Tsukamoto (Kiyoshi Yamamoto's niece) because "he wanted to marry anybody who would be approved by his family." On the day after the wedding, his bride bought for him a pot of daffodils. In reaction he remonstrated her: "You should not waste money." The complaint was not really his, but his aunt's; he simply transmitted his aunt's wish. He suppressed his own feeling for the harmony of the family. His wife apologized profusely not only to him but also to his aunt.

Akutagawa gained success and fame with "Hana" [Nose], published in 1916. In this work he dealt with a priest who suffered from an abnormally long nose, which was like a long sausage hanging from the center of his face to below his chin. The priest tried various methods, following people's advice, to shorten it. When he succeeded in shortening it, he was most unhappy, and when the nose was long again, he felt relieved. The primary objective of the story was to show an inner contradiction in the Japanese mind: people are compassionate with the person who suffers, but once he overcomes the suffering by solving his problem, people feel thwarted. When they find him happy, they even become antagonistic to him; they wish to place him in the former situation again.

Akutagawa's success was, in part, the result of his skepticism and cynicism. Skepticism and cynicism appealed to the Japanese intelligentsia, who in the 1920s were tired of the romantic conception of human beings shown by the Shirakaba Group. They were also dissatisfied with works by Japanese naturalists. In Western naturalism, writers focus their works on natural desires and instincts but also, almost unavoidably, imply critical attitudes toward a society that stifles the self. Conflict between the wish to develop human potential and allow self-expression on the one hand and social control on the other is traditional in Western cultures. In contrast, Japanese naturalism is often expressed in *shi shōsetsu* ("I" novels), which are usually sentimental memoirs and detailed descriptions of the author's sex life, without an element of social criticism.

Thus, being tired of the sentimental romanticism and elitism of the Shirakaba writers and the lack of intellectual analysis of personal life on the part of Japanese naturalists, many Japanese intellectuals found the skepticism and cynicism of Akutagawa refreshing. Moreover, Akutagawa offered more. Through his criticism of actual men and women, his earlier works showed an image of ideal humanity, so gentle that it is easily hurt by wicked social reality. This criticism of society and sympathy toward man appealed to the Japanese public, who found in Ryuunosuke's work the representation of their own feeling of being victimized.

Akutagawa was an uncanny observer of human life. He was objective in the sense that he saw characters as a bystander does, although what he wrote about them was the projection of his own feelings and thoughts—that is, mistrust and anxiety. He did not place himself into the characters and trace the development of their thinking and feelings, as determined by their own unique situations. When his emotions were not controlled by his objectivity, he apparently felt himself losing creativity. In 1921, at the age of thirty, Ryuunosuke confessed that he could no longer be creative and that it was shameful to be treated as a great writer when creativity was gone. In such a case, he thought, it was better to die.

In 1922, he wrote "Yabu no Naka" [In the thicket], which later became a movie entitled *Rashōmon*. In this work, the wife of a samurai was raped by a bandit while her husband was forced to look on. Upon investigation, each presented his own interpretation, which was contradictory to the other. Akutagawa's primary objective was to show the relativity of interpretation and also the untrustworthiness of women. Before he wrote this work, Akutagawa had an affair with another man's wife. He was shocked when he found that the woman was also having sexual relations with one of his younger friends, reinforcing his prejudice that women were evil and incomprehensible.

Around this time, he suffered from *shinkei suijaku* (neurasthenia) and manifested many symptoms of mental disorder, such as illusions of maggots in his food or cogwheels in the air. He suffered from an obsession with sinfulness. He felt that people, and even dogs, were laughing at him all the time. He felt also that he was constantly watched by people who attempted to pry secrets from him.

At the age of thirty-four, Akutagawa suffered from insomnia and became addicted to sleeping pills. When he finished *Aru Ahō no Isshō* [A fool's life] in 1927, he was depressed and blamed himself for his own immorality and shortcomings. He saw before him nothing but insanity or suicide.

In January 1927 his brother-in-law's house was burned, and the brother-in-law, who was suspected of insurance fraud, committed suicide. Akutagawa knew that he would have to shoulder his sister's family and pay their debts. His already tautly strung nerves almost snapped. In May one of his most intimate friends, Kōji Uno, was institutionalized for mental illness, intensifying Akutagawa's fear of his own mental illness. On July 24 he died by taking sleeping pills.

These situational causes affected his suicide importantly, but they did so only in combination with his pessimistic view of life and his accepting attitude toward suicide. Life to him was darkness in which flickers of fireworks brighten the sky temporarily but disappear quickly. Therefore, when his first child was born he lamented, "Why did you come to be born in this hellish world—to have such a person as me for a father?" When he saw the body of a child who was killed in the great earthquake in 1923, he commented, "Everybody should die" (i.e., no Japanese deserves to live). He despised Japanese people, but he was afraid of them.

Akutagawa's view of the self was similarly dark. In *Anchū Mondō* (Questions and answers in darkness], he says, "I have no conscience; the only thing I have is nerves." His tragedy was in his inability to accept the traditional values of Japanese culture, which allowed the juxtaposition of *tatemae* (social front; words) and *honne* (actual feeling and intention). Despite his contempt for traditional values, however, Akutagawa did not have anything that he could call his own firmly established value orientation. Therefore, he told himself, "Ryuunosuke Akutagawa, Ryuunosuke Akutagawa. You should put your roots deeply in the ground. You are a reed blown by the wind."[9] He envied the people in the Middle Ages, who had at least acquired strength and hope from God.[10]

One of the greatest contributions of Akutagawa is that he, more than any other Japanese, clarified the psychological process that led to his suicide. It is very rare that a suicidal person analyzes and records his own thinking before death. Therefore, although it is long, a major part of his last note is reproduced here:

No one has yet described the psychology of his own suicide as he sees it. . . . I would like to clarify this psychology in this last letter of mine. . . . Régnier[11] described a suicidal person in one of his short stories. Its protagonist did not know why he was killing himself. You find in newspaper articles various motives for suicide—financial difficulty, illness, suffering, or others—but my experience tells that these are not all. In most cases so-called motives show the process leading to a true motive. I think most suicidal persons do not know their basic motivation, as Régnier showed. It involves complex causes, just as our actions do. However, at least in my case, the cause is just a vague anxiety. I do not know what, but a vague anxiety about my future.

These two years, I have kept thinking of death. During this period I have read Mainländer seriously.[12] The work artistically describes the process leading to death in abstract words. I want to do the same in more behavioral terms. Compared with such a wish, sympathy toward family members is nothing. I am obliged to write honestly. I have already analyzed my vague anxiety about the future in *Ahō no Isshō* [A fool's life], although I did not write about the feudalistic social conditions which affected me.

The first thing I considered is how to die without suffering. For this purpose, probably hanging is the best, but when I picture a person hanged to death, I feel an aesthetic abhorrence. . . . Drowning is not good either, because. . . . drowning will involve more suffering than hanging does. Suicide by running into a rushing train also is aesthetically abhorrent to me. Suicide by gun or knife does not seem to work well for me because my hands shake. Jumping from a high building produces an ugly sight. Considering thus, I have decided to die with pills. To do so implies longer suffering than hanging but it has advantages. My body would appear better and there would be less risk of failure than with other methods. Its only disadvantage is the difficulty of obtaining pills. Since I have determined to use pills, I have tried to acquire them at every opportunity. At the same time, I have attempted to increase my knowledge of drugs.

Then I considered the place of my suicide. My family members must depend on what I leave for them. My possessions are a piece of land of 100 *tsubo* [about 100 feet square], my home, the royalties from my books, and savings of 2,000 yen. If I commit suicide in my house its value will drop. I want to commit suicide in such a way that my body will be seen as little as possible by others—other than my family members.

Even after deciding on the method, I still clung to life. So I needed a springboard to catapult me to death. I do not regard suicide as a sin as "Red Haired People" [Westerners] do. Historically, Buddha approved of the suicide of one of his disciples as recorded in the *Agon* Scripture. People commit suicide because they see no alternative. Thus suicide indicates courage rather than necessity.

The best springboard for suicide is a woman. Kleist[13] attempted to induce his [male] friends to die with him before his suicide. Racine,[14] too, attempted drowning in the Seine River with Molière[15] and Boileau-Despréaux.[16] Unfortunately, I do not have such friends. Some women wanted to die with me but we could not come to a final agreement. In the meantime I gained confidence to die alone. It is not because I have nobody to die with but due to my compassion for my wife, who has to live on after my death. I also recognized that to die alone is easier than to die with another. To die alone enables me to choose the time of death more easily.

The last consideration was about killing myself without letting the family members know in advance. After several months of preparation, I gained confidence. . . . I coolly completed my preparation and am now just playing with death. My psychology from this point will be close to what is described in Mainländer.

We humans are animals, and all animals are afraid of death. What we call life energy is animal energy. But my being tired of eating and having sex must mean I am losing animal energy. The world I am living in now is the icily transparent universe of sickly nerves. I spent last night with a prostitute, talking about her wage. The talk made me realize the misery of human beings, struggling just to live. If we can enter eternal sleep, we may at least have peace, even if we may not enjoy happiness.

However, I am doubtful about when I can dare to take my own life. Under conditions like these, Nature herself looks more beautiful to me than ever. You may laugh at the contradiction between the love of Nature and the wish for suicide. However, Nature looks even more beautiful exactly because I am at the end of my life. This gives me satisfaction even in a life which has been a series of sufferings. Please do not publish this letter for several years after my death. I may end my life in such a way that it appears to be death from illness. . . .

We humans do not easily commit suicide because of a single incident. I kill myself as the closing account of my entire life. I admit, one of the main events in my life was the crime I committed with Mrs. X when I was twenty-nine years old. I have no qualms of conscience about the crime. I only regret that because of my poor judgment, the event led to great disadvantages in my life. I hated Mrs. X's egotism and animalistic impulses.[17] There are other women, too, who fell in love with me. However, I have had no lover in my thirties, not because of morality but because of calculation of advantages and disadvantages.

Of course, I do not want to die, but it is suffering to live. People may laugh at me for committing suicide when I have parents, a wife and children. If I were alone, I would not have committed suicide. I was reared by foster parents and I have never acted willfully. Now I am regretting my "dutiful" behavior to my parents, although I really could not do otherwise. My wish to commit suicide now is probably the only willful act in my life. I have had many dreams, as all young people do, but thinking back, I might, after all, just have been an odd person. At present I dislike everything, including myself.

This suicide note indicates the major factors that determined Akutagawa's suicide:

1. Cause of suicide: Vague anxiety and a wish to escape from suffering; obsessive fear of mental illness.
2. Method of suicide: Pills that enable a man to die easily without presenting an ugly appearance after death.
3. Place: At home, where the body will not be seen by others.
4. View of life: Human life is a miserable battle; the only salvation is in Nature.
5. View of man: Mistrust of man; women are wicked and fearsome.
6. View of the family: The family stifles individual freedom; it should not be relied upon.
7. View of suicide: Suicide is not only acceptable but is also a courageous act.

In conclusion, Akutagawa committed suicide because of "vague anxiety," which was produced by the following multiple causes:

—— Unsatisfied basic childhood needs, especially dependency, and consequent diffuse mistrust and basic anxiety.
—— Ideological conflict between traditional groupism and familism, on the one hand, and a desired emphasis on a strong ego, on the other.
—— Insecurity due to rapid social change during the 1920s.
—— Decline of creativity within himself.
—— Fear of financial insecurity, which was precipitated by his brother-in-law's suicide.
—— Poor health in combination with a highly masochistic and also narcissistic self.
—— A pessimistic view of life and a highly accepting view of suicide.

OSAMU DAZAI

Osamu Dazai remains, decades after his death, the most popular writer among Japanese college students. In their eyes Dazai is the champion of underdogs. He is a symbol of the anxiety, weakness, confusion, and suspicion from which many Japanese youth suffer. He groped for the values that they search for desperately—love, truth, sincerity and beauty—in rebellion against the traditional Japanese values (i.e., groupism and authoritarianism), which stifle individuality. What Dazai opposed most were the Japanese inclination toward pretentiousness and the wide gap between words (*tatemae*) and actual intention (*honne*).

Osamu Dazai was born in 1909 in the northernmost part of mainland Japan. The area was known for its severe winters and poor crops. People there believed in the most primitive forms of Japanese pantheism, with many magical practices. Their beliefs strongly emphasized sin and fear. They lived in the legacy of feudal Japan, probably more than people did in any other part of the country.

Dazai's father was the overbearing despot of the area. The family's relationship with peasants and merchants in the area was similar to that of a feudal lord to slaves. Dazai was surrounded by a large number of slavish maids and servants. He went to school in a family-crested coach, and at school he was given especially favored treatment by principals and teachers.

Despite their aristocratic appearance, Dazai saw in his family all kinds of evil. The family life was a system of formalities and hypocrisy, without much substance of sincerity and affection. The almost exclusive concern of his parents was in maintaining their family property and prestige, for which humanity was crushed ruthlessly. Subordinates—maids, servants, and tenants—were forced to live a life of obligation, endurance, and ignorance, and their distorted egotism found pleasure in torturing those who were weaker. They lied matter-offactly but still pretended to be honest and cheerful. These family conditions largely determined Dazai's sentiments and attitudes about the world.

In 1929, at the age of twenty, Dazai attempted suicide by taking an overdose of sleeping pills. He allegedly suffered from the discrepancy between the communistic zeal that swept Japanese intellectuals in the 1920s and his own life, which was supported by the exploitation of poor people. The next year, probably because of his involvement in an illegal Communist organization and the death of the only brother who was close to him, he attempted suicide with a married barmaid. He survived, and she died. According to Dazai, she was just a *michizure* (fellow traveler) (*Ningen Shikkaku,* or "no longer human").

In 1931, Dazai married Hatsue, a geisha. He believed that he was saving her from misery, because the geisha was regarded as a semi-prostitute.[18] Ordinarily, the marriage of a youth of twenty-two to a geisha is almost unimaginable because of the high expense involved in the "purchase" of the woman. Apparently, Dazai's family paid for it. Four years later Dazai dropped out of Tokyo University and was disowned by his family. When he failed to acquire a position at a newspaper company, he attempted to hang himself.

In 1936, when he was a rapidly rising writer, Dazai failed to receive the hoped-for Akutagawa Award, one of the most coveted awards for Japanese writers. He indulged in drugs. Because of his addiction, his friends maneuvered to have him confined to a mental institution. He complained that he just wanted to live a life of truth and trust, and he asked why such a person must be treated as insane and removed from society. When he was released and returned home, he found that his wife had committed adultery with a young relative of his. The next year, he attempted *shinjū* (double suicide) with Hatsue. It was unsuccessful, and after their recovery he divorced her. For several years after his marriage to Michiko Ishikawa in 1939, he had his happiest and most productive years. In 1948 his tuberculosis worsened, causing several hemorrhages. On June 13, he finally succeeded in committing *shinjū* with a sweetheart, leaving his wife with three children and also leaving a mistress with a daughter.

How can this series of suicide attempts be explained? Dazai's personality traits seem to be crucial. His relationship with his parents was cold, and his relationships with his siblings were, on the whole, cool. He spent most of his childhood with his maid, Také, and a maternal aunt. He was almost always surrounded by some thirty maids and servants. Those who had close contact with him were mostly females. In traditional Japan, females tended to pamper boys. Narcissism became a core element of Dazai's personality.

At high school, he was the best student, far superior to any of his brothers. His family's expectations for him were exceedingly high. Their hope produced in him a sense of mission for great success. He wished to be always at the top and to be extraordinary in achievement. He was excessively vain and sensitive to other people's reactions. Also, he was vulnerable and edgy in matters of self-esteem, and his self-confidence was so frail as to be shaken tremendously by a minor difficulty. Any behavior that he interpreted as an insult caused him to wish to die in agony; he was a "flower petal ready to fall in a breeze."[19] Since he was sure that he would be a great man, "any insult could not be overlooked in order to protect the honor of a hero." To him there were only two kinds of people: those whom he could manipulate to love him alone and those who persecuted him.[20] The latter included all who did not give him special attention and praise. To him, anybody who understood him must love him, and anybody who criticized him was hostile toward him.

Dazai's narcissism was closely related to a strong dependency need. His alter ego, the character Naoji in *Shayō* [Declining sun], was hopelessly dependent on his sister for the payment of the debts he had incurred for drugs and heavy drinking. Naoji was dependent even when he knew that his sister had to sell her clothes for payment and that her assistance might ruin her future. Dazai's own dependence is shown in the incident in which he dropped out of Tokyo University, and was disowned by his family, and then attempted suicide because the prop of his dependence was gone. He was twenty-six years old at the time.

In combination with narcissism and dependence, a lack of realistic perception is important. Dazai's lack of realistic perception is indicated by his statement that "since I had such strong pride, it was beyond my comprehension that I had to convey my thinking to anybody verbally."[21] Japanese husbands tend to take it for granted that their wishes will be understood by their wives without verbal communication.[22] Dazai apparently extended this view to all social objects.

The nonlogical tendency was a cause of his difficulty as a writer, too. When Yozo (representing Dazai) saw his wife raped by a merchant in *Ningen Shikkaku,* Dazai jumped to the conclusion that she was raped because she was genuinely innocent and trustful; virtue is always raped by evil.

Dazai's novels were revelations of his own feelings. He was relatively poor in describing characters objectively, especially in terms of their personality development.

Underlying narcissism, dependency, and a lack of realistic perception in Dazai was a strong inferiority complex. Born as the tenth of eleven children, he suffered from almost complete neglect by his parents. His authoritarian father was an object of fear. Dazai recalled, "I was scared even of God. I could not believe in a God of love but only in a God of punishment."[23] During his childhood he was the least popular among his siblings. His older brothers generally ignored him; there was often strong enmity between him and his brothers. His older sister, he recalls, used to say that no girl would want to marry him because of his "ugliness." A sense of abandonment and inferiority developed.

In adulthood, Dazai was highly suspicious. He did "not experience friendship even once."[24] He could not carry on conversations with his neighbors. Even when he was eager to converse, the eagerness was shown only in the form of antics. Antics invited misunderstandings, which, in turn, made for more isolation, the feeling that "Nobody understands me."

Some critics point out another source of Dazai's inferiority feelings, an *inakamono* (hillbilly) complex. Although the *inakamono* complex seems to be common among non-Tokyoites in Japan, where Tokyo is the center of modern culture and where subservience to the central government is unquestionable, it would have been even more tormenting to the highly narcissistic Dazai. Yukio Mishima criticized the language used by the "aristocratic" mother in *Shayō,* the most representative work of Dazai's, as not being the real language of an aristocratic lady. It is possible that Dazai was chagrined about his *inakamono* background, although his conception of aristocracy was different from Mishima's; it was a projection of his ideal. To Dazai, *aristocracy* meant innocence, kindness, and honesty without calculation and pretentiousness. His aristocracy did not refer to actual persons of aristocratic rank, as Mishima thought. Dazai clarifies this point in *Shayō:*

> The peerage does not make an aristocrat. . . . Indeed, most of the noblemen are something like high-class beggars. Real aristocrats do not need affectation. Among our relatives, probably our mother is the only aristocrat. She is genuine and unrivalled.

Whether Mishima's criticism was well founded or not, Dazai's hostility to the upper class may have been a reaction to his own feelings of inferiority toward them.

Other characteristics of Dazai's were a deep sense of sin and a fear of sinfulness. These feelings may be traced back to his childhood exposure to a folk religion with emphasis on "hell and heaven." His homeland region of Japan is known for the belief in communication with the dead through mediums. He recalled:

> At six or seven years old, I was taught to read by a maid, Také. We two read various books. Také was a devoted teacher to me. . . . She taught me morality, too. She frequently took me to temples and explained pictures of Hell and Heaven. Arsonists were carrying burning baskets on their backs and unfaithful husbands were bound in agony by two headed snakes. A pond of blood, a hill of needles, and a bottomless hole filled with white smoke, which was called *mugen naraku* [bottomless Hell]. Pale and skinny people were screaming in torment all over. When I was told that liars were to go to Hell and have their tongues extracted by demons, I cried with fear.

Dazai's sense of sin was intense because he was a habitual prevaricator in childhood. When he was caught playing with a maid in the closet, he explained that he was helping the maid to find a lost coin. He lied in order to receive attention from friends and aid from his family.

Dazai recognized his tendency to lie, and he hated it. He knew it to be an undesirable trait, and he tried to correct it. As a result, when most Japanese writers, including "liberals," readily participated in the war effort during World War II, Dazai never cooperated with Japanese militarism. Honesty to an unchanging principle is uncharacteristic of many Japanese people, because their socialization produces the tendency to adjust to the immediate situation (this is termed "situational realism" by Ruth Benedict).

Dazai's literature was an attempt to defy the Japanese tendency to hide real feelings behind a good social front. Therefore, he said, "almost all of my agony is concerned with the difficult problem posed by Jesus Christ, 'Thou shalt love thy neighbor as thyself.'" To him literature was a confession of his inability to be honest and to love. Since literature is a description of innermost conflict, to publish a literary work was to him "to shame oneself—to confess to God."[25] His keen sense of sin made him say, "It is better to be punished for honesty than to be pardoned by covering up."

When Dazai was frustrated, his primary method of tension reduction was avoidance. He escaped into his own world through antics, drugs, alcohol, and women. He avoided not only tension-producing situations but also happy ones. Happiness appeared to be a trap for greater unhappiness. Avoidance is an ineffective coping mechanism. Consequently, Dazai reacted to frustrating situations with anxiety, as indicated by his confession: "The more I contemplate, the more am I threatened by insecurity and the fear that I alone am completely abnormal" (*Ningen Shikkaku*).

Because avoidance does not dissolve frustration, aggressive impulses are bottled up inside unless some outlets are provided. When Dazai was young, one outlet for his aggression was participation in Marxist revolutionary activities. However, he could not really devote himself to revolutionary causes. The Marxist ideology intensified his internal conflicts because it emphasized a critical attitude toward the established social order. Later, Dazai's outlets for aggression were sexual escapades. Whenever he saw an opportunity for decadence he grabbed at it, although his diffuse anxiety and despair were ultimately aggravated by his debauchery.

Thus, Dazai's personality traits of narcissism, dependence, lack of realism, inferiority complex, fearful sense of sin, and avoidance produced a wide discrepancy between his wishes and reality. The result was strong frustration. When the intense frustration was combined with a pessimistic view of life and attitudes of acceptance toward death and suicide, Dazai's suicidal inclination increased. He viewed humans as having the potential to desire justice, truth, purity, and love, but these virtues are stifled in actual society. He maintained that "education" is not for the purpose of promoting these virtues but rather for covering up the evil aspects of humanity that inevitably develop in society. It is the evil aspects, not the virtuous ones, that have adaptive values in present Japan, he felt. Consequently, successful and respected people are liars, fakes, and crooks. The virtuous aspects of human nature do not emerge in life but in death, because death destroys all evils.

His mistrust of society affected his view of social resources and precipitated his suicide. Dazai had no confidence in the Japanese people's ability to assist those in need. They "talk in a vague, delicate, and complicated way" so that they can avoid being involved in other people's troubles. They show unnecessarily strict precautions and have innumerable elaborate maneuvers for that purpose (*Ningen Shikkaku*).

Dazai's mistrust was accentuated by the social conditions in postwar Japan. Temporarily, with the defeat, he hoped that the old Japanese tradition that stifled the virtuous aspects of humanity was broken and that a new morality would emerge. He represented his hope in *Shayō* [Declining sun] through Kazuko, who was a sort of women's liberation advocate, who proclaims, "Revolution? Good! Love? Good! I wish to live like the sun." Dazai's hope was, however, short-lived. The new morality did not emerge. Instead, the ugly aspects of human nature were reinforced in the turmoil subsequent to the defeat in World War II.

His enmity against the superficial interpretation of "democracy" that was prevalent in postwar Japan is expressed in Naoji's suicide note in *Shayō*:

> "Men are all the same." . . . I think this saying sprang up at public houses, just as maggots hatch. It flowed out and spread into the world, producing an unpleasant atmosphere all over. . . . The words hold in contempt not only others but oneself; they deprive man of his pride and the will to strive. Marxism insists on the superiority of workers. It does not say all are the same. Only a brothel tout says, "Aha! However pretentious you may be, you are the same as other men are."

Dazai viewed human life as a vacuum. "A man's life contains various emotions—joy, anger, sadness, and hatred. They occupy, however, only one percent of his life, and the remaining ninety-nine percent is just breathing for nothing." He also claimed that "one may be waiting desperately for happiness to approach, but life is just empty. In reality all people are wishing that they had not been born, and day after day, from morning to evening, are waiting for something desperate to happen" (*Shayō*).

Dazai not only mistrusted people and viewed life as a vacuum but also did not believe in an individual's ability to solve his or her own problems. He was a fatalist. In Yozo's words in *Bannen* [Late years], "I believe in fate and I don't struggle." Dazai confesses in *Tsugaru*, "The plan I make in exaltation ends up always as a fiasco. I was born with such an inconvenient fate."

If life is given and cannot be changed by efforts, the only way to assert oneself is to deny things around one—nihilistic negativism—which is to negate one's own life. Dazai's literature is a representation of his own nihilistic feelings. Nihilism to him meant "a disregard of conventional morality" rather than the more philosophical sense of denying any objective ground of truth. He was engrossed with his own behavior and motives, but he was little concerned with the effects of his behavior upon others, especially women, whom he exploited for his own gratification.

Dazai's nihilism was culminated in his suicide. To him, death and suicide were a form of life or a means for making a life significant. In *Ha* [Leaves], he equated dropping out from the Communist cause with death, writing, "Death is best. All people who hinder the progress of society should die." Since life must be significant, death is preferable to an insignificant life. Dazai's life became insignificant when his tuberculosis worsened and his creativity drained away.

YUKIO MISHIMA

Yukio Mishima, the pen name of Kimitake Hiraoka, was born in Tokyo in 1925. His grandmother took him away from his parents when he was forty-nine days old. She wanted to rear him as a member of her own aristocratic Nagai family rather than have him raised in her commoner husband's (i.e., Mishima's father's) Hiraoka family. Sticking to rigid class prejudice, and convinced of her superiority, she was very demanding and was dominant in family affairs.

The grandmother was "frail and sickly," "frantic and poetic," and excessively vain. Because Mishima was physically weak, she poured her affection upon him, although he was almost a prisoner in her darkened sickroom. The grandmother was highly sensitive to noise, and the boy was forced to be still and quiet. She guarded him jealously, fiercely, and hysterically against his parents and the outside world. Afraid that Mishima would learn "bad things" from other boys, the grandmother raised him as a girl, isolated from his peers. The only exceptions were three older girls from their neighborhood, handpicked for their gentleness by the grandmother. Mishima lived mostly in the fantasy world of pictures and books. This situation continued until he was fourteen, when his grandmother died.

He then returned to his parents. His father, at that time director of the Bureau of Fisheries in Osaka, was home only two or three nights a month. Mishima was the center of his mother's affection. She seemed to want to make up for the time during which she had been deprived of her son by her mother-in-law.

Upon his graduation from the Peers School, Mishima received an emperor's silver watch, given to the top student. He was graduated in 1947 from Tokyo University as one of the top students and acquired a position in the Ministry of Treasury, where the most promising future leaders of Japan gather. However, he left the ministry the following year in order to concentrate on writing. In 1949, *Kamen no Kokuhaku* [The confessions of a mask] was published, and *Ai no Kawaki*

[The thirst for love] was published the next year. *Kinkakuji* [Temple of the golden pavilion] was published in 1956. Two years later, at the age of thirty-three, Mishima was married to the daughter of a famous artist. *Kyōko no Ie* [Kyoko's house] was published in 1959, and *Yuukoku* [Patriot] in 1960. After *Yuukoku*, Mishima's works shifted from aestheticism to ideological dogmatism.

Mishima became a Nobel Prize candidate in 1968 for his earlier works. Two years later he committed *seppuku* (self-disembowelment) with one of his male admirers, following the traditional samurai ritual. He was forty-five years old. He did so after delivering an impassioned plea to 1,200 members of the Self-Defense Forces from the balcony of its Tokyo headquarters. He called for an uprising to produce a constitutional change that would revive the Imperial army.

The plea attributed the moral weakness of modern Japan to the loss of the "sword" aspect of her tradition. His speech reflected a conflict between his own feudalistic philosophy and present-day Japan's reality. Was his suicide really ideological?

Suicide is mostly a consequence of despair. What caused Mishima's despair? According to special issues of two popular magazines (*Bungei Shunjū* and *Shuukan Gendai*), twenty-seven (65%) of forty-one critics interviewed attributed Mishima's suicide to the discrepancy between his ego ideal and his self-concept, eleven (27%) to the disparity between his view of the ideal society and actuality, and three (8%) to *jōshi*, a love-pact suicide. These three issues are regarded as major causes of Mishima's suicide.

The majority view is supported by the critics' attitude toward Mishima's works: 65 percent of the critics who evaluated his works in the above issues were generally negative, while 23 percent praised them as "first class," deserving of a Nobel Prize, and 13 percent labeled them as "good." Their consensus seems to be that Mishima was a genius but that his later works showed little variation or development despite the fact that he continued to be a superb critic. Probably Vidal is right to comment that once Mishima became famous, he was "too quickly satisfied with familiar patterns and did not venture into new patterns of literary art."[26] Seidensticker pointed out the "intrinsic emptiness" of *Kinkakuji* in 1965, suspecting that Mishima might not have found what he really wanted to write.[27] In 1968 the same critic observed that Mishima seemed to have been exhausted and that his "recent works have nothing to add to what have been already published in foreign countries. He probably needs to make a new start."[28]

In the final tetralogy, after Mishima had made the decision to die, he seemed to have regained an aestheticism free from ideological dogmatism. Evidently the gap between his ego-ideal of being a great writer and his self-concept (a reflection of significant others' reactions) was an important cause of his suicide. What caused a gap between his ego ideal and self-concept so wide that Mishima despaired?

First of all, Mishima's aspiration was extremely high, primarily because of his narcissism, as expressed by many of the protagonists of his works. For example, Noboru in *Shizumeru Taki* [Sunken waterfall] "did not feel the necessity to love at all, but to be loved was always convenient." Etsuko in *Ai no Kawaki* could not allow her lover to make her feel love, because love to a narcissist implies capitulation. As one would expect from a narcissistic writer, Mishima was at his best when he wrote in the first person, as in *Kamen no Kokuhaku* or *Kinkakuji*. However, he was rather poor at placing himself in the minds of others and observing an event from their point of view.

Mishima was not hesitant to display his narcissistic egocentrism in discussions. He declared to students at Waseda University in October 1968, "Regarding the problem of humanism and egoism, I am not one who can have sympathy with other people. I am only worried about myself."[29] His explanation of why he became anti-Communist is extremely egocentric: "I felt that ideology, idea, and spirit debilitate when there is no enemy. So I wanted to have an enemy at any cost. I decided to have Communism as my enemy." His anti-Communist stance functioned as a means to satisfy his own need.

Another indication of his narcissism was his obsession with his appearance, as indicated by his body-building efforts and his wish for a hero's death. In *Taiyō to Tetsu* [Sun and steel], Mishima recalls that at the age of eighteen he wanted to die young. However, since he felt that he did not have a muscular body suitable for a heroic death, he had to build a beautiful body first. On New Year's Day 1966, he faced a dilemma between finishing his life work (tetralogy) and dying while still young (which he called a "hero's death"):

> When I finish this big work, I shall be forty-seven years old, and I
> shall have to give up forever the opportunity to die a hero's death. Shall
> I give up a hero's death or shall I complete my life work?[30]

In contrast to his high aspiration, Mishima's self-concept was characterized by inferiority feelings. His narcissism itself was primarily a reaction to his strong inferiority complex.

Mishima's inferiority feelings were produced by several factors.

First, there was a strong female identification. Female identification is suggested by his child-rearing experiences: being the center of his grandmother's and then his mother's love. His highly authoritarian father was an object of resentment and fear rather than of affection. This is the father who could declare that "a parent has to apply pressure. You squeeze and you squeeze, and any child that collapses is better off dead."[31] The physically weak Mishima was not cherished by his father. Because of this weakness, since the first grade his family doctor had advised against his being exposed to direct rays of the sun. At twelve, he looked no more than eight or nine; he was "thin as a reed and pale as the underbelly of fish."[32]

The language he learned during childhood was that of girls. Even more than in Western cultures, the language spoken by a girl is formal and distinctly different from that of a boy in Japan. A boy who speaks the language of girls becomes an object of severe ridicule in that society of male chauvinism. Particularly, the Peers School stressed masculinity. The school aimed to instill the samurai (warrior) spirit into students who were to become the leaders of the next generation. In this atmosphere Mishima's generally girlish attitude, together with his pale complexion and frail build, strengthened his inferiority feelings. The sense of inferiority was intensified by his own strong sexism, as expressed in his statement in *Taiyō to Tetsu:* "What man has and what woman lacks are muscles and intelligence."

Another source of his inferiority complex was his status consciousness. His awareness that his father was a commoner and not an aristocrat must have made him feel inferior to classmates at the Peers School, where the student body was constituted mostly of children from aristocratic or extremely wealthy families. Mishima's family was neither. His grandmother had instilled in him the importance of her aristocratic forefathers in comparison to the family of her commoner husband, but outside her family Mishima's status was that of his father's. He was conditioned for elitism, yet the gap between his wish for aristocracy and his self-image as a commoner was excruciating.

Mishima's feeling of inferiority was aggravated by an incident that left him with a strong sense of guilt. During World War II, at the height of militarism, Mishima was rejected by the army because of a questionable change of locale for his army-induction physical examination. His father let him take the test in the father's family seat in a rural area of Hyogo-ken. Here, farm boys looked healthier and stouter than Mishima, a city boy. An army doctor's misdiagnosis, taking Mishima's falsely presented bronchitis to be tuberculosis, contributed to his rejection. Mishima lied to the doctor that "I'd been having a slight fever for over half a year, that my shoulder was painfully stiff, that I spit blood, that even last night I was soaked by sweat." Mishima was conscious of his own chicanery, and the influence of his guilty conscience seems to be indicated by his ultranationalism and by his later formation of his own private army, *Tate no Kai* (Society of Shields), whose members wore uniforms resembling those of the military.

Thus, Mishima's narcissistic temperament, strengthened by his reaction against feelings of inferiority, contributed heavily to his suicide. Narcissism involves a neurotic need for attention, which in turn produces an effort to "sell" oneself beyond one's actual worth, not only to others but also to oneself. The effort leads to further ego inflation, which produces a still greater need for attention, setting in motion a vicious cycle. At the same time, a narcissistic person damages his social relations because of his egocentricity and his lack of understanding of other people's feelings.

A core element of narcissism is *amae,* the attitude that assumes that others are always ready to serve one's own needs. Because of Mishima's childhood indulgence and a series of easy successes in adolescence and young adulthood, his *amae* appears to have been close to the infantile sense of omnipotence. Consequently, when his *amae* was not satisfied, the psychological damage he received was unusually strong. This apparently happened at least three times.

In July 1957, Mishima made a trip to New York for the purpose of arranging for his Noh plays to be performed there, but nothing came of it. On Christmas Eve, as Americans were celebrating, he disconsolately left the United States for Europe. (In Japan, Christmas Eve, without religious significance, is a relatively unrestrained time of fun, especially at bars and cabarets.) Donald Keene later recalled that Mishima appeared dejected by what he must have considered "cold treatment" from the Americans.[33] And Scott-Stokes wrote, "It is well known that Mishima felt that Americans whom he had entertained royally in Japan . . . did not reciprocate properly when he visited their city."[34]

Mishima's psychological damage was dramatized by the desperate loneliness of Fujiko in *Kyōko no Ie* [Kyoko's house], which was published in 1959. Fujiko was the daughter of an executive of a large company in which her husband was an employee. She accompanied her husband to New York, where he was interested only in his own affairs. In addition, all Japanese there seemed to be her "enemies" (because they did not serve her narcissistic needs). Her association with Americans was not satisfying, because she could not impress them with her wit. She became desperately lonely:

> Her apartment room, to which she is confined by a snowstorm, looks like a prison. Loneliness, burning inside, flushes her face. Standing up with her face in her hands, she walks around the room. Finally, kneeling down in front of a window, she prays to God, in whom she does not believe: "Please help me! Please save me! I will do anything if you relieve me of this loneliness."

In order to gain attention from someone, she considered attempting suicide. To alleviate the loneliness she slept with a man in New York, hoping that her husband would become angry and punish her. Although we cannot know the degree to which Fujiko's loneliness reflected that of Mishima in New York, the feeling that he was not well treated must have hurt Mishima's narcissistic ego. The incident was probably a turning point in his literature from aesthetic eroticism to ideological didacticism, as represented by his passionately nationalistic *Yuukoku* [Patriotism], published in 1960.

Another incident that hurt Mishima's ego severely was the lack of acclaim for *Kyōko no Ie* (1958), which he thought was a masterpiece. In the work, Mishima's inability to describe characters as living individuals was revealed noticeably. After this work, critics generally dealt harshly with Mishima's writings. His works became increasingly more didactic and abstract. In 1965 he was dejected and despondent, and he was disgusted with literature. He suffered from the feeling of helplessness and thought that nothing he attempted was useful.[35]

The third situational factor was his failure to receive the Nobel Prize in 1968. The damage done to Mishima's ego was extraordinarily severe because, first, he regarded himself as the greatest Japanese writer. Shortly before his suicide, he declared, "I cannot see any cultural development in postwar Japan of any significance. Poetry? No. Sculpture? No. Theater? No. In literature, there is only myself."[36] Second, he had long hoped and worked for a Nobel prize, and for that purpose he had always bent over backward to accommodate the foreign community in Tokyo.[37]

In addition to narcissism, rooted in inferiority feelings, another major factor in the discrepancy between Mishima's ego ideal and his self-concept was homosexuality. Some critics maintain that Mishima had finally found the lover he had been waiting for all his life and had contrived to die a violent warrior's death with him. Whether this was true or not, John Nathan states that Mishima "must have felt a strong sexual attraction to Morita Masakatsu."[38] Morita was Mishima's lieutenant in the Society of Shields (*Tate no Kai*). He beheaded Mishima before committing suicide himself.

Mishima's homosexuality is described in *Kamen no Kokuhaku* and *Kinjiki* [Forbidden colors]. He was known to frequent gay bars in Tokyo, and he even flew to the United States for a tour of gay bars. According to Faubian Bowers:

> One night Mishima flew to America just for sex. He came up and had dinner with me and described quite bluntly what he wanted and asked could I steer him to the right place. I should have been the hospitable host and taken him on a tour of gay bars downtown but I didn't, I didn't want to, and really didn't feel qualified.[39]

His homosexual tendency caused Mishima anxiety and produced within him a sense of being abnormal. The anxiety produced a wide discrepancy between his ego ideal (to be the center of adoration) and his self-concept (being a despicable homosexual).

Both narcissism and homosexuality caused his fear and hatred of reality. His fear and hatred of reality was intensified by the disparity between his ideal conception of society and the actual one in which he lived. His ideal society was the society of beauty. In *Kinkakuji,* when the protagonist was going to have sex with a girl, the image of golden pavilion appeared before his eyes, and he lost his desire. He destroyed the pavilion (i.e., beauty) because it obstructed his enjoyment of the real world. By contrast, Noboru in *Shizumeru Taki* felt happy only when "he was completely shut off from the world." Mishima mused, "Was it not reality that he had been afraid of?"

In conflict with the reality of postwar Japan, Mishima's ideal society of beauty was highly feudalistic. It was a mental construction composed of feudalistic elements still noticeable in modern Japan. The word *feudalism* here implies such characteristics as "education emphasizing memorization and understanding of the elite's ideal pattern by subservient masses" and "the existence of minorities occupying a marginal position,"[40] together with a lack of a sense of responsibility for the unfortunate.

Militarism, which is another element of feudalism, was also an essential element of Mishima's ideal society. He hoped for a revival of militaristic institutions. Although militarism is not directly observable in present Japan, the fundamentally militaristic pattern of thinking is still noticeable in the Japanese people's attitude that "one lives in a group, and nothing but power can defend his group."[41] Compared with China, Japan is still a *shōbu no kuni* (a country with a high regard for military power). The samurai spirit is manifested today by a stress on purity (i.e., selflessness), nonrationalism (i.e., reason as an obstacle to faith and loyalty), action without thinking, emotional rather than moral bravery, and respect for honor, name, and appearance.[42] Japanese militarism today is channeled to business, as Rodney Clark states. "Work is a war being fought by other means. Loyalty and service to one's company is loyalty and service to the nation."[43] The "business is war" mentality is the key to the success of Japan in international competition. The Japanese language even uses war metaphors in business-related talk. Despite such a retention of militaristic psychology among Japanese people, Mishima's militarism was an institutional one. He hoped for constitutionally sanctioned armed forces under the emperor.

Mishima's feudalistic tendency was quite noticeable. He hoped for the restoration of the samurai culture and emperor worship. He professed that "in the past thirteen years, since I started Japanese fencing, I have gradually felt the old samurai spirit surging back in me."[44]

Mishima's elitism, an element of feudalism is evident in the following statement by him:

> Let the weak alone. In the present world, it is the strong who are tortured. There has been no time when the "morality of being strong" is so suppressed. Therefore, it is my task to restore the priority of the strong.[45]

In his eyes the masses were ignorant, always concerned with the status quo, accepting any ideology for economic gain, yielding to the rhetoric of Communists. Therefore, Mishima stressed the necessity for the elite to adhere to their *sogai* (i.e., separateness from main trends) and to uphold the rights of the elite minority. Japanese tradition serves as the foundation of this elitism. Mishima regarded himself as "the flower of Japanese tradition." Even assassination was good in his eyes if it followed the Japanese tradition in which the assassin commits suicide afterward.[46]

Mishima's feudalistic attitude is most strongly indicated in his view of the female minority. His ideal woman was decorative, without much intelligence. He holds in *Kinjiki* that a woman is something like a watch, which a man takes off when he takes a bath—that is, when he bares his real self. Conversely, when dealing with a woman, a man has to forget his "real" self.

Mishima's ideology thus appears to be grossly feudalistic, but it is not entirely so because of its abstract nature. While the basic unit of a feudal system is personal loyalty to the lord, Mishima's concept of the emperor was entirely impersonal. His emperor was a symbol of the "totality and continuity of Japanese culture."[47] Consequently, Mishima did not approve of the present emperor's personal contact with the public. In his mind, the emperor should not act in an ordinary human manner.

Mishima's apparent feudalism may be seen as a facade for egoism—a wish to enhance or maintain his own prestige and privileges. Despite his crusade against general egoism among the Japanese people, Mishima evinced similar traits under another guise.

Thus, narcissism and homosexuality made for the discrepancy between Mishima's ego ideal and self-concept, and his concept of the ideal society, characterized by feudalism and militarism, was in conflict with the reality in which he lived. Another factor in his frustration was his limited life experience. Mishima's limited life experience apparently aggravated the stresses he underwent as a writer. His frustration became more poignant because of his superb competence as a critic.

Mishima's childhood and adolescence were characterized by an atmosphere of limiting rigidity, fanaticism, indulgence, and detachment from reality. Donald Keene was surprised when he found that Mishima "did not know the names of trees, flowers, or animals." Once Mishima asked a gardener the name of a tree, and the gardener answered *"matsu"* (pine tree). Mishima also asked Keene one night, "What is that sound?" and Keene answered, "It is the sound of frogs croaking."[48]

As an adult, Mishima was strongly self-restrained in both heterosexual and homosexual associations. His untroubled, well-ordered, and unchallenging life affected his goal as a writer, which was to describe *tōsui* (rapture), *isshun no jōnetsu no kōyō* (a moment of frenzied passion), or *isshin no seimei no nenshō* (a moment of burning life). It hampered his ability to understand and describe a great variety of emotions.

Mishima's limited life experience is represented by gaps in his knowledge of Japanese tradition. He knew the samurai culture but not that of the merchant. The former is characterized by an emphasis on *on* (repayment of favor), *gimu* (heavier obligation to repay all through life), a fanatic belief in the supremacy of one's own group, nonrational obedience to the lord at the sacrifice not only of self but also of family members and lovers, and elitist contempt for social inferiors. Merchant culture, on the other hand, stressed *ninjō* (human feelings), *giri* (lighter obligation to repay), calculation for self-profit, and cooperation among family members and friends. Mishima understood *seppuku* (self-disembowelment) but not *jōshi* (love-pact suicide) which is an aspect of the merchant culture and requires treating the female more nearly as an equal than is done among samurai.

Even the samurai culture that Mishima knew was only that of the latter Tokugawa regime (1600–1867). At that time the samurai, composing about 6 percent of the total population, was an alienated figure entirely dependent for his survival upon the rice stipend that his lord bestowed. Cultivation of a spirit of self-sacrifice was the price for securing dependence. The samurai's anxiety over his dependence found compensation in his prejudice against and maltreatment of commoners and outcastes.

In addition, Mishima knew only the ideal abstraction of the samurai culture, disregarding the humanity underneath. The samurai was a human being, too; he had the same basic needs and wishes as anyone else. The human side of the samurai culture may be inferred from the behavior of those who lived before the establishment of the rigid status stratification under the Tokugawa regime. The samurai in that earlier period were independent figures who could support themselves on their own land. They could count on their own ability for achieving a better future. Because they were less alienated from life, they were more rational about life and death and freer in self-expression and enjoyment. Of course, the human aspect of the samurai must have been observable in the Tokugawa Era, too. If Mishima had understood the human side of the samurai, he could have written about real humanity rather than about his own imaginary world.

The negative effect of his limited life experience is indicated by Naoya Shiga's criticism: *"Are wa dameda. Yume bakari kaite irukara ikan"* (He [Mishima] is not good. He writes only dreams). Hideo Kobayashi, who is considered Japan's chief literary critic, commented that *"Kinkakuji* is not a novel. It is a lyric produced only by Mishima's imagination. Despite his superabundant talent, no characters are alive; they give no sense of reality."

Thus far, a wide goal-means discrepancy as a cause of Mishima's despair and suicide has been explained with reference to narcissism, homosexuality, a feudalistic philosophy of life, and limited life experiences. Despair, however, does not necessarily make for suicide. Suicidal tendency is promoted by a nonrational tendency whereby the despairing person jumps to the constricted judgment that death is preferable to life.

Japanese thinking is generally characterized by such nonrational tendencies as mysticism, obscurantism, and emotionalism.[49] Although Mishima appears to have been an extremely rational thinker, his nonrational tendencies toward mysticism, obscurantism, and emotionalism seem to have increasingly characterized his works after *Yuukoku*. His action was a result of intuition rather than of reasoning. Reasoning is by definition future oriented. It is the process of choosing from available alternatives the best means for attaining a certain goal, and a goal is always future oriented. However, Mishima disliked any future-oriented activity. He remarked, "What we call a revolution is based on the preference of future to present. I don't like any idea which involves such concepts as future or tomorrow. If we are future oriented we cannot achieve a great thing."[50]

Mishima's concern with ideological conflict was more emotional than rational. In his discussion with students on different campuses, Mishima showed only a fanatic conviction without making much effort to understand the students' arguments. An example of his "logic" is that freedom of speech leads to irresponsible freedom and eventually to reactionary controls, making for totalitarian suppression. Therefore, freedom of speech is to be avoided. To criticisms by students who clamored for freedom of speech, Mishima's answer was, "Then you must like the secret police" or "You must be for concentration camps."[51] In this way he squelched opposition. The dogmatic nature of his thinking is exemplified by a discussion with Waseda University students about society: "Ever since I started as a novelist, I have regarded society as my enemy. There will be no writer who is so foolish as to think otherwise."[52]

Toward the end, Mishima's disaffection with logic grew with his sense of the inadequacy of words. His autobiographical *Taiyō to Tetsu* (1968) begins with the statement:

> Of late, I have come to sense within myself an accumulation of all kinds of things that cannot find adequate expression via an objective artistic form such as a novel. . . . Words constitute a medium that reduces reality to abstraction for transmission to our reason, and in their power to corrode reality inevitably lurks the danger that the words themselves will be corroded too.

Indeed, it is a handicap imposed upon writers (in contrast to musicians and artists) that they have to rely on words for expressing their deepest experiences. However, writers have to discipline themselves to use concepts and words, so that what they want to communicate can be understood by other competent thinkers. When writers quit using words they can no longer communicate. Because of this difficulty, writers are appreciated for their capability to communicate, and literary works are welcomed as contributions to the understanding of humans and society.

Mishima's mistrust of words at the time of writing *Taiyō to Tetsu* must indicate his inner difficulties and loss of confidence, at least temporarily. With the mistrust of words, he gradually discarded his artistic detachment and became emotionally involved in an ideological conflict, even though ideological writings had been objects of his earlier attacks.

Along with nonrational tendencies, another factor in converting suicidal motivation to action is a lack of social resources, especially meaningful communication with significant others. Shohei Ooka recalls that Mishima had no friends among literary colleagues and that Mishima felt that "he had been betrayed by his seniors and friends one after another."[53] The fact that Mishima's wife heard about his dramatic death on a car radio while driving and that she had no idea about his current activities may show the lack of Mishima's meaningful communication with his family members. His contempt for the "ignorant masses" prevented him from developing meaningful communication with ordinary people, although his yearning for it is shown in his writings.

Mishima had young people, members of *Tate no Kai,* who could kill themselves with him, but they were not "others"; they were Mishima's creations, only the reflection of his own will and ideology. They were simply his toys. *Tate no Kai* was an expression of Mishima's desperate attempt to regain the meaningful communication that he had lost among "significant others." However, his creation turned out to be his alter ego and not a social resource for his problem solving.

In combination with nonrational tendencies and a lack of social resources, Mishima's chance of suicide was enhanced by a pessimistic view of life. He was pessimistic about the human capability for self-control. Therefore, he emphasized the importance of a guide for the spirit, such as the samurai code of behavior, to regulate human life. This emphasis occupies a focal point of his literature after *Yuukoku.*

Mishima's pessimism took the form of nihilism. He asserted that "you cannot really perform a significant work without being a nihilist. All those activists who appear to be optimistic are fakes."[54] Regarding *Kyōko no Ie,* he wrote that "the characters in this book ran about in this direction or that, as their individual personalities, their profession, and their sexual preferences commanded them, but in the end all roads, no matter how roundabout, led back into nihilism." A nihilistic denial of existence appears to be quite common among Japanese intellectuals, although their nihilism tends to be more a mood than an ideology; Japanese intellectuals tend to conduct their exploration of selfhood "through an attitude of negation, through the mood of nihilism."[55]

Mishima called his ideology "active nihilism." It is the philosophy that the ultimate significance of life is in attaining the "great nothingness." In order to achieve this, it is necessary to reject oneself for a great cause. "Nothingness" meant being selfless, devoid of selfish desires, and the "great cause" was Japanese tradition.

Although Mishima maintained that sixteenth-century Chinese philosopher Wang-Yang-min's "great nothingness" was the root of his active nihilism, there was a great difference between the two. The "great nothingness" is, as Mishima describes, "the root of creation and the fundamental truth beyond good and evil." When a person attains it, his action becomes "justice beyond life and death." Heihachiro Oshio, a scholar of the Wang-Yang-min school, was one of the few scholars whom Mishima respected. In 1837, a time of terrible famine, Oshio demanded that the government open its storehouses to the starving people of Osaka. The government officials refused, and in desperation Oshio and his men broke open the storehouses. The triumph was short-lived. Oshio dismissed his followers and killed himself. In his mind, the fundamental truth was that of human welfare and the individual's right to survive, and the "great nothingness" was the root of justice for which he died.

The difference between Oshio and Wang-Yang-min's philosophy on the one hand and Mishima's on the other is the matter of suprasocietal (or universal) value. To Chinese Confucian scholars, including Wang-Yang-min, "Heaven" was the central concept. It was a suprasocietal value under whose mandate the ruler ruled people. Therefore, at a time of natural disaster, people could evaluate whether the ruler was fulfilling Heaven's mandate. They could even dethrone him. Although the evaluation was formally done through scholars' divination, there is no doubt that the people's resentment and wishes were reflected in the scholars' interpretations. The concept of Heaven thus implies a conception of the ideal value (i.e., human welfare and the individual's right to survive), against which the established social order may be criticized.

The concept of Heaven was diffused to Japan mainly through the Chu Hsi school of Confucianism, which was the official religion of the Tokugawa administration. This school was more conservative than the Wang-Yang-min school. Gradually the suprasocietal connotation of Heaven was lost. "*Tenchū*" (*Ten,* "Heaven" and *chū,* "killing as punishment"), which originally meant "punishment by Heaven," was shouted by the samurai, who killed anybody inimical or inconvenient to their own interests (or to the interests of their group). Japanese people were particularistic and had difficulty in understanding the universal value implied in the Chinese conception of Heaven. In the Japanese people's eyes, the emperor took the place of Heaven. After World War II, Japanese tradition seems to have replaced the emperor as a sacred object, at least on the *tatemae* level.

Thus, Mishima was less concerned with a universal and more concerned with himself and with the particular group he belonged to—Japan and her tradition. What he wanted seems to be the satisfaction of his own narcissistic need and the need of his society as an extension of his own ego. His nihilistic denial of reality for a great cause turned into the denial of reality for his own need.

Finally, frustrated persons cross the line to suicide when they have more accepting attitudes toward death and suicide. Mishima's attitude toward death and suicide was determined by samurai values. To samurai the highest value was that of selflessness, being ready to die for loyalty. Killing, whether homicide or suicide, was considered justifiable when it was committed for loyalty. According to Mishima, assassination was good if it followed Japanese tradition, with the assassin later committing suicide. Suicide was good if it was done to atone for what the person considered to be his own shortcomings, to pay for a crime he had committed, or to avenge his lord. The manifest motive of Mishima's suicide, as indicated in his final plea, was *kangen* (remonstration) to a modern corrupt Japan.

On another level, Mishima's suicide was a restitutional act in that he was seeking to restore or to create a positive sense of identity. True to his preoccupation with the samurai, he chose the samurai identity. Indeed, because of his creative powers as a writer, he was able to shape a group of young men into his army, his followers in the samurai tradition. Mishima's aim was to assert his own samurai identity as a reaction to the anxiety rooted in his ambivalent sexual identity.

For Mishima the act of suicide was a final act of manhood, courage, and advocacy of a return to traditional values of high importance in a nation so tied to the past. In his final act, he was the samurai, he was a hero, he was Japan calling for a return to its glorious and powerful past. A basic motive of his suicide was self-assertion.

In this respect Mishima's suicide was a consequence of his conception of beauty. In the 1960s many Japanese intellectuals, including Mishima, lost their sense of identity. They were alienated from their prewar tradition but did not yet have a new philosophy with which to identify. They had a deep sense of mistrust about human potential. To some of them the only meaning of life was beauty in contrast to truth or goodness. Some of them, such as Mishima, Shintaro Ishihara (the writer), and Masahiro Shinoda (the movie director), maintained that beauty could be experienced only in violence and in its corollary of rapture, whether sadistic or masochistic. For them the utmost representation of masochistic ecstasy and, therefore, of beauty is suicide.

YASUNARI KAWABATA

Yasunari Kawabata was born in Osaka in 1899. When he was two years old, his father died, and his mother died the next year. At that time he was separated from his only sister. She died at the age of seven. When Kawabata was seven years old, his grandmother died, and eight years later his grandfather, the only remaining member of his family, also died.

Kawabata started to write for publication while in middle school (comparable to today's high school). By 1924, when he graduated from Tokyo University, he had become an established writer. In the year of his graduation, he and others initiated a new school of literature, *Shin kankaku ha* ("new sensualism"). The school was directed primarily against socialistic and naturalistic writings. In 1926, *Izu no Odoriko* [Izu dancers] was published, and *Yukiguni* [Snow country] in 1937. Kawabata was elected president of the Japan Pen Club in 1948, at the age of forty-seven, and *Senbazuru* [Thousand cranes] was published in 1952. In 1958, he was elected vice president of the International Pen Club. *Nemureru Bijo* [Sleeping beauty] and *Fushi* [No death] were published in 1962 and 1963, respectively. Kawabata was awarded the Nobel Prize for literature in 1968. On April 16, 1972, he routinely left his home in Kamakura for his workroom in nearby Zushi. That evening, in a room that commanded a magnificent view of ocean and mountains, he was found dead with a gas conduit in his mouth. He was seventy-two years old.

A characteristic of a successful writer's suicide is extraordinarily high aspiration. When successful persons attain the gratification to their self-esteem, their exhibitionism and relative omnipotence actually create a wider gap between their ego ideal and their actual self-concept. The gap becomes wider in the case of writers because of their introspective tendency. Self-generated anxiety becomes a source of achievement when it is combined with creativity and a certain degree of adequate physical conditions. Otherwise, it may lead to intense frustration.

In contrast to his grand aspirations, Kawabata's health was very poor. He was never really healthy, and he called himself *byōki no tonya* ("wholesaler of illness").[56] In his later life he often suffered from insomnia and needed sleeping pills to ease his tension and anxiety. He was often seen in a daze.[57] The habit of taking sleeping pills accelerated his physical deterioration. Shortly before he received the Nobel Prize, Kawabata felt that his body was "crumbling down all over," and he said that he was "almost giving up."[58]

His physical deterioration was aggravated by the Japanese custom of visiting. In many situations in Japan, there is little tradition of respect for other people's time and privacy. Kawabata wanted to be alone. He wrote:

Always we had so many visitors that I was tired and irritated. They disturbed my work and sleep. They deprived me of most of my working time during the day. Often, waking up or returning home, I found visitors waiting for me. It was disgusting. I complained frequently to my wife that "I am not an innkeeper. I am not living for visitors." Tired of entertaining them, my wife got ill, too.[59]

Because of visitors, he worked at night. His wife stayed awake with him while he worked, and she was often seen tired and falling asleep even while talking with visitors.

Receiving the Nobel Prize made the situation worse. Politicians were eager to exploit Kawabata's enhanced popularity among the general public. At the same time, the prize may have unconsciously strengthened his sense of omnipotence, as he became increasingly imperious. He was naively enticed into participating in an emotional campaign for Hatano, a conservative candidate for the 1972 Tokyo mayoralty. Hatano's opponent, Ryokichi Minobe, against whom Kawabata was "unusually emotionally hostile,"[60] was a progressive candidate. Minobe was very popular among intellectuals, including most of Kawabata's friends. The political involvement sapped a good deal of Kawabata's time and energy. With physical exhaustion, his mental stability also declined.[61]

These situational factors aggravated the natural process of deterioration due to aging. The biological deterioration apparently made for anxiety and a lower degree of flexibility, which in combination contributed to a lowered tolerance for frustration. Kawabata's anxiety was probably reinforced by "anticipatory anxiety."[62] Generally, because an old person anticipates his further deterioration, what Victor Frankl calls hyperintention (which demonstrates potency) intensifies his anxiety. Moreover, anxiety is reinforced by experiences of observing other people's deterioration. Probably more than anything else, Kawabata's feeling that he did not publish any meaningful work after winning the Nobel Prize nagged him to the despair that his creative days were over.

His frustration over the discrepancy between high aspiration and poor health was intensified by the gap between his ideal world of mystical beauty, self-restraint, and harmony, on the one hand, and the actual social conditions in postwar Japan, on the other. In his mind, the latter were characterized by materialistic pragmatism, selfishness, and chaos. Kawabata rebelled against these conditions.

He was an inveterate rebel. He repeatedly maintained that "literature is rebellion; the writer is a *burai no to* [villain]."[63] Apparently, by *burai* he meant nonconformity to conventional morality. Kawabata's literature was characterized by three forms of rebellion.

First, he rebelled against the feudal tradition of Japan, which had been strong until World War II. Japanese rebellion against the feudal tradition generally took the form of Communism, Christianity, or nihilism. All of these responses attempt to uphold the individual self against the oppressive society. Kawabata, like Dazai and Mishima, chose the last. His rebellion was expressed in reference to sensual gratification. He did not hesitate to write about what appears to be immorality in the eyes of traditional Japanese. An example is *Senbazuru,* in which incestuous relationships are symbolized.

Second, Kawabata rebelled against the tradition of modern Japanese literature, which, following modern Western literature, aimed at a realistic description of the individual oppressed by society. He also denigrated Japanese "naturalists," who tended to indulge in detailed descriptions of sex. Denying both ideological and naturalistic emphases, Kawabata advocated *shin-kankaku-ha* ("the new sensualism") in 1926. He stressed sensuality as opposed to ideological involvement. But sensuality, he maintained, must be beautiful. Beauty is subtle and cannot be depicted by a superficial description of animalistic behavior. His emphasis on the description of beauty through the senses is exemplified by his famous description of a girl reflected in a window of a moving train:

> Outside it was growing dark, and the lights had been turned on in the train, transforming the window into a mirror. . . .
> In the depths of the mirror, the evening landscape moved by, the mirror and the reflected figures like motion pictures superimposed one on the other. . . . When the light in the mountains shone in the center of the girl's face . . . the reflection in the mirror was not strong enough to blot out the light outside, nor was the light strong enough to dim the reflection. The light moved across the face, though not to light it up. It was a distant, cold light. As it sent its small ray through the pupil of the girl's eye, as the eye and the light were superimposed one on the other, the eye became a weirdly beautiful bit of phosphorescence on the sea of evening mountains. [From *Yukiguni,* translated by Edward Seidensticker]

Third, Kawabata rebelled against postwar conditions in Japan. Deprived of their traditional values of emperor worship and militarism, the Japanese people returned to a basic motive of the human animal—biological gratification. It might have been a natural reaction to the traditionally stifled individuality. Japanese masses were conditioned to respond to social expectations. When social expectations broke down, they had little to follow but the most primitive needs. The self-interest motive was reinforced by the concept of democracy, as imposed en masse from American GIs. Since American democracy was interpreted by the Japanese as a claim for the individual's rights (even at the expense of others, while disregarding social responsibility), this "democracy" produced people without principle.

To such conditions, Kawabata reacted with intense hostility:

> Since the defeat in the last war, I have nothing to return to except *Nihon korai no kanashimi* [traditional pathos of Japan]. I neither believe in postwar conditions nor in reality.

He wanted to embody in his literature "*Furui utsukushii Nihon*" (old beautiful Japan). His emphasis on harmony and tradition was rooted in his admiration of Heian literature, developed by courtiers in the ninth through the twelfth century, and was in conflict with the modern tendency toward *anomie.* His stress on an intuitive and mystical comprehension was in conflict with the new tendency toward materialistic rationalism.

Like Mishima, Kawabata was a traditionalist, although they represented different aspects of Japanese tradition. In contrast to Mishima, who symbolized the "sword" aspect of Japanese culture, Kawabata represented its chrysanthemum aspect. The Japanese people have been known for their militarism and also for "the pleasure they get from innocent things: viewing the cherry blossoms, the moon, chrysanthemums, or new-fallen snow."[64]

Kawabata's traditionalist aspect, however, should not be over-emphasized. If he were living in a society where Japanese tradition was alive and well, he would have rebelled against that society, too.

Thus, Kawabata's frustration over the discrepancy between his aspiration and his deteriorating physical strength led to despair, and his despair was aggravated by his inclination to rebel. The conversion of despair to self-destructive behavior is a function of one's philosophy of life and death and of the availability of social resources contributive to tension reduction and problem solving.

As influenced by Heian literature, Kawabata's philosophy of the world was pessimistic. Toward the end of the Heian Period, the power of the courtiers was rapidly waning because of uprising warriors, rampant bandits, and a series of natural disasters. It was also endangered by the commoners' resentment of the inept, extortionate government.

Heian literature reached its apex in *Shin-Kokinshu* (compiled in 1206). It is characterized by (1) an almost exclusive concern with sensual gratification; (2) an animistic belief in the existence and influences of spirits; and (3) the view that life is suffering and death is sweet. The literature was a collective representation of the courtiers' wish for escape. Similarly, the dominant traits of Kawabata's literature are those of loneliness and the wish to escape from it. Kawabata believed that human fate is predetermined and that there is no way for humans to control their future.

Kawabata's fatalism is represented by one word, *torō* (futile). The word appears twelve times in the relatively short but representative novel *Yukiguni*. The futility of any effort for future welfare is indicated by the protagonist of the novel, Komako, a geisha. She loves a traveling writer, Shimamura, but his feeling toward her is never clear. She fears that her love will never be rewarded and that it will bring her only desperate loneliness. Despite the fear, she cannot help waiting for Shimamura. She represents the beauty of feminine affection and the ultimate aloneness and helplessness of all humans.

Kawabata's pessimism was probably rooted in his yearning for his mother, a yearning that could never be satisfied. The loss of parents, sister, and grandmother at a very early age and the lack of emotional involvement with family members probably produced in him a strong sense of deprivation and loneliness. The sense of deprivation and loneliness was intensified by the idealization of family life, especially of the mother-child relationship, in Japan. Kawabata's yearning for his mother was generalized to other women. *Nemureru Bijo* [Sleeping beauty] symbolizes his wish to cuddle with and to be warmed by a maternal figure. In that work, an old man patronizes a place where he can sleep with a young girl; she is drugged and asleep during the encounter, and he is not allowed to have sex with her, suggesting an Oedipal relationship.

Kawabata's attitude toward death is highly accepting. Influenced by the animism, mysticism, and fatalism of Heian literature, he recognized little difference between life and death. Both are seen as aspects of the same Nature. While he was being massaged during his campaign for Hatano, he suddenly rose and said, "Welcome, Nichiren-sama!" (Nichiren founded the Nichiren sect of Buddhism in 1253). At another time, also during a massage, Kawabata leaped up and said, "Mishima-kun. Did you come to help me campaign?" Mishima had been dead for more than a year. Recalling that Kawabata often disappeared from his friends for long periods, Tōkō Kon theorizes that Kawabata might have left this world as casually as he took off on a trip.[65] It is probable that Kawabata wanted simply to return to Nature rather than to terminate his life.

Moreover, death contained an element of beauty to Kawabata. Beauty was only in the world of phantasm—that is, between life and death. In a short story, "Fushi" [No death], Kawabata wrote about a couple who attempt a double suicide. The girl dies, but the young man lives for forty more years of travail. After he dies, his spirit, as a haggard old man, unexpectedly meets with the eighteen-year-old spirit of the girl. Their short conversation is full of calm affection and pathos. This short story suggests Kawabata's feeling that death is beautiful, while life is not only ugly but also full of suffering.

Not only was Kawabata intimate with death, because of his childhood experiences, but he also lived with a suicidal wish. Shinichiro Nakamura reports that "except when he was on a trip abroad, there was no day when he did not wish to die."[66] Why? The combination of Kawabata's physical illness (worsened by his habitual use of sleeping pills), his pessimistic conception of life, reinforced by the social conditions in postwar Japan, and his romanticized conception of death must have been a strong inducement to suicide. There was, however, another factor, that of his lack of social attachment.

Kawabata's sense of social isolation was rooted in the Japanese prejudice against orphans. Because of the close-knit family structure in that country, there is a belief that without parental supervision and discipline, and with the economic insecurity generally expected from a fatherless family, an orphan's personality is believed to be too warped to allow him or her to be a reliable employee. "Good" companies, especially banks, do not employ orphans. People tend to regard them as untrustworthy and inferior. Understandably, the expectation of such rejection and discrimination causes insecurity and paranoid mistrust in the orphan, a condition that Kawabata called *koji konjō* (orphan mentality). The *koji konjō* and the negative expectations of others make it difficult for an orphan to relate comfortably to others. All his life, Kawabata never had a really intimate friend. He begins *Izu no Odoriko* with the statement:

> Desperate because of the suffocating depression from my severe self-examination, I felt that my personality at the age of twenty has been warped by the *koji konjō*. I started on the trip to Izu [a peninsula south of Tokyo].

In addition to *koji konjō,* Kawabata was a self-sufficient, independent thinker. As a result, his social interaction was even more difficult. In Japan, where social extroverts (those attentive to others' responses) and field-dependent people (those high in social sensitivity) are the norm, self-sufficient and independent persons may be looked upon as strange. Kawabata was called *bukimina hito* (a weird person) even by one of his closest friends.[67] Sohachi Yamaoka, who served with Kawabata as a war writer at navy kamikaze pilot bases, reported about Kawabata's weirdness and his indifference to other people's feelings:

> Every day, without writing anything himself, Kawabata gazed rudely at the papers that I was working on. The gaze from this master writer made me so uneasy that I begged him to stop. He grinned slightly, but did not stop.[68]

When a group of young musical dancers visited Kawabata and had a merry time, one of the girls noticed that Kawabata "was observing their frolics in the same way he would have observed fifty birds."[69]

His detached observation is what really made Kawabata a great writer. His skill and detachment are illustrated by the tragic ending of the novel *Yukiguni*. The scene is a burning theater. At the sight of Yoko's body falling from a balcony through the flames "quite horizontally," Shimamura started back. It was not from fear, however—if he felt even a flicker of uneasiness, "it was lest the head drop, or a knee or a hip bend to disturb that perfectly horizontal line." At the same time, Kawabata's capability for emotionless observation made for a lack of real intimacy in a society where personal cohesiveness is emphasized. Kawabata was unable to merge his ego into one "collective we." His lack of social involvement made for an egoistic suicide in Durkheimian terms. He preferred death to "unbearable, lonely, empty, and meaningless" living.

七

VII

JAPANESE
VALUE
ORIENTATIONS

The discussions of suicide among Japanese youths, women, and writers showed the importance of social structure in relation to suicide. The concept of anomic suicide (as indicated by a wide discrepancy between ego ideal and self-conception, the sense of relative deprivation, greed, disillusionment, and jealousy) facilitates the understanding of college-student suicides. Because of the high emphasis on education and ambition, the importance of a wide goal-means disparity as a cause of suicide also applies generally to Japanese youths.

A UNESCO study by Jean Stoetzel in 1951–52 found Japanese youths to be highly ambitious, hankering after fame, but unable to give any details about how to attain their goals. The Japanese youth was very self-confident, but his self-confidence was based on "faith in his star, not belief in his present judgment, will-power, and efficiency." His personality was characterized by high ambivalence, ambiguity, passivity and resignation, lack of imagination, insecurity, and escapism.[1] These characteristics also appear to be important elements of the Japanese youth's personality today.

Many Japanese women's suicides were fatalistic, due to sex prejudice, with resulting resentment, fear, and resignation. Some others were of the anomic type, due to role conflicts that produced a wide goal-means discrepancy and disillusionment. Writers' suicides are difficult to categorize because they appear more various in motivation. Arishima's suicide seems to show more elements of egoistic suicide (e.g., a desire to find meaning in life), Akutagawa's suicide shows elements of fatalistic suicide (e.g., his strong sense of family obligation, resentment, and resignation), and Dazai's suicide shows elements of anomic suicide (e.g., his inflated ego ideal and dependency). Mishima's suicide may be categorized as an altruistic one, at least on his conscious level, because it was a remonstration against the "corrupt" Japan of the postwar period. He showed a high degree of integration into Japanese tradition. Kawabata's suicide was egoistic, because he was a self-sufficient thinker. In his case, physical illness seems to have been the most important factor. (If there is a rational suicide—that is, suicide as a result of thorough contemplation of all alternatives—Kawabata's suicide appears to have come close to it.) However, on a deeper level, the suicides of all these writers may be attributed to the discrepancy between their ego ideal and self-concept (for example, losing creativity).

Suicide is mostly caused by a failure to attain personal goals because of inadequate means. Inadequate means include "inimical" behavior, illness, declining creativity, and weak ego. Weak ego is characterized by a strong dependency need, a tendency toward emotionalism, high susceptibility to group pressure, a lack of reality testing, and weak impulse control.

Some of the data used in these discussions were from studies done in the mid-1950s, when Japanese suicide rates were highest (in 1958, 25.7 per 100,000: 30.7 for males and 20.8 for females). However, as Christopher observed in 1982,[2] feudalistic remnants of behavior patterns—such as education characterized by memorization, a strong stress on power and status difference, and sex and ethnic prejudices—are still prevalent in present-day Japan. Compared with the 1950s, there is even a sign of the strong revival of traditionalism in the 1980s, with the decline in prestige of their model—American democracy. The revival is marked by the governmental control of Japanese education.

Discussed in this chapter are the components of Japanese social structure that largely determine the goal-means discrepancy—that is, the

TABLE 32.

A COMPARISON OF JAPANESE AND AMERICAN VALUE ORIENTATIONS

Problem of life	Japanese	American[a]
1. Man–Nature relationship	Monism Polytheism Mysticism	Dualism Monotheism Rationalism
2. Valued personality type	Groupism	Individualism

Emphasis on:	Harmony
	Selflessness
	Competition for
	   group goals
		Ego-strength
		Self-assertion
		Competition for
		   self-interest

3. Time orientation	Accommodationism "Field dependent" Short-time perspective	 "Field independent" Future orientation
Emphasis on:	Adjustment	Development, change
View of future:	Insecurity about future	Optimism about future
4. Mode of social relations	Familism Authoritarianism	Mechanistic view of society Egalitarianism
Emphasis on:	Faith, loyalty	Efficiency, cleanliness, orderliness
Values counterbalancing individualism for social integration		Love, fair play, coopera- tion, conscience, group sport, humanitarianism

[a]Adapted from John Gillin, "National and Regional Cultural Values in the United States," *Social Forces* 34 (December 1955): 107–113.

value orientations that produce unrealistically high aspirations and inadequate means to achieve them.

At the risk of oversimplification, table 32 describes Japanese culture in comparison with American culture. The American material has been adapted from John Gillin's characterization of American culture.[3] The comparison is made of the basic problems that all peoples have to solve: the Man–Nature relationship, the valued personality type, time orientation, and the mode of social relations.[4]

The American view of the Man-Nature relationship is dualistic: man versus nonhuman, including Nature and God. The separation of man from Nature promotes rationalism; eventually, everything, including God, has become the object of reasoning. At the same time, an ideal is separate from natural phenomena—that is, the law ("what ought to be") versus existence ("what is").

The valued personality type among Americans is individualistic, with emphasis on self-interest, self-development, and self-reliance. The modality of social relations is revealed in principles for social integration and collateral values. The American view of social integration is mechanistic, holding that society is like a machine. It operates well only when its parts are clean, efficient, and coordinated in an orderly fashion. Hence, values of cleanliness, efficiency, and orderliness are expected. Since "efficient" Americans use reasoning for attaining self-profit, their social integration requires values that counterbalance self-profit—for example, Americans place strong emphases on love, cooperation, conscience, fair play, humanitarian assistance, and group sport. The American culture is also characterized by future orientation. It aims at future success and development. Because of American faith in development, together with the historical experience of their frontier, Americans are optimistic about life and change.

In comparison, Japanese culture is characterized by monism, groupism, familism, and accommodationism, as explained on the following pages. Of course, these are persisting elements of Japanese tradition. The more traditional are Japanese persons, the more strongly they manifest these traits. These elements of Japanese tradition are quite applicable to explanations of Japanese behavior patterns, whether of suicide or of economic success.

MONISM

Monism is the doctrine that there is only one ultimate substance or principle, whether mind (idealism) or matter (materialism) or some other thing that is the basis of both. It holds that reality is an organic whole without independent parts. Within the framework of monism, Japanese regard both man and natural phenomena as of the same substance, that is, Nature. To the traditional Japanese, Nature is absolute, and they reject "the recognition of anything existing over and above the phenomenal world."[5] Therefore, "the natural sciences have almost never been established on the foundation of traditional Japanese thinking. . . . The natural sciences were begun only in modern times through the introduction of sciences from Holland."[6] Science requires the human mind to observe phenomena with detachment. To traditional Japanese, Nature includes society. Therefore, society is natural, and individuals must adjust to it rather than analyze it.

To Japanese, "natural phenomena" also include biological drives. In the Western dichotomy of ideal and real, Christianity emphasizes the control of biological drives for religious goals. Marxism does the same for ideological purposes. The Russian Revolution turned Soviet society into "perhaps the most puritanical in the world."[7] In contrast, in Japanese monism, biological drives are natural (although just for males, in practice) and are for man to be in harmony with rather than to control. When Takeo Arishima was studying at Harvard University, he dropped Christianity because he did not like its puritanical attitude toward sexual desires which dominated New England churches then, although he himself was highly puritanical in comparison with most other Japanese. The difficulty is explained by a Christian Kyoto University student who attempted suicide:

> Marxism and Christianity make me incapable of any action, because they cause conflict with my natural desires. . . . I attempted to stifle my desires by reasoning. . . . I have too many desires to be a Christian. The more I have come to know Christianity and the more I read the Bible, the more painful becomes the awareness of my own ugliness, evilness, and sin.
>
> Christianity is intolerant. Since it mistrusts human nature, it is a burden on man. . . . Christianity is dysfunctional. It generates guilt, affecting social relations adversely, and hampers man's natural development.

The Japanese tendency to accept sexual desires as natural is expressed by their positive attitude toward prostitution. An example is their practice of visiting houses of prostitution as part of their itinerary when traveling abroad. "Each year about 1 million Japanese sign up and head for sexual binges in Taipei, Bangkok, Seoul or Manila, often conducting their revels at Japanese-only bars and brothels."[8] The Rev. Sir Alan Walker, president of Life-Line International, urged the Japanese government to cease the "disgraceful exploitation of women" and "violation of human rights."[9]

In addition to their attitude toward Nature, society, and human nature, the attitude of the Japanese toward the "ideal"—whether law ("what ought to be") or divinity ("ego ideal")—is also monistic. In the West, the law is separated from existence; justice as an ideal supersedes everything, including the established social order, even if the world were to perish on the course of justice's attainment (*Fiat iustitia pereat mundus*).[10] In contrast, Japanese laws are for humans to use. Since the human being in traditional Japan is a carrier of statuses rather than an embodiment of humanity, laws tend to be influenced by the individual's statuses.

In contrast to a Western God, who is absolutely separate from man, Japanese gods are either ancestors or personalized spirits who are supposed to exist in natural phenomena. Thus, an expression of Japanese monism is animism, the tenet that holds that spirits reside in all things and influence human activity. The deceased person's spirit becomes a guardian angel of his family. The living members can pray to the spirit for protection.

Animism is the basic element of Shintoism. Shintoism was the national religion of Japan until the U.S. Occupational Armed Forces forced the Japanese to abandon it after World War II. The Shinto follower worships unusually awe-inspiring or fear-provoking natural phenomena, together with ancestors of the imperial family and cultural heroes. The function of Shinto priests is ritual purification, intended to purify people from the influence of evil spirits and to make them attractive to beneficial ones. Because all human miseries, including illness, are considered to be caused by evil spirits, it follows that "purification" is the only cure. The Shinto laxness of distinction between god and human, Jared Taylor contends, can shade into what appears to Westerners to be just plain superstition:

> Shinto charms and amulets, for example, are big business. Wives who want to get pregnant wear them, mothers buy them for their children at exam time, and people about to go into the hospital take them along for speedy recovery. Practically every vehicle in Japan has hanging from the rearview mirror a small, embroidered pouch which contains a special charm to prevent traffic accidents.[11]

Animism is polytheism. The majority of Japanese people are dominated by polytheistic folk religion in their personal lives as well as in their social, family, and work activities.[12] A unique aspect of Japanese culture and personality is the coexistence of highly developed technology and polytheistic beliefs. In 1981 alone, some 7,000 Japanese companies built new office shrines for Inari (fox god), the patron deity of business prosperity.[13]

Sometimes animistic beliefs can cause international embarrassment, as exemplified in the following report:

When the British ambassador, Sir Michael Wilford, inspected construction of the world's longest undersea tunnel in northern Japan, his wife got no further than the entrance.

Politely, but firmly, a construction site official insisted, "No women are allowed in the thirty-two-mile Seikan Tunnel." Lady Wilford was told, "It is said that the gods will become angry if a woman enters the tunnel, and a bad accident will occur. It may only be an old superstition, but the workers still get very worried about it."

The ambassador's wife accepted the rebuff with good grace and could at least be consoled that she joined a growing list of women in public life who have run into the same problem at construction sites up and down the country.[14]

A corollary of animism is nonrational tendencies, which include "regarding reason as an obstacle to faith and loyalty." Through analysis of the Japanese language in comparison with Indian, Tibetan, and Chinese with reference to Buddhist concepts, Dean Nakamura Hajime of Tokyo University found the following attributes of nonrationality to be typical of Japanese culture: indifference to logical rules, emotionality, avoidance of complex ideas, fondness for simple symbolic expressions, and lack of knowledge concerning the objective order.[15] Rationality develops through the effort to find the most effective means for solving a problem. For problem solving, however, Japanese people traditionally rely on customs rather than reason—for example, relying on a go-between or *oyabun* ("parent-role person"). *Oyabun* also includes governmental officials. Many Japanese "just acquiesce to the opponent's demands, if the opponent has more power."[16]

Japanese nonrational tendencies are expressed in intuitive and obscure thinking. The best leader in Japan is the person capable of *haragei*, that is, of expressing his feelings directly to his audience without saying or doing anything. He is the person who is able to transcend logic and solve problems with intuition or spirit.[17] The prototype of intuitive thinking among Japanese people is the *Hagakure,* written for samurai around 1715. The book exhorts, "Reason not, set your mind on the way you choose and push on." The teaching is accepted as the essence of the "samurai spirit."

The intuitive tendency was broadly spread among Japanese people by the Zen teaching of *kuu* or *mu* (emptiness). The philosophy teaches that anything that has form has no substance. All things observable are relative, and the real meaning is hidden behind surface matters. Zen is an attempt to grasp the meaning behind the interacting confusion of particular matters. The real meaning is universal, like a universal law, and cannot be attained by an individual's conscious reasoning. The way to grasp the real meaning is for a person to become "mindless" or "purposeless," unconscious not only of himself but of all phenomena surrounding him. His mind must be perfectly purged of all egocentric desires. Only then can the activities of the universal mind be displayed to the utmost extent. There is no room for reasoning in this process. Since the deliberation surely interferes and stops the course of the flowing mind, Zen masters admonish disciples to "have no deliberation, no discrimination." Reasoning localizes one's capacity and freezes the mind, and, therefore, one should let the mind "go all by itself, freely, unhindered and uninhibited."

Obscurity is a characteristic of the Japanese language that structures the thought process of Japanese people. In the following quotation, Junichiro Tanizaki, one of the greatest writers in Japan, points out the obscure nature of Japanese language by comparing a section of *Genji Monogatari* [The tale of Genji] with its English translation by Arthur Waley:

> As you see, what is covered in six lines in the original is extended to thirteen lines in the English translation. There are many words which do not correspond to the words in the original. The English version is more detailed than the original; it has no part which is unclear in meaning. English writers make an effort to make clear sentences clearer. In the Japanese language a few words provide and provoke the reader's imagination, and make the reader himself supplement what is not really clear. The writer's function is only to stimulate the reader's imagination. Japanese people do not rely upon language as much as Chinese or Westerners do. They believe that as long as a person is sincere, his feeling and thinking are conveyed to another, even when they sit together without words. They are convinced that mutual agreement without words is more important than ten thousand words.[18]

Regarding this nonrational tendency, a question may be raised as to why Confucianism and Buddhism, which were originally highly rational, did not contribute to the development of rational thinking in the Japanese people in general.

Chinese Confucianism contributed to Japanese culture through its emphasis on "the cultivation of filial piety, honesty, and loyalty, and the idea of honoring the virtuous and repaying the services of outstanding men."[19] The difference between Japanese and Chinese ways of thinking in respect to rationality seems to be rooted in the nature of rulership. While China has been under civilian rule, Japanese society has been controlled by military men, first by the imperial family and then by a series of military lords. In modern times Japan was controlled by military leaders until the defeat in World War II. These experiences, over thousands of years, have formed the Japanese culture and personality.

While civilian control perceives law as superior to individuals, military control sets military leaders above laws. For example, the Chinese emperors, as well as the common people, were evaluated against the "will of Heaven." The emperor's evaluation was done by scholars' divination, but the interpretations were greatly influenced by the masses' general welfare and opinions at the time of natural calamities. Chinese emperors could be dethroned. On the other hand, Japanese emperors, originally military leaders, became "sons of God" and could do nothing wrong, depriving people of any ground to criticize them. The concept of the inviolability of the emperor was later transferred to the shogun and was used by other military leaders for the purpose of social control.

The psychology of a people rooted in long tradition does not change easily under external pressures, even those of the "revolution" that the Japanese experienced after the defeat in the last war. Japanese "revolutions" have always been imposed upon people from above, and her institutional change has not been correlated with psychological change. A group of Japanese tourists, who follow the leader in line, and employees of big Japanese companies, who devote themselves to their companies at the sacrifice of their families, appear like people under military control.[20]

Indian Buddhism, which became the prototype of Japanese Buddhism, was called "a metaphysic generating a religion" by A. N. Whitehead (*Religion in the Making*, 1926). Reasoning is the primary means for attaining its ultimate objective, *satori* (enlightenment). *Satori* is indicated by the realization that all phenomenal appearances are lost and that the things a man craves have no more reality than a dream—the realization, that is, of Nothingness or Emptiness.

In order to attain the enlightenment, Buddhists must learn the Four Noble Truths and practice the Noble Eightfold Path and the Middle Way. The doctrine of the Four Noble Truths, a common property of all schools of Buddhist thought, holds that (1) all life is inevitably sorrowful, (2) sorrow is due to craving, (3) sorrow can only be stopped by the cessation of craving, and (4) cessation of craving can only be accomplished by a course of careful disciplined and moral conduct, culminating in the life of concentration and meditation led by Buddhist monks.[21] The Noble Eightfold Path consists of Right View, Right Resolve, Right Speech, Right Conduct, Right Livelihood, Right Effort, Right Mindfulness, and Right Concentration. The Middle Way doctrine teaches the avoidance of two extremes: the pursuit of desires and the pursuit of pain and hardship. The Middle Way brings clear vision, makes for wisdom, and leads to peace, insight, enlightenment, and Nirvana. Thus, Indian faith in Nothingness or Emptiness is not to deny reason but to attain a stoical and noble equanimity through thorough reasoning.

Buddhism, as advocated by Shakyamuni (historical "Buddha"), rejects magic and ritual because they serve man's craving.[22] Indian Buddhism does not believe in such supernatural phenomena as "soul" or "spirit" and does not accept the idea of Heaven or Hell, where the soul is supposed to go.[23] When a man dies, he becomes nothing. Burial is not a Buddhist tradition; the dead body is burned, and the ashes are scattered. The sole purpose of original Buddhism is not salvation but *gedatsu,* the freeing of the mind from illusion. This purpose is quite akin to that of science.

By contrast, Japanese Buddhism is filled with magic and ritual and with ideas of souls, spirits, Heaven, and Hell. Funeral and burial are major sources of income for Buddhist priests in Japan. Buddhism was originally welcomed in Japan for its artistic appeal and magical functions (e.g., healing). It was transformed into a system of faith and rituals with little doctrine. Shingon Mikkyō, which Kuukai taught to courtiers as a means for spiritual emancipation in the ninth century, was a composite of arts, magic, and rituals as well as philosophy.

Philosophy was largely gone and personal effort as a requirement of salvation was denied when Shinran taught in the thirteenth century that salvation truly depended on nothing but the grace of Amida Buddha and that it was needless and perhaps dangerous to act as if one's conduct could have any bearing on ultimate redemption.[24] Shinran even declared that "If even a good man can be reborn in the Pure Land, how much more so a wicked man!" Salvation came from paying homage to Buddha only by repeating the *Nembutsu* ("*Namu Amida-Butsu*"). The idea of salvation through the *Nembutsu* was not an element of Shakyamuni's original teachings. In Shinran Buddhism ("Shin-Shu" or "True Pure-Land School"), which exerted the greatest influence upon Japanese personality, "virtually nothing remained of the Buddha, as manifested by Shakyamuni, or the Law as embodied in scripture, or of the religious company as represented by a celibate clergy following monastic discipline. Gone, too, was the traditional emphasis on enlightenment through strenuous personal effort."[25] Shinran's nonrational tendency is shown in his statement that "whether the *Nembutsu* brings rebirth in the Pure Land or leads one to Hell, I myself have no way of knowing. But even if I have been misled by Hōnen and go to Hell for saying the *Nembutsu*, I have no regret." This emphasis on faith and loyalty at the expense of reason is the essence of the Japan spirit.

Like Shin-shu, Nichiren-shu (the Nichiren school), which is the most nationalistic among Japanese Buddhisms, stresses the need for complete faith in something beyond oneself: the Lotus Sutra. One of its offshoots, Soka Gakkai, teaches that simply by chanting the sutra *Namumyo hō rengekyō* over and over, the believer will get whatever he wants.

Zen Buddhism, however, which is the closest to the historical Buddha's teachings among Japanese schools of Buddhism, stresses that every man has a Buddha nature and that in order to realize it he needs only to look within. Self-understanding and self-reliance are the keynote of Zen. Therefore, Zen appears to emphasize reason and to develop rationalism. Nevertheless, it teaches that Buddhahood is realized in life by "selfless" action and strenuous effort, with no thought of achieving an end apart from the means. It emphasizes intuition at the expense of reason. Dogen, the founder of the Soto Zen Sect, which provided the essence of the samurai spirit and *yamato damashii* ("Japan spirit"), exhorted that only when one let go of the mind and ceased to seek an intellectual apprehension of the Truth was liberation attainable. He also taught that to do away with mental deliberation and cognition and simply to go on sitting was the method by which the Way was made an intimate part of our lives.

Regardless of their affiliation, lay Buddhists in general are taught to have faith in the established social order and to practice thanksgiving to society, filial piety, and ancestor worship. The unquestioning faith in the established social order prevents the development of reasoning. Moreover, reasoning is not encouraged by Japanese Buddhism as a tool for problem solving. The primary function of Japanese Buddhism in the mind of lay members is the same as that of Shintoism—magical problem solving.[26] What its members pray for in front of the *butsudan* (miniature household Buddhist altar) is Buddha's help for the safety, comfort, and prosperity of themselves and their family members rather than for the development of their own potential. In this respect, the ultimate goal of Japanese Buddhism in lay members is opposite to that of Protestantism. In Protestant movements, secular activity (according to Max Weber) was regarded as a "calling," in which an individual proves his competence and his primary qualities of character. These Western religious movements, far from positively sanctioning materialism (including economic greed and biological gratification), were fundamentally otherworldly and suspicious of the temptations of the flesh. On the other hand, lay Japanese Buddhists pray for *genze riyaku* ("this worldly profit")[27] and readily accept the temptation of the flesh as "natural." The inclination to rely on external objects and their magical power (e.g., Buddha or the chanted *Nembutsu*) for goal attainment (e.g., *genze riyaku*) or tension reduction does not facilitate the development of reasoning.

Thus, neither Confucianism nor Buddhism developed rationality among Japanese in general. It is difficult, moreover, to call Confucianism and Buddhism "Japanese religions," in the sense of faith in a supernatural or superempirical entity that regulates the daily lives of a majority of Japanese people and provides a rallying point for them. Of a representative sample of Japanese people, 75 percent in 1973 and 66 percent in 1978 stated that they did ot have any religious faith (table 33). Although 62 percent of the Japanese had a miniature Buddhist temple (*butsudan*) and 63 percent a miniature Shinto shrine (*kami-dana*) in their household in 1981,[28] in 1978 only 2 percent had a personal faith in Shintoism and only 25 percent in Buddhism. One percent were Christians, and 4 percent had "personal religious faith" but not that of an established sect.

It seems that to a majority of Japanese people, Confucianism is a

TABLE 33.

"DO YOU HAVE ANY PERSONAL RELIGIOUS FAITH?"

	Total	Have %	Have not %
1958	920	35	65
1963	2,698	31	69
1968	3,033	31	69
1973	3,055	25	75
1978	5,400	34	66
Persons of Japanese ancestry in Hawaii (1971)	434	71	29

SOURCE: Tōkei Suuri Kenkyūsho [Institute of statistical mathematics], *Nihonjin no Kokuminsei* [National character of Japanese people] (Tokyo: Shiseido, 1975), p. 448.

system of ethics, Shintoism a system of rituals for supplicating gods for beneficial influence, and Buddhism a system of rituals dealing with ancestor worship, funeral, and burial. Japanese Buddhism, which many people believe to be the primary religion of Japan, has virtually no moral principle (*kairitsu*) of its own. The moral influences that Japanese Buddhism exert upon Japanese people are traditional ancestors worship and authoritarian familism, reinforced by Confucian ethics.

Although Confucian and Buddhist concepts provided the core elements of Japanese culture, if one were to name the primary faith that regulates the daily lives of a majority of Japanese people, the closest would be what BenDasan calls "Nihonkyo."[29] BenDasan maintains that Nihonkyo is the strongest faith in the world because it so thoroughly permeates all aspects of Japanese life and personality that its followers are not even conscious of their adherence to its doctrine, and that Confucianism, Buddhism, and even Christianity as believed by Japanese are versions of Nihonkyo.

The doctrine of Nihonkyo is a simple, indefinable system of concepts characterized by the worship of tradition—that is, shamanism and the worship of ancestors and cultural heroes. Its theme is clearly embodied in Yukio Mishima's act of suicide, which was committed in order to "defend Japanese history, culture and tradition under the emperor."[30] Today, although the qualifier "under the emperor" may be less stressed, the worship of Japanese tradition is essential in the Japanese personality. The concept of Nihonkyo fits nicely with Christopher's contention that "the Japanese people as a whole have only one absolutely immutable goal—to ensure the survival and maximum well-being of the tribe."[31] The unquestioning acceptance of tradition does not develop rationalism.

GROUPISM

All five writers discussed in the preceding chapter sought a firm sense of selfhood. Their desires for selfhood under the influence of Western thought unavoidably caused an internal conflict with their firmly established groupism—the emphasis on group goals at the sacrifice of individuality.

Japanese groupism is reflected in the concept of sincerity, or *makoto*, the primary value of the Japanese. While sincerity in the West means the capability of following one's own conscience even against social expectations, the Japanese conception means the elimination of all selfish (and even self-oriented) desires, enabling social expectations to dominate one's thinking. Sincere Japanese join "forces with like-minded people in order to further historical goals."[32]

An expression of Japanese groupism is ethnocentrism. In studies conducted by Tōkei Suuri Kenkyusho (the Institute of Statistical Mathematics of the Premier's Office) from 1958 through 1973, representative samples of Japanese individuals were asked to respond to the question, "If you had to make a generalization comparing Japanese people with Westerners, would you say that the Japanese are superior or inferior?" The percentage of "Japanese superior" was 20 percent in 1958 (shortly after the defeat in World War II), 33 percent in 1963, 47 percent in 1968, and 39 percent in 1973 (table 34). Japanese ethnocentrism appears to be increasing. When the subjects were asked to designate "superior people or peoples" among a list of peoples, the percentages of Japanese who regarded themselves as "superior" was 57 percent in 1958, 52 percent in 1963, 59 percent in 1968, and 60 percent in 1973 (table 35). In contrast, the percentage of Japanese people who regarded Americans as superior people decreased from 47 percent in 1958 to 46 percent in 1963, 43 percent in 1968, and 25 percent in 1973. The comparable figures for Britishers in the same years were 31, 27, 21, and 15 percent. The corresponding figures for French people were 17, 15, 13, and 9 percent. Japanese hold Germans in high esteem, second only to themselves. Even their respect for Germans, however, has declined greatly in contrast to the rise of the Japanese respect for themselves. The percentage of those regarding Germans as "superior people" was 52 percent in 1958, 45 percent in both 1963 and 1968, and 36 percent in 1973.

Groupism is also expressed in the intense desire to hide shameful aspects of one's own group. The revelation of the seamy aspects of one's own community is reason enough to ostracize the disclosing member. Kawashima observed a family that was completely shunned by other families in a farming area in Tokyo. When he questioned the members of the community about this, they consistently replied that a great-grandparent (long deceased) had once taken neighbors to court over a boundary dispute.[33] Such an act, in Japanese eyes, is in clear violation of the implicit rule of saving group honor.

The emphasis on group harmony makes Japanese reluctant to take legal action in traffic accidents involving damage and/or injury. The number of cases brought to court was 20 out of 4,645 (0.4%) in 1953 and 24 out of 6,317 (0.4%) in 1959. Only 2 out of 2,567 taxi accidents causing injury and/or damage (0.08%) were taken to court in 1960. This extremely low proportion is in marked contrast to the situation

TABLE 34.

"IF YOU HAD TO MAKE A GENERALIZATION COMPARING JAPANESE PEOPLE AND
WESTERN PEOPLE, WOULD YOU SAY THAT THE JAPANESE PEOPLE ARE
SUPERIOR OR INFERIOR TO WESTERNERS?"

	Total	Japanese people			
		Superior %	Inferior %	Same %	Other %
1958	2,254	20	28	14	38
1963	2,698	33	14	16	37
1968	3,033	47	11	12	30
1973	3,055	39	9	18	34

SOURCE: Tōkei Suuri Kenkyūsho [Institute of statistical mathematics], *Nihonjin no Kokuminsei*
[National character of Japanese people] (Tokyo: Shiseido, 1975), p. 493.

TABLE 35.

"WOULD YOU NAME ANY OF THE PEOPLES ON THIS LIST
WHOM YOU THINK ARE SUPERIOR?
YOU MAY NAME AS MANY AS YOU LIKE."

	1958	1963	1968	1973
Japanese	57%[a]	52%[b]	59%[c]	60%[d]
German	52	45	45	36
American	47	46	43	25
British	31	27	21	15
Russian	20	16	12	5
French	17	15	13	9
Chinese	9	6	9	21
Jewish	8	6	8	12
Indian (East)	7	3	3	3
Korean	1			
Arab	0			
Micronesian	0			
Other	2	6	7	10
Don't know	20	21	17	18

[a-d]The totals of Japanese samples were 1,449, 2,698, 3,033, and 3,055 in the respective year.
SOURCE: Tōkei Suuri Kenkyūsho [Institute of statistical mathematics], *Nihonjin no Kokuminsei*
[National character of Japanese people] (Tokyo: Shiseido, 1975), p. 494.

in New York City, where 77,000 (40%) out of 193,000 taxi accidents were tried in court in the same year.[34]

The reasons for the avoidance of court solutions in Japan include the paucity of lawyers, the inconvenience incurred by a lawsuit, and the people's ignorance of legal matters. More important are the concern with group harmony and the sensitivity to other group members' reactions. A comparison of 932 Japanese in Osaka (representing urban areas) and 569 in Shimane Prefecture (representing rural areas) was made in 1960–1961, regarding how they felt about taking someone to court.[35] Fifty-five percent of Osaka subjects and 81 percent of Shimane subjects indicated that their overriding concern would be the mainte-nance of harmony, and the taking of legal action would therefore be rejected. Twenty-one percent of Osaka and 34 percent of Shimane subjects answered, "Both parties are to be blamed in any dispute," indicating their opposition to court trial. The percentage of subjects who answered that "I would feel bad afterward" was 17 percent for Osaka and 34 percent for Shimane. Seventeen percent of both popula-tions responded, "People would frown upon me if I took the case to court." The degree of groupism is higher for rural areas, but it is also considerable in city subjects.

The strong group orientation of the Japanese tends to impede them from developing beliefs in abstract, universalistic ideological systems. Within a particularistic framework, the demarcation between insiders and outsiders shifts easily according to the immediate situation. In international conflict, all Japanese are insiders, but in interfamilial con-flict, only one's own family members are insiders. Therefore, cliquish-ness is very prominent among Japanese people. National goals, how-ever always supersede other group goals.

AUTHORITARIAN FAMILISM

Law is the basic instrument for social integration for the mechanistic Americans. The comparable Japanese mechanism is authoritarian fam-ilism. Familism, a form of groupism, refers to the supremacy of the family goal over individual goals and to the emphasis on close family ties. The strength of family ties in present Japan is indicated by the Oigawa *shinjū* (multiple suicides) in 1978. The bankruptcy of H. Heikichi (age fifty-five), a businessman and prefectural assemblyman, precipitated not only his own suicide but also the deaths of his family members: his wife (fifty-one); his oldest son, Hiroshi (thirty-one), and

Hiroshi's wife (thirty) and daughter (six); his third daughter (twenty-three) and her daughter (one); and his fourth daughter (twenty-one). The fourth daughter was a successful third-year medical-school student. Why, with a secure future, did she have to die with her parents? The emphasis on family ties and parental affection, along with the insecurity that results from the loss of parental protection, appears to have been the major motivation behind the collective suicides (and the murders of the children).

Several years ago, a married university professor in Tokyo murdered his pregnant student mistress. When the scandal was revealed, he was not remorseful but professed that "she loved me, and therefore she must be happy to be killed by me." Nonetheless, he was compelled to resign from his post. A few days later, he committed suicide. His wife and two children died with him, too. Why was the death of his wife necessary, considering that the man was unfaithful to her? Why were the children killed? The explanation is that shame and insecurity subsequent to the breadwinner's dishonorable death were inevitable in light of the Japanese emphasis on family name and family ties and of the antipathy shown toward relatives of one who violates social norms.

The uniqueness of Japanese familism in contrast to groupism in general is its vertical relationship between superordinate and subordinate, as represented by parent and child. The Japanese community is a family, as shown by the *buraku* (small neighborhood community) in which writer Minoru Kida lived. The village, under a single chief, is a system of groups. Each group, under a *sewayaku* (caretaker), consists of from ten to sixteen families (from fifty to eighty persons).[36] The *sewayaku* is responsible for finding a bride or groom for each member, for acting as a *nakoodo* (go-between) in their marriages, for solving criminal problems before requesting police aid, and for negotiating with outside authorities to improve the group's welfare. If the police arrest a member for any reason, the *sewayaku* must be able to free the member via his personal influence and skills. He is a sort of parent figure, providing security while serving the larger community as a supervisor of each member's behavior. If a member offends the *sewayaku* of his group, he may not be able to live in the village.[37]

As this *buraku* structure illustrates, Japanese community and family structures are vertical (i.e., built on status differences). The nature of social relations is authoritarian. Although Japanese society appears to have become democratized since World War II, authoritarianism is still a major component of Japanese social and political life. Using the California *F* Scale as a measure of authoritarianism, Lewis Austin

TABLE 36.

"WHAT DO YOU THINK ABOUT DEMOCRACY? WOULD YOU POINT OUT
ON THIS LIST THE OPINION THAT COMES CLOSEST TO YOURS?"

	Total	Good	Depends	Not good	Other
1958	1,449	55%	a	17%	b
1963	2,698	38	49	3	10
1968	3,033	38	52	3	7
1973	3,055	43	46	2	9
Persons of Japanese ancestry in Hawaii (1971)	434	74	21	0	5

a,b The total of "depends," "others," and "don't know" is 28%.

SOURCES: Tōkei Suuri Kenkyūsho [Institute of statistical mathematics], *Kokuminsei no Kenkyū* (Tokyo: Shiseido, 1975), p. 485; idem, *Hawaii ni okeru Nikkeijin* [Persons of Japanese ancestry in Hawaii] (Tokyo: Shiseido, 1973), p. 32.

found that young Japanese were significantly more authoritarian than young Americans.[38] In contrast to 74 percent of persons of Japanese ancestry in Hawaii who favored "democracy," less than half (43%) of Japanese subjects in Japan held this view (table 36). A large percentage of Japanese subjects (30% in 1968 and 23% in 1973) thought that "the best way to improve the country is for the people to leave everything to good political leaders rather than for people to discuss things among themselves," in comparison with 13 percent of people of Japanese ancestry in Hawaii in 1971 (table 37).

The authoritarian stress on power and status difference is also shown by the finding that 52 percent of Japanese respondents in 1958 thought that "because there are differences in ability among races and peoples, it is only natural that superior races and peoples should dominate inferior ones," while 31 percent disagreed (table 38). This item was dropped after 1958 as a survey tool by the premier's office researchers, probably because of its obvious racist overtone.

Familism functions as a means for social control. When Japanese and Americans were compared in terms of the life situations that require greatest adjustment, "detention in jail" and "minor violation of the law" were both given significantly higher scores by the Japanese than by Americans (table 39).[39] Going to jail, for whatever reason, or even being suspected of a crime impose a great sense of shame on the family and of guilt for loss of prestige and status on the Japanese individual. A mortgage or loan is considered by the Japanese to be shame-

TABLE 37.

"Some people say that if we get good political leaders,
the best way to improve the country is for the people to leave
everything to them, rather than for the people to discuss things
among themselves. Do you agree or disagree with this?"

	Total	Agree %	Depends %	Disagree %	Other %
1953	2,254	43	9	38	10
1958	2,367	35	10	44	11
1963	2,698	29	12	47	12
1968	3,033	30	10	51	9
1973	3,055	23	15	51	11
Persons of Japanese ancestry in Hawaii (1971)	434	13	10	70	7

SOURCES: Tōkei Suuri Kenkyūsho [Institute of statistical mathematics], *Nihonjin no Kokuminsei* [National character of Japanese people] (Tokyo: Shiseido, 1975), p. 484; idem, *Hawaii ni okeru Nikkeijin* [Persons of Japanese ancestry in Hawaii] (Tokyo: Shiseido, 1973), p. 31.

TABLE 38.

"Some people say that since there are differences in ability among
races and peoples, it is natural that superior peoples should
dominate inferior peoples. Do you agree or disagree with this?"

	Total	Agree %	Disagree %	Other %
1958[a]	1,449	52	31	17

[a]This question was deleted in the subsequent surveys.

SOURCE: Tōkei Suuri Kenkyūsho [Institute of statistical mathematics], *Nihonjin no Kokuminsei* [National character of Japanese people] (Tokyo: Shiseido, 1961), Appendix, p. 28.

ful, regardless of the sums of money involved, since a mortgage loan means one has mortgaged one's honor and family name. Therefore, although Americans consider a major change in financial state to be of more consequence than do Japanese, the Japanese show significantly higher scores on the stressfulness of both "a mortgage loan over $10,000" and "a mortgage loan less than $10,000." The significantly lower score for Japanese than Americans on "major change in arguments with spouse" also indicates the familism of the Japanese. In Japan, arguments between individuals are not as important as responsibilities to the family. Arguments should, and usually do, end with

TABLE 39.

COMPARISON OF RANKING AND ITEM SCORES DERIVED FROM THE
SOCIAL READJUSTMENT RATING QUESTIONNAIRE BETWEEN
JAPANESE AND AMERICAN SAMPLES, 1967

Crisis requiring readjustment effort	Japanese (N: 112)		American (N: 168)	
	Rank	Geometric	Rank	Geometric
[a]Death of spouse	1	1,079	1	880
[b]Detention in jail	2	721	6	474
[b]Major personal injury or illness	5	542	7	426
[a]Marital separation	7	459	3	541
[a]Marital reconciliation	15	272	10	362
[c]Mortgage loan over $10,000	17	252	28	158
[a]Son or daughter leaving home	18	247	22	204
[b]Major change in financial state	21	210	15	288
[c]Minor violation of the law	28	138	43	34
[c]Mortgage loan less than $10,000	30	170	39	78
[c]Major change in arguments with spouse	33	118	16	281

[a]Items scored significantly different: $P < 0.05$.
[b] $P < 0.01$.
[c] $P < 0.001$.

The item scores of the American and the Japanese samples were compared by the Mann-Whitney U tests supplemented by student t tests using log scores.

SOURCE: Minoru Masuda and T. H. Holmes, "The Social Readjustment Rating Scale: A Cross-Cultural Study of Japanese and Americans," *Journal of Psychosomatic Research* 11 (1967): 227–237.

the wife's yielding to the husband's wishes, primarily because of the great difficulty that she would have in case of divorce.

Familism is not unique to Japan, but its extension to all social institutions seems to be characteristic of that country. Its pervasiveness is shown by the *iemoto* (literally, "root family") system, which is "a giant kinship establishment with the closeness and the inclusiveness of international links, but without kinship limitations on its size—an application of the patriarchal family system to nonfamilial, especially artistic organizations."[40] The *iemoto* is the central individual of the quasi-kinship establishment.

The primary authority of the *iemoto* is to issue licenses certifying the achievement of followers at various levels of progress. The recipients of a certificate above a certain level of progress become teachers of their own students, who in turn receive certificates to teach and also have students of their own. In some cases, the total number of students in such a pyramidal hierarchy reaches several million. The recipients of certificates directly from the *iemoto* form a higher echelon of the hierarchy.

Crucial in this structure is the fact that whatever high achievement a student may attain (and in some cases, his ability may be even higher than that of the *iemoto*), he is never allowed to issue certification on his own authority. Related to the certification, the *iemoto* also have the exclusive authority of bestowing professional names (*geimei*). In addition, the *iemoto* has exclusive authority over many other aspects of artistic life, such as the use of necessary facilities (e.g., theaters), choice of costumes, determination of programs, copyrights of scripts, and other necessities for public performances of all members in his entire organization.

One component of the *iemoto* system is the maintenance of *nawabari*, or boundaries that outsiders are not allowed to cross. Within an *iemoto* organization, a teacher's boundary of influence is determined by the *iemoto* or his delegates. The content that is taught by the organization is kept secret from outsiders. The essential parts of teachings are orally transmitted so that outsiders cannot steal them.

The *iemoto* system is most marked in the fields of Japanese music, Japanese dance, Noh, flower arrangement, tea ceremony, and martial arts, but its equivalent is noticeable in virtually all aspects of Japanese life—in religion (e.g., *Go-Monshu* system), politics, underworld organization, craftsmen, laborers (*oyabun/kobun*—parent role/child role relationship). The system also extends to scholars, although one might expect this group to be resistant to this kind of particularistic relationship. In the presence of a professor, the lower-status scholar generally cannot express any thought or opinion that conflicts with his professor's view. The *iemoto* system obviously clashes with the basic values of science, which assert that thinking must be independent, unbiased, analytical, and critical and also tolerant of dissident opinions.

ACCOMMODATIONISM

Regarding time orientation, are Japanese people past, present, or future oriented? Although all peoples at all times deal with all three time dimensions, they differ in relative emphasis.

Japanese people almost worship tradition, but they are not necessarily past oriented. Their traditionalism is for the purpose of attaining "the survival and the maximum well-being of the tribe," which is future oriented. Japanese people are obsessed with the goal of success, suggesting a future orientation. *Time* (March 1981) counts future orientation as one of the causes of Japan's great success in international economic competition:

> Individuals are seen to benefit only through the elevation of the entire group. Corporations are not after the quick pay-off or big quarterly imputs in shareholder dividends, but a solid market position that will be rewarded over the longer time. Businesses and government look five, ten, even twenty years ahead and try to build a prosperity that can last. . . . The long-haul mentality is reflected in Japan's dedication to savings.

In contrast to a future orientation, Japanese people are also strongly concerned with the immediate situation, suggesting present orientation. This concern is called by Ruth Benedict "situational realism." When situations change, she holds, "the Japanese can change their bearings and set themselves on a new course."[41] Ideological conviction is not a Japanese concern. Benedict explains:

> In Japan the constant goal is honor. It is necessary to command respect. The means one uses to that end are tools one takes up and then lays aside as circumstances dictate. . . . Changing does not appear to them the moral issue that it does to Westerners. We go in for "principles," for convictions on ideological matters. When we lose we are still of the same mind. . . . Except for a few diehards, the Japanese . . . feel no moral necessity to hold to the old line.

In order to look "honorable," Japanese people often say something that is not exactly true. Because of this tendency, Westerners sometimes regard Japanese as liars. Japanese people generally do not intend to lie, but their intense concern with the other's reaction in the immediate situation produces the well-known tendency toward a gap between *tatemae* (what they say) and *honne* (what they do, or what they want to do).

"Honor" in this context is the highly subjective feeling of being honored by the other in a particular situation, which may not be substantiated by long-lasting esteem. It is more a matter of appearance in the eyes of the other than of the ego's quality or achievement. For example, Japanese people in general are very sensitive to even the most trivial of "apparent" defects.

The Japanese concern with the other's reaction in the immediate situation is pointed out in a different way by Shichihei Yamamoto, who maintains that Japanese culture is a culture of *hanashiai* (negotiation) rather than of *keiyaku* (contract).[42] Contract "presupposes a commitment to some abstract (long-lasting) principle, while "negotiation" presupposes a greater concern with the immediate interaction, to which the ego adjusts for tension reduction or for short-range problem solving. Once, a Japanese company refused to accept a shipment of raw sugar from Australia, despite their long-term contract. The reason was that since the price of raw sugar had declined, there should be a new negotiation. This attitude caused a serious conflict between the two national governments.

The predilection to adjust to the immediate situation is also illustrated in the following excerpt from Lifton's description of a young Japanese:[43]

> As the youngest son in a professional family, he was brought up to be a proper middle-class Japanese boy. He was a fiery young patriot who was convinced of the sacredness of the Japanese cause, revered her fighting men . . . accepted without question the historical myth of the Emperor's divine descent, and hated the Americans. Japan's surrender came as a great shock and left him temporarily confused in his beliefs. . . .
>
> He soon became an eager young exponent of democracy, caught up in the "democracy boom" which then swept Japan and which seemed to most youngsters to promise "freedom" and moral certainty. During junior high school and high school he was an all-round leader, excelling in his studies. . . . Yet he also became the outspoken critic of society at large (on the basis of Marxist ideas, current in Japanese intellectual circles).
>
> He took advantage of an opportunity to become an exchange student for one year at an American high school. During that year he became a convert to many aspects of American life . . . he made a sudden, emotional decision to be baptised [sic] as a Christian.
>
> He returned to Japan reluctantly. Eager to regain acceptance, he re-immersed himself in Japanese experience—sitting on *tatami*, indulging in quiet melancholy moods, drinking tea, and so on.
>
> (After graduation from high school and one year of preparing for the entrance examination, he was admitted to Tokyo University.) Once admitted, he found little to interest him and rarely attended classes. Through the influence of a Marxist professor . . . he became an enthusiastic *Zengakuren* activist (participating in radical student movements).
>
> But when offered a position of leadership during his third year at the university, he decided that the best path for him was a conventional life of economic and social success within the existing society.
>
> He drifted into a life of dissipation, devoting his major energies to heavy drinking, marathon mahjong games, and affairs with bar girls. But when the time came, he had no difficulty in gaining employment

with one of Japan's mammoth business organizations (and one of the *bêtes noires* of his Marxist days) and embarking upon the life of a young executive or *sarariman* (salaried man).

How do these contradictory traits—future orientation and the tendency to adjust to the immediate situation—coexist in the Japanese personality? An explanation is that when a Japanese behaves as a group member he may become more future oriented than an American, because his supreme goal is the "survival and maximum well-being of the tribe." The adjustment of Japan to international competition requires a long-range perspective on the part of Japanese leaders. When the leaders make plans for international competition, they decide upon the priority of industries and companies for governmental cooperation and assistance. Because of the government's assistance and influence, as long as particular companies have a good rating in the eyes of the bureaucrats and political leaders they do not have to worry about their immediate achievement (e.g., shareholders' dividends) as do companies in the United States. Government leaders, in cooperation with their economic counterparts, are future oriented in the matter of international competition. Other Japanese follow. Japanese people in general work most effectively when they are ordered to do a certain thing. It is to be noted, however, that Japan is not rigidly totalitarian. The rating of companies in the eyes of government officials is largely determined by the achievement of the companies themselves.

In contrast to his future orientation when acting as a group member, a Japanese behaving as an individual tends to adjust to the immediate situation. His preoccupation is with other people's reactions to his behavior and status. Lifton proposes three modes of imagery that coexist in the Japanese personality: transformationism (or a vision of making social and individual existence into something that is fundamentally, if not totally, new), restorationism (with a strong urge to return to the past), and accommodationism (which is "a wide category of compromise"). Accommodationism includes muted elements of transformation and restoration, and it is the category that encompasses all those who do not fit into either of these two modes.[44] However, says Lifton, "These patterns of imagery are, to a surprising degree, interchangeable according to the immediate situation,"[45] Thus, accommodationism seems to be not only a coordinate concept to transformationism and restorationism but also a superordinate concept, regulating all three modes of imagery. There seem to be very few Japanese who are genuinely transformationists or restorationists.

TABLE 40.

ACTION OF "LAST TWENTY-FOUR HOURS"

	Japanese		German	
	197	100.0%	197	100.0%
1. I would remain calm.	23	11.7	45	22.8
2. I would spend my time with somebody else.	54	27.4	68	34.5
3. I would set out on a journey.	25	12.7	17	8.6
4. I would look back upon my life.	17	8.6	19	9.6
5. I would be disturbed.	16	8.1	0	
6. I would be carried away by the impulse of the moment.	53	26.9	18	9.1
7. I would make my will.	6	3.0	12	6.1
8. I would put all in order.	6	3.0	8	4.1

SOURCE: Heizo Toriyama, "Death and Personal Value Orientation: A Comparative Study between Japanese and German Cultures (unpublished MS).

Since the accommodationist "places greatest imagery closest to his own life—upon the present, the immediate future and perhaps the recent past,"[46] the typical time orientation among Japanese people seems to be "short-time perspective," whether they are past or future oriented. Dedication to savings, which *Time* referred to in the beginning of this section on accommodationism, is not entirely future-oriented behavior. Eighty-two percent of Japanese who were asked about the reasons for saving answered "as protection against illness, injury, or damage,"[47] indicating their reaction to insecurity—a present state of mind.

Accommodationism enables Japanese people to freely accept foreign ideas and to allow the coexistence of contradictory ideas—that is, tradition and modern values—without endangering social integration. However, accommodationism also tends to prevent the development of strong selfhood. Moreover, Japanese accommodationism contains an element of impulsiveness. Heizo Toriyama[48] compared 197 Japanese university students (165 males and 32 females) with 197 German university students (77 males, 100 females, and 20 with sex distinction unknown), who averaged 23.9 years of age. These subjects were asked, "If you were to die without fail tomorrow, how would you spend your last twenty-four hours?" The greatest difference between the two groups was that 27 percent of the Japanese answered, "I would be carried away by the impulse of the moment" in contrast to the 9 percent of the Germans who gave the same answer (table 40).

八

VIII

JAPANESE CULTURE AND SELF-DESTRUCTIVE ADJUSTMENT

WIDE GOAL-MEANS DISCREPANCY ─────────────────

The major characteristics of Japanese culture—monism, groupism, authoritarian familism, and accommodationism—contribute much toward producing a wide goal-means discrepancy, leading to the feeling that "there is no other way out."

In combination with the governmental effort to induce young people to apply for leadership positions, an authoritarian social structure produces high aspiration among Japanese people. The authoritarian emphases on power and status differences, together with the misery that accompanies failure in Japanese society, where feudal remnants are still manifest, cultivate *shusse shugi* (the "success principle," or obsessive success orientation). The success goal is intense because of both emotionalism (a corollary of monistic nonrational tendencies) and a keen sensitivity to other people's reactions (from groupism), together with parental pressures. Parental pressure is particularly effective in Japan because of the typically strong dependency need among young Japanese, resulting from close contact with affectionate, generally indulgent, and often self-sacrificial mothers.

However, despite their high ambition and their hankering after fame, Japanese youths are characterized, as Stoetzel found, by a lack of realistic planning and self-confidence and by ambiguity, passivity, insecurity, and escapism. These traits are to a large extent applicable to Japanese people in general. Japanese value orientations make for inadequate means in many individuals of meeting their high aspirations. Nonrational tendencies due to monism are not effective for goal attainment. Groupism, authoritarian familism, and accommodationism stifle individuality and foster dependency need. They also tend to produce a lack of resourcefulness. Accommodationism contributes to short-sightedness. The combination of nonrational tendencies, dependency, lack of resourcefulness, and short-sightedness produces weak ego, and weak ego is a key factor in a wide goal-means discrepancy and eventually in suicide among Japanese.

A wide goal-means discrepancy does not necessarily lead to suicide. The conversion of the discrepancy to self-destructive behavior requires restraint on outwardly directed aggression, negative perception of social resources, and accepting views of death and suicide.

RESTRAINT ON OUTWARDLY-DIRECTED AGGRESSION ————

Japanese people have been traditionally socialized to stifle aggression in the interest of group harmony. Not only self-restraint but also self-negation is often required for adaptive adjustment in Japan. When aggression is not directed at an external object, it may be directed at oneself.

The political system in the Tokugawa regime (1600–1867) was characterized by "unescapable absolutism and sumptuary control of individuals."[1] The police state, the elaborate espionage system, the principle of collective responsibility, and the enforcement of severe punishment unavoidably developed a highly inhibited personality. The individual self had to be negated in order to attain complete identification with role expectations. Even a demonstration of affection to one's own wife and family members was disapproved of as *memeshii* ("womanlike," unworthy of man).

Since the modernization of Japan in 1868, the samurai spirit became the ideal of all Japanese through nationalized education. Self-restraint for the purpose of furthering national goals has become the primary aim of socialization. The restraint on self-expression affects not only verbal but also neuromuscular functions. According to Miyagi, emotional expression through glands, especially tear glands, provides a substitute form of self-expression and even becomes a source of masochistic pleasure.[2] This interpretation explains, at least partly, why traditional Japanese like maudlin plays and stories and why the dominant themes of Japanese popular songs are "sadness, loneliness, helplessness, parting, and relinquishing."

SOCIAL RESOURCES

When a person defines a situation as providing no way out but death, the attitude of people surrounding him, or the person's perception of their attitude toward him, is crucial. If they are concerned with the victim's welfare and attempt to help him, suicide may be avoided. Even when people are sympathetic with the victim, if they are pessimistic about their own capability to help, their lack of self-confidence adversely affects the attitude of the suicidal person toward others,[3] and his perception of alternative means for problem solving becomes increasingly constricted. In this respect, Japanese people have been known for their predilection to avoid being involved in other people's trouble.[4]

The Japanese attitude of avoiding being involved in other people's trouble is represented by an incident that occurred on September 24, 1984.[5] A 21-year-old university coed was sexually molested for a full hour by a delinquent armed with a razor while about eighty passengers in the same railway car coolly ignored her distress. The man continued to molest her from Yokohama, where she got on the train, to Shinagawa Station, Tokyo. In response to her tearful plea to be allowed to proceed to her job interview in Tsurumi, the man took her onto another train. He continued to molest her until the train reached Tsurumi. The man was later arrested. The police said that the girl would have been saved from her attacker if even one person had reported the situation to the conductor.

A Japanese-American journalist who goes to Japan almost every year and who understands the Japanese personality as well as the natives do comments that this incident gives insight into the mentality of most Japanese. In an overcrowded society, he says, "most Japanese are concerned about the small space around their own bodies. Everything that goes on beyond that small space is of no concern. They all seem to follow the philosophy of 'letting well enough alone.' Here in America, in most instances if someone tried to molest a woman in public, [as in the preceding situation], dozens would come to her aid." The journalist supports his observation by citing his own experience. In Shibuya a purse snatcher grabbed a woman's purse and did not even run from the scene; he just walked a little faster. Even though the woman was yelling that she was robbed, nobody made an effort to stop the culprit. The snatcher walked near where the journalist was standing, but by that time "[the journalist] had also developed the 'when in Rome . . . ' type of thinking."

Japanese may avoid being involved in other people's trouble not because they are indifferent or cold but rather because they are afraid of the consequence of the involvement. Or, they may lack confidence in their own capability to solve problems and to help. They are not reared to be independent and resourceful. Japanese education aims at memorization for entering a university but not at developing the capability to solve problems in life situations. The Japanese seem to be more concerned with their own tension reduction than with problem solving, much less with helping others to solve problems. For problem solving they count on those with more power, such as government officials or parent-role persons (*oyabun*). This attitude is related to *amae,* which Dr. Takeo Doi calls the key to understanding the Japanese personality.

The Japanese lack of self-confidence is shown by Irwin Mahler's studies. In one study, he compared 345 Japanese university students (160 females and 185 males) with 75 American university students (37 females and 38 males) using the Tennessee Self-Concept Scale.[6] The subjects were compared in terms of self-feelings (i.e., identity, self-satisfaction, and behavior) and of self-description from an external frame of reference (the physical self, the moral self, the personal self, the family self, and the social self). The differences between the median scores of the Japanese and American samples were subjected to the *t* test, and the differences in all categories were found significant at the .01 level. Mahler concludes, "The Japanese subject sees himself as less adequate than the American subject sees himself" and is "a highly guarded and defensive individual who does not wish to reveal himself to others."

In another study, Mahler queried whether happenings were conceived to be controlled by the individual himself or by external forces that might be thought of as powerful people or as chance and fate.[7] A Japanese university sample of 109 women and 85 men was compared with an American university sample of 61 women and 59 men, who were then living in Japan, by the use of Levinson's IPC control scale.

TABLE 41.

ANNUAL AMOUNT SPENT PER PERSON 65 AND OLDER BY SOCIAL SECURITY
AND WELFARE IN SELECTED COUNTRIES

	Amount	Percentage of Japan Amount
Japan	$174	100
West Germany	978	562
United States	942	541
Sweden	795	396
Britain	486	279
Italy	447	257
France	432	248

SOURCE: National Life Center, 1972; Palmore, Erdman, *The Honorable Elders* (Durham, North Carolina: Duke University Press, 1975), p. 88.

In this scale, *I* stands for "inner control," *P* for "control by powerful others," and *C* for "control by chance or fate." The finding was that "Japanese university students scored significantly lower on the *I* scale than did the American students. The mean score on *C* was significantly higher for Japanese students. Although there was no significant difference on "control by powerful others" between the two samples as a whole, Japanese women perceived things as "being controlled by powerful others" to a much higher degree than did Japanese men, American men, or American women.

The Japanese public's predilection to avoid being involved in others' troubles is a reflection of the attitude of the Japanese government. The government is traditionally less concerned with people's welfare than are governments in Western countries. For example, it spent $174 per person annually from 1964 to 1967 on social security and welfare for the aged. The amount was far less than the comparable assistance paid by the government of France (2.5 times more), Italy (2.6 times), and Britain (2.8 times). Sweden spent 4.0 times as much, and the United States and West Germany spent 5.4 and 5.6 times as much, respectively (table 41).

In addition to the tendency to avoid being involved in other people's troubles, Japanese people may be so insecure that they become hostile against those in need, in case their own security is threatened. The groupistic stress on selflessness ironically produces the attitude of "no self, no sin." Being selfless or egoless justifies being indifferent to, or even antagonistic toward, others in need. An example is given by the the experiences of W. Eugene Smith, a noted American photographer. When Smith revealed by his photographs to outsiders the Minamata disease—a form of mercury poisoning, producing paralysis, deformation, brain damage, blindness, and sometimes death to hundreds of residents—he reported the following in *Newsweek* (April 2, 1973):

> Those who are directly or indirectly connected to the chemical company [Chisso, which was the source of the mercury contamination] for their livelihood . . . have a real antagonism for the victim.

Smith became an object of attack. He said that as he was shooting pictures of a protest by victims of Minamata disease, "A gang of company employees smashed his camera and beat him so brutally that he still suffers from it." Smith could survive the attack, but any Japanese who defied the power would not be as fortunate as Smith was. The hostile attitude of Japanese people toward the revelation of the culprit in this incident is unbelievable when we consider the effects of the poisoning: more than 100 persons had died by 1977 and another 1,500 were officially designated as patients suffering from the Minamata disease.

With the lack of self-confidence and resourcefulness, together with such attitude of indifference toward, and antagonism against, the victim, the Japanese persons, who are in the position of the victim, may easily give up any hope for help.

ATTITUDES TOWARD DEATH ————————————————————

When frustrated, Japanese people seem to be highly susceptible to a death wish. Akutagawa noted in his suicide note that life was a continuous battle, and that if a person failed he should die. Dazai regarded life as a system of pretension and "double-talk"; sincerity was found, he thought, only in death. For Mishima, death was a part of life. Meaningful life existed only when a person constantly strove for a meaningful death. His idea of meaningful life was that of "no tomorrow." For Kawabata, meaningful life existed only in beauty, which, in turn, existed only in the sphere between life and death, in a spiritual world. Arishima was the only one who did not have a death wish. However, since he saw love and honor as the only meaning in life, death became welcome when it was necessary for the fulfillment of his romantic love and for the avoidance of dishonor.

In the West younger people are expected to have few thoughts about death. However, about 40 pecent of high-school and about half of college students in Japan have a "wish to die," as shown in table 4. This probably shows the generally acceptable attitude toward death among Japanese people, because the elderly are expected to think about death more than the young are.

In addition to the susceptibility to a death wish, Japanese people seem to have less fear of death as a biological termination than do Westerners. In a study, Heizo Toriyama asked 197 Japanese university students in comparison with 90 German and 93 Austrian students about why death was feared.[8] Toriyama let them rearrange the following list of "consequences of their own death" according to importance to them:

A. I could no longer have any experiences.
B. I am uncertain as to what might happen to me if there is a life after death.
C. I am afraid of what might happen to my body after death.
D. I could no longer care for my dependents.
E. My death would cause grief to my relatives and friends.
F. All my plans and projects would come to an end.
G. The process of dying might be painful.

Toriyama found that the Japanese subjects, both male and female, ranked the fear of death as biological termination significantly lower than did the German-Austrian subjects i.e., C (fear of body change) and G (fear of pain) (table 42).

The primary cause of the Japanese students' fear of death is the loss of the individual as the agent of work (A) and that "my plans and projects would come to an end" (F). In contrast, German males were found to be more concerned with death as "giving grief to my relatives and friends" (E). This finding suggests an egocentric nature of Japanese intellectuals' philosophy of life in contrast to more affective and affiliative views among German intellectuals.

The Japanese acceptance of death is facilitated by their various views of death. First, death is a philosophical concept based on the idea of *mujō* (a sense of eternal change and the ephemeral quality of all things, including human beings). Because everything is changing constantly, death is just one moment of cosmic change. To acquire the knowledge of *mujō* is the purpose of Japanese religions, and to develop the capacity for meeting death with complete equanimity is a sine qua non of Japanese maturity.

TABLE 42.

Mean Rank Scores for Students in Japanese and German–Austrian Culture Groups on "Consequences of One's Own Death"

Total	Japanese (N: 197)		German-Austrian (N: 183)		
	M	SD	M	SD	t
A	2.91	1.87	3.81	2.29	17.62[a]
B	4.37	2.01	4.23	2.26	2.91[b]
C	4.72	2.03	4.01	2.02	11.59[a]
D	4.19	1.82	4.14	2.03	0.06
E	4.21	1.65	4.11	1.88	0.30
F	3.45	1.85	3.89	1.82	5.44[b]
G	4.14	2.16	3.80	1.57	9.17[b]

[a]$P < .001$.
[b]$P < .01$.

Males	Japanese (N: 165)		German-Austrian (N: 71)		
	M	SD	M	SD	t
A	3.01	1.90	3.83	2.37	7.83[a]
B	4.33	2.04	4.56	2.12	0.61
C	4.60	2.05	4.39	1.89	0.54
D	4.28	1.80	4.20	2.04	0.09
E	4.29	1.63	3.83	1.96	3.45[a]
F	3.45	1.89	3.52	1.84	0.07
G	4.04	2.15	3.63	1.39	2.17[b]

[a]$P < .001$.
[b]$P < .05$.

Females	Japanese (N: 32)		German-Austrian (N: 94)		
	M	SD	M	SD	t
A	2.44	1.60	3.84	2.24	10.50[a]
B	4.56	1.87	3.86	2.29	2.39[b]
C	5.34	1.78	3.86	2.04	13.13[a]
D	3.72	1.86	4.10	2.03	0.86
E	3.81	1.67	4.29	1.76	1.80
F	3.44	1.64	4.21	1.81	4.48[a]
G	4.69	2.10	3.86	1.69	4.97[a]

[a]$P < .001$.
[b]$P < .02$.

TABLE 42. (*Continued*)

A. I could no longer have any experiences.
B. I am uncertain as to what might happen to me if there is a life after death.
C. I am afraid of what might happen to my body after death.
D. I could no longer care for my dependents.
E. My death would cause grief to my relatives and friends.
F. All my plans and projects would come to an end.
G. The process of dying might be painful.

SOURCE: Heizo Toriyama, "Death and Personal Value Orientation," in *Annual Report of Health Administration*, no. 8 (Kyoto Technical University, 1981), pp. 190–199.

A second view sees death as emancipation from the illusion and anguish that are the substance of human life. Our life is an illusion because we take as stable such ever-changing phenomena as life, love, and possessions. Because we become attached to illusory human or nonhuman objects, life is a series of anguish-filled experiences. In medieval times, according to the Shin-shu teaching of *onri edo; gongu jyōdo* ("Forsake the filthy world; joyfully seek the Pure Land"), hundreds of priests and their followers confined themselves in nailed boxes on small boats and were left adrift in the ocean. Their purpose was to reach the Pure Land, which was believed to exist somewhere beyond the ocean. These suicides were called *fudaraku tokai.* Buddhist teaching is particularly reassuring to a person who suffers from shame and guilt. *Tanishō,* one of the major scriptures of Japanese Buddhism, offers assurance that a wicked man is more likely to be saved than is a righteous one, because the former will be more likely to "abandon his reliance on his own power and put his trust in the power of Amida Buddha."[9]

Third, death is ethical. It means the return of a soul to its natural habitat after it has fulfilled its obligations and duties on earth. Therefore, when one feels that he has done his best, he should be able to feel satisfied. Even those who have had miserable lives may consider their lives as necessary obligations and duties. Death is particularly ethical when it is a suicide for self-sacrifice, remonstrance, or apology.

A fourth point of view sees death as creative. Arishima saw self-fulfillment in his love suicide. Life is natural, and so is death. To accept death as natural is creative, because "natural forces in man become fully operant." When man realizes the approach of his own death, he can make the most of his remaining life. At the age of nineteen, Akutagawa assumed that, with his poor health, he would not live past the age of twenty-five, and he determined to experience whatever possible.[10] He became one of the top writers in the nation. Masaaki

Yamagata had a bad lung hemorrhage at the age of twenty-eight. One night he found himself in a hospital bed, desperately lonely. Suddenly he realized that he had his hand over his heart, and underneath the hand his heart was thumping regularly. For the first time in his life, he realized that some natural force was constantly working within him in order to keep him alive. It was not he himself but rather some external force that enabled him to live. He also recognized that it was his own ignorance of the natural force that caused his misery. From then on, he was determined to behave only in accordance with Nature. His tuberculosis was eventually healed, and he helped many people to overcome their suffering and misery by his philosophy of "being natural."[11]

Fifth, death is perceived as beautiful. A young chemical engineer who sat next to Dr. Edwin Shneidman on a bullet train in Japan said, in English, "Cherry blossoms are blooming quickly and scattering at once. Better to come to fruition and die like the blossom." He added, "We have many great men among our forefathers whose deeds remind us of the noble characteristics of cherry blossoms."[12] The primary themes of Japanese literature are love and death. They are most beautiful because they are both peak experiences. In both, a person negates himself and does not know what he will get in return or where he will go. The complete negation of the self and the sense of impermanence are what Japanese people consider most beautiful and attractive.

The beautification of death is promoted by mysticism, a characteristic of Japanese thinking. The slight separation between this and the afterworld, typical of mystical thinking, is illustrated by the title of a short story, "Fushi" [No death] by Yasunari Kawabata. To Kawabata, there was no separation between life and death. He perceived the most beautiful sensations when he was in the twilight zone between consciousness and unconsciousness. In order to experience this sensation, he habitually used sleeping pills.

The sixth way of viewing death is through familism—that is, identifying the self with the family. The concept leads to the tendency to make light of one's own life, because an individual's death means his continuing life ("postself") as a family member. As Lifton holds, "The biological mode of immortality is epitomized by family continuity, living on through one's sons and daughters and their sons and daughters, with imagery of an endless chain of biological attachment."[13] The sense of continuity is more concrete in the Japanese mind, which holds that the deceased person's soul can actively participate in his family's daily affairs. Most Japanese homes have in the *butsudan,* or

Buddhist household shrine, mortuary tablets (*ihai*) for deceased members. Special solace is acquired when Japanese people literally talk to deceased family members at the *butsudan*. It is a ritualized effort to hold on to at least part of those relationships and to maintain an unbroken sense of family continuity. Every morning and evening, many Japanese pray to the deceased members in the *butsudan* for their protection of the family's living members and for their assistance in promoting family prosperity.

These various views of death provide what Lifton calls "symbolic immortality," that is, "a continuous symbolic relationship between one's finite individual life and what has gone before and what will come after."[14] By satisfying the compelling inner quest for symbolic immortality, Japanese culture lessens the fear of death.

ATTITUDES TOWARD SUICIDE ───────────────────────────

When overwhelmed by difficulty, Japanese people not only have an accepting attitude toward death but they are generally susceptible to a suicidal wish. Half of the replies of college students and about a quarter of the replies of high-school students indicated that they regarded suicide as justifiable. Such responses as "Suicide is a matter of individual freedom," "I envy the person who commits suicide," "I feel sympathetic toward the victim," or "Society is to be blamed" (table 43) were typical.

Generally, about one of every five Japanese persons justifies suicide in such situations as "a conflict between obligation and love," "extreme poverty," "love without parental approval," "when a person loses face," and "for self-sacrifice" (table 44). From this list we can generalize that Japanese people tend to justify suicide on two grounds: (1) a sense of responsibility (as indicated by "a conflict between obligation and love," "when a person loses faces," and "for self-sacrifice"), and (2) a sense of helplessness and hopelessness (as exemplified by "extreme poverty"). "Love without parental approval" in traditional Japan involves not only responsibility but also helplessness, because Japanese people generally feel responsible for satisfying parental wishes as well as highly dependent upon their parents emotionally and financially. They tend to become easily overwhelmed by difficulties. Today, the situation has not changed very much.

The sense of responsibility as a cause of suicide may sound contradictory to Westerners. Responsible Westerners try to live and work hard for their causes. The difference between Japanese and Westerners in

TABLE 43.

JAPANESE STUDENTS' ATTITUDES TOWARD SUICIDE

	High school (1960) %	College (1961) %
Negative attitudes		
"Cowardly"	19.6	19.2
"Not good"	3.6	6.2
"Shallow thinking"	20.7	20.0
"No excuse to make to parent"	7.8	5.8
Subtotal	51.7	51.2
Accepting attitude		
"Individual freedom"	4.5	20.2
"I envy the person who can commit suicide."	2.7	4.0
"I feel sympathetic toward the victim."	3.7	11.7
"Society is responsible."	13.3	9.0
Subtotal	24.2	44.9
No Response	24.0	1.9

SOURCE: M. Kosaka and N. Usui, *Nihonjin no Jisatsu* [Suicide of Japanese people] (Tokyo: Sōbunsha, 1966), p. 225.

TABLE 44.

ATTITUDE TOWARD SUICIDE: "IS SUICIDE ACCEPTABLE IN THE FOLLOWING SITUATION?"

	Total (N:355) %	Acceptable %	No %	Other %
A conflict between obligation and love	100	20	61	19
Extreme poverty	100	18	65	17
Love without parental permission	100	17	80	3
When a person loses face	100	17	75	8
Self-sacrifice for group	100	19	70	11

SOURCE: Tōkei Suuri Kenkyūsho [Institute of statistical mathematics], *Nihonjin no Kokuminsei* [National character of Japanese people] (Tokyo: Shiseido, 1961), pp. 413–414.

this respect seems to be that while the Western responsibility is to a cause, Japanese responsibility is to social superiors or to the group. While Westerners stress performance, Japanese emphasize quality—integrity and sincerity, or selfless devotion to superiors or the group. When a Japanese cannot satisfy his superior's expectations, he may show his sincerity by "selfless devotion to his group." The most selfless action is suicide.

In such cases, an individual's judgment about responsibility is subjective. Therefore, a Japanese person may commit suicide in an unexpected situation. An example is that of a twenty-seven-year-old man who burned himself to death because he could not fulfill his conceived responsibility to his group. According to his father, the man was depressed over his inability to help remove snow that had totaled nearly thirteen feet that winter. He could not do so because four of his fingers had been amputated three years earlier, following an accident.[15]

With modernization the Japanese attitude toward suicide is expected to change, but traditional types of suicide are still dominant. In order to see the trend, suicides in Japanese literature were classified. Applying Durkheim's classification of suicide types (table 1) to Japanese literary works, it was found that suicides in the pre-Kamakura Period (i.e., before 1185) were dominantly fatalistic (69%), followed by altruistic ones (26%). The former include "fear of punishment, incest, etc." (25%), "unescapable dilemma between obligation and love" (19%), "defeat in battle" (16%), and "loss of protector" (9%). Those who were defeated in battle were usually hunted and killed by the victor. The altruistic suicides include "self-sacrifice" and *junshi* (following a deceased master or husband) (table 45).

During the Kamakura-Sengoku Period (1185–1600), the Japanese feudal system was completed and the country was torn by incessant wars among feudal lords. This period also shows a predominance of fatalistic suicides (61%). However, the proportion of altruistic suicides—that is, those committed for self-sacrifice, *junshi,* remonstration, and for apology—increased to 39 percent. It appears that the Japanese social structure was firmly established and that social norms were thoroughly internalized in individuals.

In the Edo Period (1600–1868), the number of altruistic suicides rose to almost equal the number of fatalistic ones (43% and 53%, respectively). The percentage of suicides from "regret, shame, or guilt over own mistake" (15%) became marked. This change may suggest a more effective moralistic education during this period.

The Meiji Period (1868–1911) was characterized by a sharp decrease

TABLE 45.

SUICIDES IN JAPANESE LITERATURE BY DURKHEIMIAN TYPES AND HISTORICAL ERAS
(in percent)

	Pre-Kamakura Period (before 1185)	Kamakura-Sengoku Period (1185–1600)	Edo Period (1600–1868)	Meiji Period (1868–1911)	Contemporary (since 1911)
	32	33	123	68	35
	101%	100%	100%	100%	100%
I. Fatalistic: excessive regulations and fear about future: Total	69%	61%	53%	66%	43%
1. Dilemma between obligation and love; obstacle to love	19	27	27	42	12
2. Crime; fear of punishment	25	0	20	9	6
3. Loss of protector	9	0	0	0	0
4. Defeat in battle	16	34	2	3	3
5. Failure in work; ill health; poverty	0	0	4	12	22
II. Altruistic: excessive integration to society: Total	26%	39%	43%	25%	23%
1. Self-sacrifice	13	12	13	7	11
2. Follow the deceased master, husband, or lover	13	27	15	12	9
3. Regret, shame, guilt over own mistake	0	0	15	6	3

III. Anomic: lack of external regulation; wide goal-means discrepancy: Total	6%	0%	4%	10%	20%
1. Revenge	0	0	0	5	0
2. Unrequited love	6	0	4	5	20
IV. Egoistic: little integration to society; loss of significance of life: Total	0%	0%	0%	0%	14%

SOURCE: Joji Hirayama, "Nihon Bungakuni Arawareta Jisatsu" [Suicides that appeared in Japanese literature], ed. K. Ohara, *Gendai no Esupuri* [L'esprit d'aujourd'hui]: *Jisatsu* [Suicide], November 1, 1965, pp. 239–254.

in altruistic suicides and an increase in suicides for "failure in work, ill health, and poverty" and for "revenge." The change may show the individuation of Japanese people under the influence of Western culture, although individuation (or awareness of self-society conflict) was attained without providing a corresponding increase in social resources or in the individual's ability to solve problems. Such motives as "the conflict between obligation and love" were quite high during this period, and they show a more conscious conflict between individuality and an oppressive society than in preceding periods.

Individualism becomes more noticeable in contemporary Japan (since 1911). The percentages for both fatalistic (43%) and altruistic suicides (23%) declined, and the percentages for more individualistic ones, whether anomic (20%) or egoistic (14%), increased. However, still dominant are fatalistic and altruistic types.

Thus, these two types—altruistic suicides from the sense of responsibility and fatalistic suicides from the sense of helplessness—have characterized Japanese suicides since the beginning of the nation's history. They were still dominant in prewar Japan, and they seem to be prevalent today, too, with the exception of college students' suicides, among whom anomic suicides occupy the dominant place.

These altruistic and fatalistic suicides were romanticized and glorified by Monzaemon Chikamatsu, who set the tone of the Japanese attitude toward suicide. He wrote thirty-three major plays from the end of the seventeenth century to 1723, including eleven plays about love-pact suicides. An analysis of the motives of suicides that Chikamatsu glorified will show the motives of traditional Japanese suicides. The inferred causes of the suicides of the sixty major themes of these works are as follows:

Altruism	20
Failure	16
Love forbidden by parents or employer	12
Other conflicts between obligation and love	5
Unavoidable situation	5
Anxiety about the future	1
Other	1

The twenty altruistic motives include: avenging the deceased master with the full knowledge that one would be executed; *migawari,* or assuming responsibility for a misdeed committed by a lord, husband, or lover; suicide for remonstration; suicide out of sympathy for a master or lover; and *junshi* (also called *ato-oi shinjū*), or suicide in order to follow a deceased master or lover.

Sixteen "failure" motives include not only actual failures but also more subjective judgments of failure in fulfilling social expectations. They include, for example, suicide for inflicting injury on a lover unintentionally; the suicide of a prostitute who found that her patron-lover was her biological father; suicide due to guilt because of unwittingly driving a child to crime; suicide for an unavoidable illegitimate sexual relationship; and suicide for failure to kill an enemy when ordered to do so by one's master. Conflict between obligation and love includes informing the police of a husband's crime and receiving (and rejecting) sexual advances made by a stepmother. The latter implies a motive of guilt for having disobeyed the stepmother's wish and also for having produced an atmosphere that invited the stepmother's sexual advances. An unavoidable situation includes being defeated in battle, having one's pride hurt, being beaten by the master, and being suspected of a crime.

Considering "failure," "love forbidden by parents or employer," "other conflicts between obligation and love," and "unavoidable situation" as "fatalistic," fatalistic suicides comprise 38 percent of Chikamatsu's suicides. These suicides indicate the unbelievably oppressive nature of Japanese feudal society, which Douglass Haring described as "unescapable absolutism and sumptuary control of individuals." Especially, suicide for guilt because of unwittingly driving a child to crime and suicide for receiving (and rejecting) sexual advances made by a stepmother are characteristic of feudal Japan. Both show the importance of guilt, which Ruth Benedict regarded as unimportant for Japan. While Westerners' guilt is related to God's commandments, Japanese guilt is related to such social expectations as "obedience to parents," whether parents are worthy or not. In the Japanese mind society takes the place of the Westerner's God.

The protagonists of Chikamatsu's plays were ordinary men and women who were victimized by the social structure. Their "sin" was that they were powerless. The plays, which highly romanticized and glorified not only altruistic but fatalistic suicides, appealed to the masses who were themselves victims of hardships. The masses could easily identify themselves with the protagonists. The plays provided an outlet for resentment toward the oppressive society which could not be overtly expressed. Because of popular identification with characters and motives, Chikamatsu's influence upon the Japanese people's attitude toward suicide is both extensive and intensive even today.

Assuming that fatalism is a more or less universal ingredient of suicide, the most characteristic type of Japanese suicides is the self-sacrificial one, and the most typical Japanese attitude toward suicide is romanticization. These two characteristics are exemplified by the contemporary cases described in the following sections.

ROMANTICIZATION OF SUICIDE

Japanese people are inveterate romantics. Even revolutionaries, who are expected to be highly rational in Western countries, are romantics in Japan. Feuer describes the nature of Japanese student leaders in radical movements:[16]

> The student leaders were young romantics seeking to lift their people out of submissive attitudes and abnegation before authority; they had a faith in the sheer force of their own will. . . . They seemed poised between a politics of revolutionary romanticism and a Bakunist blend of self-destructiveness together with the sheerest aggressive adventures. They lived in a world peopled in large part by unrealities born of their own real frustrations.

Kōzō Okamoto, a university student from Japan, and two of his revolutionary friends raided Tel Aviv's Lod Airport on May 20, 1972, killing twenty-six tourists and injuring seventy-five others. His two friends killed themselves with grenades, but Okamoto failed to do so. He was arrested. In his memoirs, Okamoto wrote, "It is an established racial trait of the Japanese not to fear death for the attainment of a high goal." When he was asked by a Japanese Embassy official in Rome about the reason for his having killed innocent tourists, Okamoto replied that "I wanted to die a beautiful death for a great cause, but since I am a human being, there are some things I cannot quite explain reasonably." He attributed his behavior to fate: "No matter how hard I tried to escape from such a fate, I could not help it."[17] The wish to die a beautiful death for a great cause was also the motive for Yukio Mishima's suicide. A strong undercurrent of Japanese culture is devotion to the company, and to the nation, even at the sacrifice of the family. (If I remember correctly, Okamoto's father committed suicide in order to show his apology to society for his son's misbehavior.)

For the purpose of romanticizing death, Japanese people often attempt to make their suicides appear to be based on philosophical motives. An eighteen-year-old boy left this note:

> I wish to live longer, but I cannot know why I should live. During the three years in high school, I just lived to find an answer to it. It is easy to live an ordinary life, but without knowing its significance, it is hard to live.

"I think; therefore, I am." I regret that I was born. The animal that is endowed with the capability to think is sure to suffer. It is possible to live without suffering, like a cat or an insect. Unfortunately, being born as a man, I am leaving here sadly.

In Heaven, I would ask Socrates about the question. I would hear Bergson and Kierkegaard about the philosophy of life, see Schopenhauer and Kant, and then converse with Misao Fujimura. You may live human life without understanding it, but you can die for it, too. Peacefully I am rising to Heaven. I will drink with friends and smoke a cigarette with my father there.

This note appears to be a poor imitation of the famous suicide note written by Misao Fujimura in 1903:

How immense the universe is!
How eternal history is!
I wanted to measure the immensity with this puny five-foot body.
What authority has Horatio's philosophy?
The true nature of the whole creation
Is in one word—"unfathomable."
With this regret, I am determined to die.
Standing on a rock on the top of a waterfall,
I have no anxiety.
I recognize for the first time
Great pessimism is nothing but great optimism.

Because Fujimura died by jumping from the top of a waterfall, his suicide was hailed as a "symbol of human emancipation," unifying the human self with Nature.[18] The philosophizing of suicide, however, may often be a disguise for another motive. Despite his philosophizing, Fujimura's suicide was said to have been the result of his unrequited love.[19] A suicidal Kyoto University student stated in his note:

Truth, I will pursue truth even against a million foes. Otherwise give me death. Death is pure and life is foul. Nobody is reliable on this earth.

His life history, however, revealed that he had had an unhappy family life as a foster son and that his love affair with an older woman had resulted in his failure in schoolwork along with financial difficulties.

In addition to beautifying and philosophizing suicides, the romanticization leads to imitative suicide of which there have been many in Japan. In the seven years following Fujimura's suicide, about 200 persons jumped to death in the same place. The "unification with

Nature" became a fashion. In May 1932, a university student and his sweetheart, both from wealthy families, participated in a love-pact suicide (*jōshi*) on a mountain near Tokyo. Later their tombs were opened by vandals. When the police investigated, it was reported that the girl was a virgin. The report caused frenzied excitement among the people. What stirred their imagination was the "purity" between the lovers, in addition to the *jōshi*. Poems were written about the pure lovers; movies were made. A song about the lovers became a top hit. After a college coed jumped into the crater of Mount Mihara in 1933, 944 persons (804 males and 140 females) imitated her death in the same place within the same year.

SACRIFICIAL SUICIDE

The Japanese accept the established social order as natural, group ties as sacred, and strong dependency as normal. The result is that individuals are emotionally identified with their group. Another consequence is that individuals sacrifice themselves for the group. The willingness to die for the group is strengthened by the neo-Confucian concept of honorable death.[20] If death occurs for a group goal or as an apology, it is honorable.

At the end of World War II, Admiral Onishi and Defense Minister General Anami killed themselves in order to protest the declaration of the termination of the war. About ten army officers followed Anami to death. There were, in all, more than 584 suicides of the same nature at that time. There were also about 150 civilians who committed suicide in order to follow the demise of the old sacred Japan. Three right-wing organizations provide examples: sixteen members of Sonjō Gigun, thirteen members of Meirōkai, and thirteen members of Daitō Gijuku. The last group committed *seppuku* (self-disembowelment) in front of the Imperial Palace.

Among the ninety-seven suicide subjects in my Kyoto study, five cases appear to indicate a basic element of altruism, a concern with group welfare that overrides individual goals and even life itself. One of them is an example of suicide for the purpose of remonstration—here, remonstrating his older brother, who had neglected the family business and squandered family property. Other cases involved both apology to the families and the wish to lighten the families' financial burdens by committing suicide.

Recently, there have been several cases of sacrificial suicides. S. Shimoda was an executive of the Nissho Iwai Co., the company prosecuted in the Lockheed bribery scandal. He admitted that he was involved in the bribery but denied any wrongdoing. In his mind, he simply acted in behalf of what he thought was a great cause—his company. He died by jumping out a window in 1979. His suicide note emphasized that "the life of our company is eternal. For eternity we should sacrifice ourselves."

K. Yamaguchi made several foreign trips accompanying the president of his company (Kokusai Denshin Denwa Kōsha). The purpose of the trips was to smuggle millions of dollars' worth of jewelry and paintings through customs. The assets were to be used to bribe politicians and officials of the Transportation and Communication Ministry (*Unyushō*) for the purpose of rigging international telecommunication rates. When police investigations began, Yamaguchi hung himself (on January 2, 1980). He was a minor employee of the company. Therefore, if he was ordered by the president to smuggle, he could not disobey. He might have stated that fact to the investigator, but he could not. Instead of blaming the company superiors, he blamed himself. The note he left reads:

> I am not an exception in making too small a declaration at the custom house. I am sorry that I gave much trouble to my company.

A. Goto, a staff member at Waseda University, was suspected of having sold entrance examination questions. He committed suicide by jumping in front of a train on March 22, 1980, leaving a note claiming his innocence:

> I can no longer stand being regarded with the eye of suspicion. I feel my heart torn to pieces every day. Any further police investigation will end up in exaggerating trivial points and confusing groundless allegation with fact. There is nothing this fainthearted man can do other than to die. Facing death, I swear that I have nothing to do with these bribery incidents. . . .
> The scandal is about what happened such a long time ago that I have nothing with which to prove my innocence. I have never personally received a bribe. If there is anyone who entered the university through such means, please come out and tell the university. I swear I have nothing to hide. I am clean.
> Banzai [Hurrah] for Waseda University!
> Cowardly Me.

In his note, Goto wished to show his integrity by his suicide and thought that his university would be cleared of suspicion by his death.

To commit suicide in order to clear oneself of a false charge seems to be uniquely Japanese. If it was a false charge, why does one need to die? Goto's suicide makes us suspicious that it might not have been a false charge after all, because his wish to stop further police investigation is evident in the note.

The preceding three cases are typically altruistic and sacrificial suicides. There is no display of resentment toward superiors and companies, following Japanese tradition. However, the following note deviates from this pattern, suggesting some change in Japanese society. A few days after Yamaguchi died, T. Yasuda of the same company (Kokusai Denshin Denwa Kōsha) hung himself in order to escape the police investigation into smuggling and bribery. He left a note dated January 31, 1980, and addressed to Kazuo Tamaki, a member of the Diet:

> I thank you for the favor you have given me just because I am from the same prefecture as you. I have regarded you as a god.
>
> Since the revelation of this incident, you have given me kind support. I am thankful for it and I feel sorry that I gave you much trouble. You told me to be patient and endure. . . . Please laugh at me who could not be courageous enough to endure.
>
> I saw many wrongdoings by the president (of Kokusai Denshin Denwa Kōsha) and the director, and I thought "just this much will be all right." Then I found myself the whipping boy, as reported in newspapers and on television. I feel something is wrong. I have been framed; I am the victim.
>
> I cannot forgive the president and the director. They led me to destroy the proof of their misdeeds, and still they behave as if they have nothing to do with me. I cannot but feel angry.
>
> You have told me not to have rancor against others, but the fact is that the director bought jewelry, art, antiques, and paintings from the Seibu department store. Why am I alone to be picked out? I have worked hard in the matter of gift giving to outsiders. I took upon myself much trouble just for my company. And now I am the one who is blamed for everything. After all, I was stupid to be used, because I worked hard to adjust myself to the atmosphere in the president's room under the direction of the director. Please laugh at me.
>
> May I take the liberty of asking your favor for my family members?

This note shows resentment and anger. Traditionally, the note writer in such cases does not express his resentment in order to insure protection of his family members by the superiors whom he is protecting.

Any display of resentment might incur punishment on his family members. Apparently, Yasuda could air his resentment because he was addressing the note to a member of the Japanese Diet, whose status and influence are superior, or at least equal, to those of Yasuda's company president. Because of Tamaki's influence, Yasuda's family would be able to avoid the punishment that otherwise might be administered by his immediate superiors.

If Yasuda was resentful, why did he not clarify how he was used? Newspapers report that Yasuda had received telephone calls from the president of the company reminding him that he should not cause trouble to politicians and government officials.[21] It is said that Yasuda had a list of names of politicians and government officials who had received bribes from his company, totaling more than 2,200 million yen (about $10 million) in 1978. At the same time, Yasuda was warned by his immediate superior (Director Sato) that he could be sued for misusing company money unless he "behaved."

Yasuda had two mistresses on whom he apparently spent part of the money that he was to use for bribery. Yasuda insisted to his lawyer that he had used the money with the approval of Sato, but Sato denied this. Yasuda's wife accused Sato of "framing" her husband and driving him to suicide.

Sacrificial suicide in contemporary Japan usually involves an employee sacrificing himself for his superiors by eliminating a key witness (himself) who might be used against the superiors. Such suicide has several ingredients:

1. The concept that the company is more important than one's family or oneself.
2. The idea that one's responsibility to the company is better fulfilled by dying than by living.
3. The public's attitude that death purifies a person's wrongdoings.
4. The public's tendency to regard the person as a "victim" of the situation, implying that he himself is not responsible, especially if he shows his sincerity (i.e., "selflessness") by suicide.
5. The Japanese personality structure, which is easily susceptible to a constricted perception of the situation in a crisis, to depression, and to a wish to escape.
6. The realization that the violator of social expectations and his family members will be severely punished and that no public support can be expected.
7. The awareness on the part of the victim that even if he does not kill himself he might be eliminated in some way.

This fear of being killed is an essential element of the self-sacrificial suicide involved in Japanese scandals. In such cases it is sometimes difficult to know whether the death is suicide, "being forced to die," or even homicide. This is so even when suicide notes are left. In traditional Japan, where government officials, business leaders, politicians, the police, and *yakuza* bosses were close allies, a person who might provide evidence against an important individual could easily be "erased." *Yakuza* is a large organization of professional gamblers, extortionists, and hoodlums, together with members of criminal organizations. *Yakuza* could be hired as professional killers. Fear of *yakuza* is traditional in Japan. While ordinary Japanese are not allowed to have any weapons, *yakuza* members carry them. Legality is not their concern. If *yakuza* do not carry weapons, they are quite adept in other methods of violence, using brass knuckles, crowbars or knives. They are generally physically strong. They are also daring and are disciplined to die at any time for their group or boss.

Yakuza's threat to ordinary Japanese is enhanced by their power and accepted status, despite their antisocial behavior, in Japanese society. In the 1960s, *yakuza* movies (with *yakuza* as heroes) almost single-handedly carried the Japanese movie industry.[22] The movies glorified *yakuza* as the embodiment of the samurai code of behavior. They highlighted the sense of obligation and loyalty and suppressed love, tolerance, and patience. Their appeal was also in the compassion that *yakuza* heroes showed to those struggling at the bottom of Japanese society, in contrast to general Japanese who lost themselves (or "Japan Spirit") in materialistic prosperity, allegedly under American influences. *Yakuza* movies were favorites of Yukio Mishima.

Yakuza business has been thriving. In 1983 a Mainichi newspaperman interviewed a Yamaguchi-gume (*yakuza* group) boss and reported that the annual income of a *yakuza* leader (say, a syndicate head with a thousand men under him) was estimated at about $360,000. (The total *yakuza* membership today is about 110,000—larger than half the entire Japanese police force.) Their income is almost tax-free because of the difficulty involved in its calculation. Their illegal income from gambling, narcotics peddling, prostitution, massage parlors, Turkish baths, loan-sharking, extortion, and other sources was estimated at $22 billion in the same year.[23]

The accepted status of *yakuza* is shown by their relationships with government officials, politicians, and businessmen. The close tie between *yakuza* and local government officials is exemplified by the reaction of the officials to people's complaints about the intimidation tactics used by the Yamaguchi-gumi (the *yakuza* organization headed by Yamaguchi). The *Asahi shimbun* reported the following on September 6, 1966:

> When the local people were opposed to the construction of a boarding house for harbor laborers, we [of the Kobe Harbor Administration] asked Yamaguchi to help, and the opposition stopped immediately. When we needed an extra 35,000 yen, we asked for Yamaguchi's help again. He immediately donated the sum. Therefore, the administration's attitude is that as long as he did not violate laws, we could not revoke his permit as a labor contractor.

The relationship between *yakuza* and government officials on the national level is suggested by the fact that Yoshio Kodama, who boasted freely of his power as "boss of the *yakuza* world,"[24] recently received one of the highest-order decorations from the government for his services to the nation. He was the behind-the-scenes founder of today's dominant political party in Japan, the Liberal Democratic Party. He was the one through whom Lockheed channeled its bribes to then Premier Kakuei Tanaka.

Many politicians need *yakuza* bosses for raising money and getting votes in elections. *Yakuza* leaders often have stronger influence on local populations than do politicians. When rival politicians need to cooperate against common foes, a *yakuza* boss often functions as an intermediary, or "fixer." It is said that Premier Tanaka was one of the most effective users of intermediaries of this sort. In return *yakuza* need politicians, too. When a *yakuza* was arrested, for example, his boss asked a politician to use his influence on the local police chief to bring about the release of the criminal, with a lighter punishment than he deserved. When the man was released, his prestige among *yakuza* was enhanced. He then took revenge on those who had been instrumental in his arrest. Thus, *yakuza* are troublesome to the public and are greatly feared. The fear enhances the *yakuza*'s influence.

The *yakuza*-businessmen coalition is exemplified by the institution of *sōkaiya,* that is, *yakuza* specializing in handling shareholders' meetings. Through them, company executives may either reject protesters by force or prevent their presence at the meetings. The *sōkaiya* buy one or two shares of a corporations stock, giving them the right to attend the firm's meetings. They approach corporate executives, threatening to disrupt their meetings if they are not paid. They also use "dirt hunters," who try to dig up compromising information on company officials. They can threaten to sell the information to yellow journalists.

The practice of *sōkaiya* is exemplified by the following report on the Mitsubishi shareholders' meeting immediately after the revelation of the IBM espionage scandal:[25]

> Mitsubishi president Nihachiro Katayama opened the meeting and apologized to the shareholders for the bad publicity the company had received over the IBM scandal. He then proposed pay raises for company executives. The impeccably attired men believed to be *sōkaiya* punctuated Katayama's brief speech with shouts of "Good, good! No objections!" and the annual meeting was over in eighteen minutes.
>
> The Hitachi shareholders' meeting the previous day followed a similar scenario, and the business was wrapped up in seventeen minutes.

At a meeting of stockholders of the giant Marubeni Corporation, *sōkaiya* violently cut off inquiries about Marubeni's role in relaying bribes as Lockheed's formal agent in Japan.[26]

Probably the most marked difference between Japanese and American democracies is the lack of genuine debate in Japan. The lack is largely due to Japan's educational system, which does not develop an analytical and critical attitude, and to Japanese religions, which do not develop a suprasocietal value and principle on which lay members can base an evaluation of the status quo.

The use of *sōkaiya* is extensive. According to a 1982 survey conducted by the state-run NHK Broadcasting network, 40 percent of the business firms in Japan use more than 100 *sōkaiya,* 10 percent use more than 500, and 2 percent use more than 1,000. A separate police study showed that only 5 percent of Japanese firms claimed to have no dealings at all with *sōkaiya.*[27] A well-known *sōkaiya* received 20 million yen from a steel-making company for his services.[28] It is estimated that the total hush-money given to *sōkaiya* in 1976 amounted to $400 million.[29]

In October 1982 a business law went into effect that would make companies, as well as *sōkaiya,* punishable for manipulating stockholders meetings for a fee. However, it is difficult to eliminate the traditional practice in a short time with a law. A *yakuza-sōkaiya* boasted that "*Yakuza* are inheritors of the old *bushidō*—the samurai code of behavior. This [*sōkaiya*] is a God-given job. Besides, Japan is not a communist country and as long as there are corporations, we will be there."

The fortune of *sōkaiya* reflects the fortune of *yakuza* in general, who are doing quite well. Because of their affinity for politicians and businessmen, *yakuza* traditionally enjoy a considerable degree of satisfaction and pride concerning their own status. They often flaunt their antisocial calling. A young, earnest *yakuza* leader, dressed conservatively in white shirt, tie, and dark slacks, proudly told Donald Kirk that he had killed more than ten people in the past year in gang fights. Oda Hidemi, a director of the Yamaguchi-gumi says, "As long as there are *yakuza,* it is a free country. . . . The police come here and say 'Hello' to me. We are like relatives. In the daytime the police protect the citizens, and at night I protect them."[30] *Yakuza* indeed contribute to Japan's low crime rate by keeping a fairly tight control on petty crime. They will not allow punk criminals to pull any scams against people who are in the good graces of the *yakuza* boss.

Yakuza enjoy not only pride and satisfaction but also considerable power in their extortion business, as indicated by the following examples.[31] The owner of a nightclub in Shibuya, Tokyo, refused to knuckle under to the *yakuza* group that controlled the area. Instead of resorting to violence, the *yakuza* would go into the nightclub and occupy every table and refuse to order anything. Naturally, other patrons stayed away from the club because of their fear of *yakuza.* Night after night, the nightclub had virtually no income. Finally, out of desperation the owner "paid his tribute" to the boss. After that he was able to run a successful operation.

However, if the promoter of an entertainment event has an understanding with the *yakuza* group in the area where the event is to take place, the group will send out its members to hustle tickets. They do not *ask* people to buy but simply drop off "quotas" to businesses and shops in their "territory" with the proviso that "this is your share and you must buy." The Japanese police seem to be relatively tolerant of *yakuza* as long as the *yakuza* are not engaged in drug trafficking or gun smuggling.

Yakuza, who are proud of their affinity to the samurai code of behavior and who can incite fear in ordinary people in Japan, are extremely obedient to authorities. They may willingly use intimidation tactics or even kill people when they are asked to by persons in high positions.

After the threat of *yakuza,* the last ingredient of self-sacrificial suicides is the extreme importance of Japanese bureaucrats. Self-sacrificial suicides are often committed for the purpose of protecting the victim's company superiors and the government officials whom the company superiors want to protect. As mentioned earlier, T. Yasuda had a list of politicians and government officials whom his company bribed. The involvement of government officials in bribery is a natural product of the Japanese social structure, which is characterized by the ubiquity of central governmental control, the importance of bureaucrats, and the necessity of personal connections.

The central governmental control is exemplified by the necessity of government permits "for more than 120,000 varieties of everyday endeavor."[32] If a bus company wishes to relocate a bus stop somewhere in the countryside, approval is needed from the Transportation Ministry in Tokyo. The Japanese economy is virtually run by bureaucrats, who "draw up decisive plans determining which industries, branches, or companies will receive what, and how much, support from the government," but there is no highly objective procedure used in making such decisions.[33] Whether a company is approved by bureaucrats or not largely determines its future. The lack of objective procedures for evaluation makes companies intensely competitive for the favor of bureaucrats. It is bureaucrats, supreme operators of the legal machine, who run the Japanese government, whether legislative, executive, or judicial. Diet members are mostly helpless in lawmaking without assistance from bureaucrats. Cabinet members, except former bureaucrats, are also helpless in administering laws without the assistance of bureaucrats.[34] The strong control or coordination by bureaucrats makes Marvin Wolf attribute Japan's success to a "Japanese conspiracy."[35]

Because of the great importance placed on personal connections, businessmen attempt to cultivate personal connections with bureaucrats and politicians, through whom bureaucrats can be reached. For that purpose, lavish entertaining and handsome gift giving are customary. The "year-end gift" (*oseibo*) and the "middle-year gift" (*ochūgen*) to social superiors are so deeply institutionalized that Japanese people are not sensitive to the difference between gift giving and bribery. The amount of money that Japanese companies spent on tax-exempt entertainment totaled $5 billion dollars in 1972—about 1.5 percent of Japan's Gross National Product. The amount was larger than the total national defense budget and also larger than 20 percent of the total spent on education by the entire nation.[36]

The close personal connection between business leaders and bureaucrats is epitomized by the institution of *amakudari* (literally, "descent from heaven"), in which a government bureaucrat who has served a company well is brought into the company on retirement (which occurs, on average, at about the age of fifty) as an adviser or counselor. Therefore, bureaucrats attempt to cultivate good relations with big companies for future security. Some bureaucrats who wish to eventually enter politics try hard to be on good terms with business leaders, whose financial support would be indispensable. These factors make bureaucrats vulnerable to bribery.

Generally, the role of the superordinate in Japan is to raise money, to take a personal interest in his followers, to be loyal to the group, and to have close personal connections with other high-echelon officials. When such a person has skills in bargaining and in achieving behind-the-scenes deals, he is regarded as a good leader. When such a bureaucrat moves to his new business position, his personal connections with high-ranking government officials are utilized for the purpose of acquiring special favors for the company. Entertainment and gift-giving tactics become especially effective when there are already direct personal connections.

The form of *amakudari* that shows Japanese bureaucrats' greed most blatantly is the establishment of many semigovernmental corporations (*kōdan* or *kōsha*) upon which the bureaucrats can descend after retirement. For example, "the Audit Bureau often employs its retired staff in the very same corporations it is supposed to audit."[37] There are about a hundred of these bodies, and in 1977 they cost the government over 9.5 trillion yen in subsidies. The Kokusai Denshin Denwa Kōsha, for which K. Yamaguchi and T. Yasuda died, is one of these semigovernmental corporations.

Because of such structural causes as the ubiquity of governmental control, the importance of bureaucrats, the necessity of personal connections, the lack of objective criteria for governmental assistance, and the institution of gift giving, political and social scandals in Japan are called *kōzō oshoku* (structural corruption). Japanese government officials are probably as corrupt as, if not more corrupt than, those in many other countries. After World War II, Seizo Shigemasa, Takeo Fukuda, and Eisaku Sato—all top-ranked bureaucrats—were involved in Shōden and Zōsen scandals, but none of them were punished.

However, despite the tendency toward corruption which is built into the Japanese social structure, Japanese bureaucrats are seldom known to be involved in scandals. That Japanese bureaucrats are not generally connected to bribery unless there is a personal connection seems to explain, at least partly, their relative immunity.

Another important reason why so little is known of their corruption is the "extraordinary finesse and discretion of those concerned."[38] Japanese bureaucrats' knowledge of laws is far superior to that of other Japanese, so it is difficult for others to find holes in it. This extreme finesse is aided by the institution of gift giving, the noncritical attitude toward authorities among Japanese, and the ubiquitous Japanese tendency toward the discrepancy between *tatemae* (what one says) and *honne* (what one feels and does). Not only bureaucrats but also most other Japanese speak according to *tatemae*. They give lip service to values such as honesty, even when they behave according to *honne* (e.g., self-profit by bribing). However, *honne* must be satisfied in such a way as not to mar *tatemae*. In most cases Japanese are not aware of the discrepancy in their behavior.

This tendency toward a disparity between words and action is especially marked when Japanese people talk to outsiders. People's desire to put up their better front to others may be universal, to a certain extent. However, Japanese people who have lived a long time in the society of "unescapable absolutism and sumptuary control of individuals" have been conditioned to hide their own weaknesses for fear of punishment. In addition, when Japanese talk to outsiders, their groupism operates to hide their group's seamy aspects. Top Japanese leaders, whether in business, politics, or government (including the judicial sector), are mostly from the same university (Tokyo University), and their *gakubatsu* (educational clique) is extremely tight and strong. Because of personal connections, they may do favors for each other, sometimes illegally, but they carefully guard against any occurrence that might reveal their dark sides to outsiders.[39]

The expectation of tacit collaboration among government officials, politicians, businessmen, and *yakuza* bosses in traditional Japan made many Japanese pessimistic when they were placed in the position of scapegoat. The pessimism made them highly vulnerable to the wish to escape through suicide from such possible danger as murder or harm to themselves and to their family members. As long as the collaboration among political and business leaders is strong and *yakuza* are available for their services, self-sacrificial suicides will remain one form of Japanese suicides.

九

IX

JAPANESE
ECONOMIC
SUCCESS

Japanese economic success has been explained in terms of such situational factors as completely rebuilt and modernized factories and mills after their destruction by bombs during World War II. Situational factors also include the economic booms produced by the Korean and Vietnam wars and Japan's small military expense due to American commitment to Japan's defense. The money saved because of this and the experts freed from military research can be used for research and development in the economic sector. Some writers attribute the success to favorable exchange rates. According to Dr. Paul McCracken at the University of Michigan, labor costs in Japan are about two-thirds of the U.S. level when the exchange rate is 240 yen to the dollar. The differential in the Japan-U.S. car-production gap is somewhat in excess of $1,500.[1]

Still others stress social structural factors such as lower labor costs and the distribution system. Lower labor costs are possible because of disadvantageous positions of females and subcontract firm employees, who are hired last and fired first. Their wages are lower, their promotions are slower, and their fringe benefits are poorer than what elite employees enjoy. The Japanese distribution system is often called "the ultimate nontariff barrier."[2] Generally, between manufacturer and retailer, there are levels of wholesalers through which goods wend their circuitous way. Since the relationship between manufacturer, large wholesaler, small wholesaler, and retailer is connected by personal ties and loyalty, it is very difficult for foreign goods to intervene. There are also writers who point to the government's industrial policy as the key factor in Japan's success.

Such situational and structural factors are important, but they are not sufficient. It must be explained why Japanese utilize the given situation so well and why structural factors work so effectively in that country. For example, Japan is not the only country that has a nationalistic industrial policy. France and Canada also have such policies. Why does the Japanese type of industrial policy work more effectively? In addition, the Japanese governmental policy (e.g., on agricultural products), like the distribution system, results in higher prices for consumers. Why do Japanese consumers accept such inconveniences as high prices and still cooperate with the government's policy wholeheartedly? A similar question may be asked about the low labor cost. If the labor cost is really lower for Japanese people, why do they work hard for less wages than do Americans? Some say that when hidden fringe benefits, such as housing subsidies, are counted, the cost difference between Japanese and American companies is not as large as is commonly thought. If this is so, why do fringe benefits work better than higher salary in Japan?

A more convincing explanation of Japanese success probably is in terms of such social interactional factors as a good labor-management relationship, participative decision making, and voluntary quality control. These factors, however, are not really Japanese in origin. Ironically, they were introduced into Japan by American engineers. In 1948 the Occupation administration had top Japanese executives removed from corporate and government positions because of their prior association with the wartime regime. As part of an effort to help rebuild the country's industry, Charles Protzman, Homer Sarasohn and, later, E. E. Deming, conducted a series of seminars for top company executives on the policy, organization, control, and operation of what they considered to be a model American company. These seminars emphasized quality control, management leadership, teamwork, and cooperation between management and workers. Why could Japanese learn from the American model so well that they made it work more effectively? An answer will be attempted here with reference to coordination, motivation, and mobilization.

COORDINATION

An example of effective Japanese companies will help our understanding. When the U.S. subsidary of the Kyoto Ceramic (Kyocera) plant[3] took over a troubled ceramic packaging plant from Fairchild Camera and Instrument of Mountain View, California, it inherited monthly losses in the range of from $100,000 to $200,000. American managers retained by Kyocera during the takeover could not accept the new company's philosophies, and they left, one after another. Kyocera replaced them with Japanese who worked seventeen hours a day, seven days a week, to turn the plant around. It took the company two years to make the operation profitable. Today it is the leading ceramic packaging company in the United States. Salaried personnel at the plant work at least fifty-five hours a week, while managers and salesmen put in sixty hours and more. The company's president works about fifteen hours on weekdays and another six or seven hours on Saturday.

Work at Kyocera begins with a ritual. Neatly lined up in columns, workers gather for a 7:00 A.M. pep talk. The president of the company tells them the company gospel: "We must win. We must accomplish our ambitious master plan and win against our invisible enemies." He tells them that the economy is weak and that everyone must continue to forge ahead unselfishly if Kyoto Ceramic is to continue to stay on top. Moments later employees begin a round of exercises, rotating their arms and lightly twisting their torsos in unison. When they go to their own departments, they are greeted with another pep talk before they throw themselves into the tasks of the day.

The pep talks always emphasize the common theme of "winning the war." This goal is to be upheld by all employees, whether Japanese or not. The two top executives of the 1,300-employee plant are Japanese, but five of the company's ten executives at the vice-presidential level are Americans. The ratio is similar among Kyocera's forty middle managers. The president of the company states that he wouldn't mind if everybody were Caucasian, "if he understands our philosphy"—that is, selfless devotion to the company's success. Employees are taught to set goals for a distant future rather than for short-term profitability.

This example shows the necessary ingredients of effective coordination: groupism and hierarchical organization (based on authoritarian familism).

<hr/>

GROUPISM

The common goal of Kyocera workers is that "business is war," fought for the company and for the nation. Group identification is fostered by doing physical exercises in unison and by working close together in the same room. With the sole exception of the company's two top executives, none of the employees has his own office. Group orientation is indicated by an emphasis on worker loyalty, which is measured by the employees' commitment to extraordinarily long hours of work. Japanese employees work overtime without concern about extra payment. The company's hierarchical organization is represented by employees wearing different-colored jackets or smocks, corresponding to their ranks. Social relations among them follow established norms regulating the behavior of persons of different status. The regulation produces a high degree of predictability of behavior, minimizing personal conflict.

These characteristics are typical of Japanese companies in general. True to groupism, the Japanese company is a community. The company is a unit of management and is very frequently the unit of an industry. It is also the unit within which labor associations are confined.[4] All employees are connected by the common goal of the company's well-being. The well-being of the company is also the primary purpose of Japanese unions. Unions believe that only the company's well-being insures benefit to the worker. Cooperation with other unions is rare.

Group orientation is insured by several means. Union leaders are usually appointed by the company management as a step in their careers. Promising employees, who are regarded as future leaders, have nonspecialized careers. They frequently transfer to other departments and to other branches, promoting group identity within the company as a whole. Other institutional mechanisms for cultivating group orientation include communal living in company houses, frequent dining and drinking together, recruitment through particularistic ties (especially from the same prefectures from which company leaders came[5]), and the *nenkō joretsu* system. In the *nenkō joretsu* system, workers are paid according to age and length of service, alleviating competition among individuals. A bonus is not contingent upon individual achievement but instead upon group performance. The slow rate of salary increase and promotion for the first ten years of employment promotes personal intimacy and understanding among workers, regardless of future promise. The intentional ambiguity about a locus of responsibility for decision making reduces the possibility of conflict between decision makers and followers.

HIERARCHY

A Japanese company has a highly centralized administration with autocratic decision making, although the autocratic control in Japan is more flexible than in the typical totalitarian system. The flexibility comes from the Japanese leaders' sensitivity to the reaction of others, both coordinates and subordinates. Before they make a decision they usually tap other people's opinions and ideas carefully. They "ensure that no one who really needs to know something is overlooked."[6] The sensitivity to subordinates' feelings is based on the Confucian teaching that real leaders are men of exemplary moral courage, self-sacrifice, and benevolence. The superordinate-subordinate relationship within a company is regarded as similar to the relationship between parent and child or between elder brother and younger brother. The superordinate is expected to be concerned with the welfare of his subordinates.

Hierarchical organization also applies to the relationship between companies. Japanese companies are typically included in a larger group—for example, a bank group in which companies are centered on a bank, or an industrial group formed around a large manufacturing company. Companies within a group are under the close direction of the central bank or company. Within the large group, companies are hierarchically organized. Ranking is determined by size, which is correlated with productivity, the level of wages paid, the number of university graduates employed, the prestige of the universities from which graduates are recruited, the stability of the labor force, the rate of interest charged on loans, and a number of other measures of the firm's quality.[7] Cooperation among members of the large group is secured by specialization and shared common stocks, which make for interdependence.

These industrial groups, in turn, are coordinated by careful and long-range government investment and planning, in cooperation with business leaders. Japanese society has been an oligarchy par excellence since the unification of the country under the Tokugawa regime in the seventeenth century. The concentration of decision-making power in a few, in combination with a loyal majority, makes for effective coordination. Oligarchical leadership is in the hands of top bureaucrats, politicians, and businessmen.

Along with bureaucrats, another enduring group of leaders is the *Zaikaijin* (financiers) of Keidanren, the Federation of Economic Organization. They number about two or three hundred, and within the group there is a marked hierarchy under a few top leaders. The Keidanren people are powerful, aged capitalists, working unobtrusively behind the scenes to control Japan's broad financial, economic, and industrial policies. They are mostly graduates of law or economics from Tokyo University, with a small number from Hitotsubashi University. They represent such key industries as steel, banking, shipbuilding, electric power, and oil—areas absolutely basic to the nation's economy.

These key business leaders see a good deal of one another as they exchange opinions concerning a broad range of issues affecting the country as a whole. They are also in constant informal contact with a smaller number of government bureaucrats and political leaders, with whom they determine major decisions for the future of the nation. The *Zaikaijin*'s influence is exerted through tremendous political contributions. Its influence is so great that scandal is only rarely attached to the group.

The interaction between groupism and hierarchy produces effective organization of Japanese workers for their common goal.

MOTIVATION

SEISHIN EDUCATION

The major motivational method is education. New employees are more apprentices than they are individual workers. They must be educated to the company's ways of doing things. An example of this education is *seishin kyōiku* (spiritual education). Employees are evaluated more in terms of the degree to which their personal characteristics contribute to group goals and integration than in terms of their technical and intellectual ability. The primary criterion for the evaluation is *seishin*, "the complex of loyalty, discipline, *esprit de corps,* and indomitable perseverance."[8]

Seishin is the essence of the historical accomplishment of Japanese civilization, from art to economic growth. Art is evaluated according to the degree to which *seishin* is represented. *Seishin* seems to mean to Japanese what *humanity* means to Westerners. Even today Frager and Rohlen found the value of *seishin* to be flourishing and providing criteria for recruitment and training in all kinds of social groups.[9] Usual methods of *seishin* training are *zazen* (meditation), marathons, other endurance tests, or brief training visits to Japan's Self-Defense Force camps. Although the following description of "Japan's largest outdoor management school" at the foot of Mount Fuji depicts an extreme case, it reflects the core of Japanese national mores.

The school trains about five thousand businessmen a year. Such Japanese companies as Nissan, NEC, Matsushita, Toyota, NTT, and Sanyo, as well as other companies throughout the nation, are willing to pay over a thousand dollars a person for the thirteen-day course. (The bank that Frager and Rohlen studied had a *seishin*-oriented training program lasting three months.) When companies are thinking of promoting someone, they send him there to acquire the personality strength necessary in a manager. Failure at the school would probably result in no promotion, demotion, or even dismissal.

At the school, trainees are not taught how to maximize profits and reduce overheads. Instead, they are subjected to unrelenting military discipline, forced marches, and intensive brainwashing. The school prides itself on putting managers through hell. The motto of the school is "Business is War." To win the war, the selfless devotion of managers is necessary. The school teaches that a good manager must understand people's feelings. In order to do so he has to be "naked," without pride. He must know his own weaknesses. Only when he becomes selfless and identifies himself with the group does he become a worthy person. One of the methods used for making the trainee admit his own weakness and evil is a ritual of "telephone reporting," i.e. in a corner of the room trainees pour out to an examiner all their wrongs and weaknesses. Instructors purposely humiliate trainees.

Another virtue to cultivate is persistence. Trainees are assigned many words of meaningless text to learn and recite to the instructor. For the same purpose, trainees are forced to march twelve miles in the dark and to participate in a twenty-five-mile march to test the limits of their strength. Also important is self-sufficiency. Administrators must always face solitude, instructors say, so that they can pass on directions and obey orders from the president in spite of what junior staff members might think. Therefore, fellowship is discouraged. Discouraged also is reasoning. Instructors stress, "This place wants bodily reaction, not thinking."

Because the school's purpose is to change businessmen into spirited "soldiers," the first task of new recruits is to exchange business suits for white smocks modeled after the uniforms of the Imperial Japanese

Navy. The day's routine begins at 4:30 A.M. with the appointment of a new leader for the group. Martial arts exercises are held in the dormitory at 5 A.M., followed by brisk toweling of the torso with a cloth. From 5:30 A.M. until breakfast at 7:00, students are given written and dictation tests by the instructors, each of whom wears a stopwatch around his neck. Spontaneous reaction is required. Most tasks assigned to students involve painful rote memorization. For example, they are required to repeat endlessly and "from the heart" assigned songs as well as "the ten commandments of being a manager."

One day, after lunch, sixteen manager trainees changed back into their blue serge business suits and piled into a bus to go to the nearest town for "singing practice." The businessmen stood in front of the Fujinomiya station and took turns belting out the following "Salesman Song" in their loudest voices in order to satisfy their instructor, who was standing fifty feet away among members of the bemused public:

> You have sweat on your forehead.
> The product you have made with the sweat of your head
> You have to sell with the sweat of your hands.
> What you produce with tears
> You have to sell with tears.
> Don't feel down, Salesbird.

A middle-aged manager bellowed, face crimson with effort. "Not good enough. Do it again," ordered the instructor.

Everything is controlled, even the taking of a bath. The bath was a huge communal tub in a room lined with picture windows facing out onto the lawn. Trainees lined up naked before entering and read the "bathing instructions" four times in a loud voice: Pour one or two buckets of hot water on your head. Wash your head with shampoo or soap. Pour cold water on your head four times.

After exactly five minutes in the tub, six minutes is allowed for washing and shaving and eight minutes for warming up. Five splashes of cold water bring the affair to an end.

The *seishin* program, as described here, reflects characteristics of Japanese socialization and education in general. It aims, first, at single-mindedness and a highly oversimplified understanding of events, as shown by the motto, "Business is war." The attitude in which business is viewed as war was also observed by Rodney Clark: "Work is a war being fought by other means, and loyalty and service to the company is a form of loyalty and service to the nation."[10]

Second, the teaching emphasizes selfless devotion to one's own group. A Japanese should not only be selfless but should also have a strong sense of gratitude to others and to society. He should not only be devoted to the cause of Japan but also to its hierarchical organization and group activities. Therefore, the material disadvantages of an individual should be disregarded. This view is exemplified by *naikan* (introspection), which is one of the major methods used in *seishin*-oriented training. Some companies require everyone from the president to the newest hireling to go through it.

Naikan is a one-week program of directed meditation. A *sensei* (teacher) first guides the trainee into greater devotion for the trainee's mother. Then the contributions of others to his life are examined. The *sensei* steers the trainee away from abstract comments and complaints and focuses on his ingratitude toward the sacrifices of other persons. Many trainees break down crying, and some even want to commit suicide out of guilt and regret. The final message from the teacher is that the only escape from mental anguish is to plunge into acts of service.[11]

Third, the program produces an inclination toward psychological change rather than toward putting forth effort for problem solving. One should change to adjust to the situation rather than attempt to change environments. Because of this tendency, Japanese people can combine traditional sentiments and values with modern science and industrial society without attempting logical and ideological integration. The capability enables them to modernize without losing social integration. However, because of this capability conflict may be built into their social structure and social character.

The fourth characteristic of the *seishin* program is the belief that personality strength is cultivated only by fortitude and strict, painful discipline. One of the reasons why the entrance examination system, which is criticized as "examination hell," does not change is that the system tests young people's fortitude and their capability to endure strict, painful discipline. The attitude is further extended to a thirst for self-sacrificial actions, a desire most glorified among rightists.

Fifth, the teaching tends to equate self-development with self-mastery, which in Japanese contexts means blunting one's sensitivity so that one can stay calm under any circumstances. The ultimate end of self-development is considered to be self-satisfaction, self-confidence, and happiness, but these concepts are so subjective that often the effort for self-development is equated with a blissful feeling of complacency.

Seishin education, characterized by the emphasis on devotion to the group, inclination toward psychological change, maturation through painful discipline, and self-mastery, is accepted eagerly by Japanese because of their diffuse insecurity. Group identification is the primary adjustment mechanism in an authoritarian society. Although security (e.g., lifetime employment) is often pointed out as the key to Japanese economic success, we cannot ignore the other side—that is, without insecurity the worker may not become a "workaholic" for a group goal. Insecurity generates energy that is directed against outsiders, whether in war or in business.

The diffuse anxiety of the Japanese samurai businessmen, who are among the most successful in that country, is produced by "the deep desire of the individual for group acceptance, a consciousness of helplessness, and cut-throat competition."[12] The consciousness of helplessness is rooted in the social structure. There is an authoritarian stress on power, with a keen sensitivity to status difference. The stress and sensitivity combine with a knowledge of the misery that accompanies failure in a society where status prejudice is strong and public assistance is underdeveloped. Thus, success becomes a compulsive goal. Japanese people as a whole are highly ambitious. If they themselves cannot succeed, then their children must. Group pressure, particularly family pressure, makes a person feel obliged to have a high goal even when he does not have adequate means for attaining it (e.g., good school grades, good working habits, health, confidence, financial security, etc.).

Japanese society is a hierarchy of authoritarian social relations, as represented by Chie Nakane below:[13]

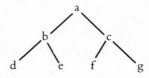

In this system, social superiors often make subjective and particularistic evaluations of their subordinates (i.e., according to personal connection). A subordinate is seldom sure about where he stands in the eyes of his superiors, because there is little specification of evaluation criteria. A formal procedure whereby a subordinate's complaints are examined fairly is one of the essential elements of democracy. There is rarely any such procedure developed in Japan.

Cooperation among subordinates is a deterrent to the possibility of the superior's abusing his power, but under the Japanese hierarchy of power, cooperation among subordinates is not developed. Coordinates (e.g., d and e, and f and g, above) compete with each other for the favor of their immediate superior (b and c, respectively).

In this system, intimacy is seldom developed between social equals in the sense of the "capability to commit oneself to partnerships, and to develop the ethical strength to abide by such commitments, even though they may call for significant sacrifices."[14] This intimacy-commitment between friends and fellow workers, called *kyō*, is highly emphasized and developed in China[15] but not in Japan. What the Japanese emphasize as *kyō* (or *ninkyō*) is limited to the attitude of *yakuza* (underworld) gamblers who are ready to sacrifice themselves for their bosses rather than for their equals. A Japanese person generally cannot count on the support of his fellow workers if he is in conflict with his superiors. This lack of support comes from the general lack of universal (or suprasocietal) values against which subordinates can criticize authority figures.

In addition to the diffuse anxiety produced by the social structure, it is also generated from an expectation of an insecure future. The alleged lifetime employment and familistic management-labor relationship do not necessarily insure security for workers. At retirement (normally at age fifty-five), according to David W. Plath, the fortunate company man will draw severance pay equivalent to two or three years' wages. Pension systems are likely to furnish little more than pocket money. About one in three company men at that age has a child or two at home, and he must therefore be prepared to meet tuition bills and wedding costs. To pay for tuition bills and wedding costs is regarded as a parental responsibility in Japan. Another one in three employees has an aged parent or parents to support. Anxiety produced by such considerations of future insecurity is quite normal in Japan and produces a strong craving for savings.[16]

The more insecure they feel about their future, the harder the Japanese work in order to get ahead of others for a very limited number of promotions. Promotions are largely predetermined in accordance with the school from which workers graduated, limiting the number of positions available for them. Particularly, the number of available higher positions in most big companies is narrowly limited because of *amakudari*, as mentioned in chapter 8.

Thus, high aspirations, social (particularly parental) pressure, authoritarian social relations, invidious competition among equals for the favor of social superiors, the lack of support from equals in case of a difficulty with superiors, and expectation of future insecurity are all contributing factors to diffuse anxiety. This is so even among white-collar (samurai) businessmen, vanguards of the Japanese economic war.

The insecurity of samurai businessmen is an important cause of Japan's economic success, but the proportion of samurai businessmen is at most 15 to 20 percent of the people with regular jobs in Japan. The real work force of Japanese production consists of subcontract workers and part-time employees, who are excluded from the privileges that samurai businessmen enjoy (e.g., lifetime employment). These workers are the ones last hired and first fired. The institutions of *shitauke* (subcontract) and part-time employees provide flexibility to the Japanese economy. The Japanese company flourishes because of the sacrifice of these underlings. Toyota and Nissan may have weathered economic storms remarkably well, but many of their suppliers have not. Small subcontractors sell virtually all of their output to a large subcontractor or a single big company. The big company controls the terms. It pays the subcontractors a price just high enough to enable them to survive if they cut costs to the bone.[17] Although the salaries of samurai businessmen may be close to American standards, it is subcontract workers and part-timers who provide cheap labor and make the Japanese economy more competitive with Euro-American economies.

The lives of these non-elite workers are very uncomfortable and insecure in comparison to those of their counterparts in other modern nations, as represented by their very constricted but expensive living conditions (which are called "rabbit hutch" housing by Westerners). Their discomfort and insecurity are aggravated by a high aspiration level, a result of economic prosperity. Despite the fact that more than 90 percent of Japanese identify themselves with the middle class, their financial insecurity is described by the Hakuhodo Life Style Research Institute study.[18] Its chief researcher, Hiraku Hayashi, has categorized the Japanese public into four classes: pretending rich (33%), well-managed poor (8%), new or quasi-poor (53%), and the real poor (6%). Although only 6 percent of the public are termed as real need-driven poor, more than half (53%) of Japanese people are the new poor, who are "highly sensitive to fashion, good taste, and art, and are attracted to quality goods, but are always living on the edge of financial disaster."

These people's financial insecurity is shown by the prevalence of *sarakin* (literally, "salarymen's finance," or loans based on future salary income). Almost every day Japanese newspapers carry articles about family suicides (parents killing children and themselves), many of which are caused by having borrowed money from *sarakin*. This borrowing usually occurs because of needs accrued from medical payments or gambling lossses or as a little supplement to regular income. The number of *sarakin* offices was estimated at 160,000 in 1978.[19] Four of these companies are so large that they gave out more consumer loans in 1982 than all the Japanese banks together.[20] Most, however, operate out of small shops, many of them gangster-connected, handing out as much as $1,250 in twenty minutes—no questions asked, no collateral demanded—as long as the customers can produce a health-insurance card for identification.

Until November 1983, *sarakin* had lent smallish sums of money at the deceptively low daily rate of interest of 0.3 percent, which added up to 109 percent per annum. The rate was official and legal, and the government only acted against those who charged more than 109 percent. When borrowers could not pay, the measures taken by *sarakin* companies were very harsh, often involving gangster-type intimidation and violence.

In November 1983, the Japanese government finally acted, with two new laws. One law set a ceiling on interest rates. Companies that had previously charged 109 percent a year had to reduce their interest to less than 40 percent within five years. The other law banned forcible debt collection. At the same time, major banks have withdrawn their funds from these credit associations. The new laws will decrease suicides caused by *sarakin* borrowing. However, the basic problem remains of why the big banks in Japan do not give loans to hard-pressed personal consumers. Traditionally, Japanese banks are not concerned with the problem of small borrowers. Public needs for smaller, softer loans probably will increase with a rising living standard.

Economic insecurity is more expected of women because of sex prejudice. Although an increasingly large number of women are employed (over 14 million in 1981, and two out of five is the national average), prejudice persists. Most women work at low-paying part-time jobs. Bright young female graduates are paid a third less than are comparable males. Particularly, university-graduating females experience severe sex prejudice in employment, as shown by the following example:

> For Emi Bessho, a recent graduate of Tokyo's prestigious Waseda University, job hunting was a nightmare. While men from her class were wooed with promises of lifetime employment and steady promo-

tions by Japan's top corporations, the same companies made Miss Bessho very different offers.

In addition to her office duties she was to serve tea and "help make working life pleasant for male coworkers," said Bessho, twenty-three years old and a political science major. She was expected to live with her parents until she married and to stop working when she became pregnant.[21]

Some large Japanese companies will not even hire female four-year university graduates, asserting that they are headstrong and will leave work shortly anyway to marry and to have children. Recruitment advertisements still separate job application by sex. Curfews imposed by national law prohibit women from working between 10 P.M. and 5 A.M., closing certain jobs to women. Thus, Japan wastes one of its greatest assets by clinging to feudal notions about the role of women.

—————————— COOPERATION

Despite such prejudice, Japanese women appear to accept discrimination willingly, as shown by the findings of the latest cross-cultural survey by the Japanese Prime Minister's Office on Women's Problems. The percentage of women who agreed to the tenet that a woman's place is in the home while the man's is at his workplace was 72 percent in Japan, 34 percent in the United States, and 26 percent for Britain. While 31.3 percent of American wives agreed that they would bring up boys as boys and girls as girls, considering the respective roles that women and men have to play, 62.6 percent of Japanese wives agreed.

In contrast to the 77.7 percent of American wives who claim that they have assets and property in their own name, the figure for Japanese wives is 11.3 percent—much lower than the 57.5 percent recorded for Filipino wives. Only 18 percent of American wives state that they ought to "look after their husband, children, and relatives," but 72 percent of Japanese wives state this. Japanese wives appear to control the household budget. In contrast to 14.6 percent of American wives, 79.4 percent of Japanese wives claim that they control the household budget. However, this control seems to be more an indication of responsibility than right—the wife's control is that of custodian, not that of co-owner.

The percentage of Japanese wives who state that they have the authority to decide what to buy is only 22.2 percent, but 46.1 percent of them say that the authority is in the hands of their husband.[22] When asked if they would divorce their husbands should they become dissatisfied with them, only 26.8 percent of Japanese wives gave an affirmative answer, in comparison with 67.7 percent of American wives.

Patience and self-sacrifice, which enable Japanese women to accept disadvantageous positions, contribute to effective coordination and economic success. An example is the practice of *tanshin funin,* in which a salaried worker sets up separate living quarters due to job transfers. Sixteen percent of Japanese salaried men are living separately from their families because of work.[23] The primary resason for *tanshin funin* is that of education. Many parents in Tokyo, where the largest majority of Japanese salaried men are concentrated, do not want to take their children out of a school because Tokyo schools are, on the whole, superior to those in other areas in preparing students for university entrance examinations. It is also practically impossible for a child to transfer from one public school to another in a different school district because of varying rules of admissions. Public schools tend to be superior to private schools. A few exceptionally good private schools are extremely expensive, beyond the means of most salaried people.

Another reason for *tanshin funin* is housing. Japanese salaried workers who do manage to purchase houses do so in their forties or later. The house is a reward for their many years of hard work. They do not like to vacate it and rent it to strangers, even for a couple of years. Besides, when a Japanese worker transfers, he usually does not know how many years he will be away. *Tanshin funin* forces Japanese people to endure difficulties because of the necessity of having two separate households, with consequent emotional insecurity. Despite the sacrifices, *tanshin funin* is such an integral part of the Japanese business world that refusing a job transfer would be a virtual declaration that one is dropping out of the race for promotion.

The burden caused by *tanshin funin* is heavier on the wife, because her husband can enjoy his work and his greater freedom. There is a large number of recreational facilities for males in any city in Japan. *Sekkyakugyō* (which includes bars, geisha houses, Turkish bath houses, cabarets, etc.) is a big industry. According to the tax authorities, more than 1 million hostesses and 35,000 geisha[24] earned more than $41 million a day in 1982.[25] This is more likely a fraction of the real amount, because *sekkyakugyō* is one of the businesses ranked high in the prosecution list for tax evasion every years. *Sekkyakugyō* is a prosperous industry, but *sekkyakugyō* women are generally not prosperous. Often they have to supplement their income by selling sexual favors. However, these women contribute to Japan's economic success by performing an effective tension-reducing function for hardworking men who are often frustrated by authoritarian work relations.

Considering the difficulties and prejudice that subcontract workers and part-time employees suffer and the ready acceptance of discrimination by women, it may be said that the real cause of Japanese economic success is the capability to motivate underlings to accept their discriminated positions and to cooperate wholeheartedly with the established authorities.

The Japanese cooperation is obtained largely because of the dependence produced by insecurity. For example, as long as the woman is dependent in general or has little opportunity for economic and intellectual independence, she will be more patient and cooperative. The Japanese mother's close contact with her children and her self-sacrificial devotion fosters a strong dependency need. Dependency, in combination with the deep involvement of the Japanese mother in her children's education, promotes effective socialization to conformity.

Effective socialization is reinforced by formal education. The content of Japanese education stresses the subordination of individual interests to group goals. The primary purpose of Japanese education is to have students memorize a great deal of rote material in order to enter a university, in contrast to the American emphasis on reasoning and problem solving. The focus on rote memory unavoidably limits the development of analytical critical thinking and also of individualism. The Japanese tendency toward conformity is a major cause of the country's economic success.

On the other hand, Japanese cooperation is also due to the more personal (i.e., familistic) attitude of the superior toward his subordinates. Japanese superiors are expected to set an example of good behavior for their subordinates. Their selfishness is curbed by groupistic and familistic concerns. Japanese education, under the strong influence of Buddhism, stresses the rulers' responsibility to foster their subjects' welfare both materially and spiritually. Buddhism was accepted by Japanese rulers primarily as a means of totalistic control. They de-emphasized the democratic aspects of Buddhism (e.g., rationalism, the notion of individual worth, and the egalitarian conception of a spiritual community). As long as status difference is observed, Japanese leaders emphasize the superior's responsibility for the subordinate's well-being. Groupism and familism cultivate in the superior the desire to control his own selfishness in the interest of the group.

As a result, the gap in average income between Japanese presidents of top-level companies and entry-level workers appears to be much less than that in the United States. According to *Nikkeiren,* Japan's Federation of Employers Association, the difference is 7.5 to 1 in Japan, in contrast to more than 20 to 1 in the United States. However, these figures cannot be taken at face value because the comparability of "new recruits" in the two countries is not known.

The recruit in a large Japanese company is usually a regular *shain* (company man), excluding subcontract firm workers and part-timers, who compose a great majority of the Japanese labor force. This new *shain* is ordinarily a graduate of one of the better universities in Japan and is expected to be a candidate to become an executive. The *shain* is an elite employee, who is called by some Western writers a "samurai" businessman. If the category of new recruit in Japan means the regular *shain,* it is not comparable to the category of new recruit in the United States, which includes not only elite but also nonelite employees.

Despite the questionableness of the numerical comparison of average income, it seems safe to conjecture that American presidents are more self-profit-minded than their Japanese counterparts are. When business is good, American executives raise their own salaries and bonuses first, and the amounts are often extreme (for example, General Motors doled out more than $181 million in bonuses to its top 5,807 executives in 1982). When business is bad, American executives lay off workers first and buy parts overseas to cut costs, depriving workers of their jobs. In general, Japanese executives feed much of the profits back into the company's capital and abstain from behavior that might incite the workers' resentment.

Japanese executives may be as selfish as their American counterparts, but their selfishness is expressed in much more subtle ways. For example, their retirement money is often quite substantial, but their subordinates are not ordinarily aware of the amount of money retiring executives get. The Japanese executives' selfishness is also shown in their fringe benefits. For example, expense accounts, which they use and often abuse, are extremely large in comparison with the comparable expenses their American counterparts are allowed. However, the benefits are not easily observable to the subordinates. Japanese workers tend to accept the executive's fringe benefits as necessary for the company.

Influenced by the Confucian ethic, Japanese people are socialized to respect "propriety" in accordance with the individual's status. The most important aspect of the feudalistic residues in modern Japan is that Japanese behavior is markedly determined by sex and by socio-economic status.

In addition to effective organization and motivation, there is another factor in Japan's success—mobilization of effective techniques and monetary funds.

MOBILIZATION OF TECHNIQUES

The mobilization of ideas (and techniques) for Japan's goal—the maximum well-being of the Japanese tribe—is attained by another characteristic of Japanese culture, that of accommodationism. Accommodationism is an attitude of compromise, or of the readiness to adjust to the immediate situation without any ideological concern. Being free of ideological concern, Japanese borrow ideas freely from other peoples, and especially from more advanced peoples because of Japanese authoritarianism. Whatever ideas they borrow are given new meanings fitted to Japanese tradition.

Accommodationism has enabled Japan, a latecomer to the industrial age, to adapt (and often to copy) ideas and techniques readily for the purpose of modernization. Consequently, there are many contradictory ideas built into Japanese culture, such as an emphasis on reasoning as a requirement for modernization on the one hand and on intuitive and mystical thinking on the other. As indicated earlier, a Japanese characteristic is the ability to juxtapose contradictions without an effort to logically and ideologically integrate them. The effort to integrate contradictions produces stress, but the effort makes for personality development. The well-developed personality (i.e., the independent thinker) is often in conflict with the status quo. On the other hand, Japanese people in general can keep contradictory ideas harmoniously and do not experience a strain for consistency. This capability contributes to the status quo and to the formation of a weak ego, although it facilitated Japan's industrialization.

Japanese accommodationism is exemplified by Japan's adaption of a Western legal system in order to rectify the inequalities in its extraterritorial rights, imposed upon it by the Western powers. These rights were abolished in 1899. According to Professor Takeyoshi Kawashima,[26] the newly accepted legal system was purely ornamental in that the leaders did not intend to adhere to the laws. In addition, the laws were incomprehensible to both the leaders and the masses. They were rarely used in resolving disputes or in exerting other forms of social control. Later, at the expense of the masses, the leaders made great efforts to restore some premodern conditions of the Japanese economy in order to develop Japanese capitalism. The primary social controls used were based on traditional mores, not on laws. The mores were derived from the principle of collective responsibility and were enforced by severe punishment in accordance with class status.

This provides the prototype of Japanese acccommodationism after World War II. Legally, Japan appears to be even more democratic than are the Euro-American nations. For example, the 1947 "Fundamental Law of Education" states that

> education shall aim at the full development of personality, striving for the rearing of the people, sound in mind and body, who shall *love truth and justice, esteem individual value,* respect labor and have a deep sense of responsibility, and be *imbued with the independent spirit* as builders of a peaceful state and society. (italics added)

However, Japanese laws are still a front that have rather little impact on actual behavior. The basic method of problem solving is not law but *hanashiai* (negotiation) and *chōtei* (arbitration), which are strongly influenced by the status difference of the parties involved. As mentioned earlier, fewer than 1 percent of Japanese people involved in traffic accidents that caused damage and/or injury take legal action. In 1973, 90 percent of divorces in the country were consummated by *kyōgi* ("agreement"), 9 percent by *chōtei,* and only 1 percent by judicial decision.[27]

Without attempting to logically and ideologically integrate ideas, Japanese people can keep contradictory ideas in harmony. This is exemplified by their idea of sovereign people, which is in conflict with the efforts of education and religions to keep people dependent and conforming. Such efforts are represented by the Japanese government's control of education through its censoring of textbooks. The *tatemae* [official announcement] of *ningen no songen* (dignity of man) is in conflict with the prevalent sexual and ethnic prejudices. There is, however, virtually no strong civil right movements for minority groups in Japan.

In many respects, Japanese people have been changing. What has not changed is the dominance of central-government bureaucrats. Bureaucrats were efficient servants of the emperor and then of General MacArthur. Now that MacArthur is gone, nobody controls the bureaucrats. They are supposed to be servants of the people, but in reality they control the people. They apparently want to educate people to be efficient conformers. Consequently, despite many criticisms against the present examination system, which places an almost sole emphasis on memorization at the sacrifice not only of critical and creative minds but also of physical and mental health, Japanese bureaucrats seem adamant about keeping the system as intact as possible.

Japanese bureaucrats are very conservative, as exemplified by the effort by those in the Ministry of Education to rewrite World War II history for the purpose of presenting only favorable pictures of Japan. They tried to obliterate the information on the "Rape of Nanking"— an orgy of murder, torture, plunder, and rape by Japanese soldiers that took the lives of an innumerable number of Chinese, including many women and children, in 1937. Most suggestive is the response by an "avowedly dovish" Liberal Democratic Diet member to foreign pressures against the rewriting: "If we have to consult with foreigners on what we want to teach our children, that is something we cannot easily swallow."[28] In this person's mind, there may be little distinction between governmental propaganda and education. Traditionally, Japanese education in humanities, history, and social sciences has been largely governmental propaganda, sometimes even at the expense of scientific validity. A basic problem in this respect is that the Japanese government pays almost 90 percent in advance for the publishing costs for textbooks and that all textbooks must get governmental censorship.[29]

The Japanese bureaucrats' conservatism has guided Japanese industrialization successfully—that is, without endangering the country's social structure. However, the question now exists of whether they can grow out of Nipponism into universalistic leadership.

———————— MOBILIZATION OF FUNDS

In addition to ideas and techniques, another important form of resources to be mobilized is capital. The flow of funds between personal and industrial sectors in Japan is controlled, or at least coordinated, by the central-government bureaucracy. Japanese people have been taught to save for future security. They are assiduous savers, saving about 20 percent of their disposable income, despite the fact that individual depositors have received only a very low interest rate on their post-office or bank deposits. They save even more at a time of a recession because of their keener sense of insecurity.

Besides these savings, which are pooled to provide capital to industry, Japanese industry has been lent money at little or no real interest.

Typically, Japanese companies operate on debt. Their debts sometimes amount to 70 to 80 percent of their funds. The government has used its influence to enable producers to take advantage of savers–consumers by raising prices beyond those that would result from a free market.[30] For instance, the Japanese consumer has to pay well above market prices for rice and other crops.

It is the Japanese government that controls, either directly or through its influence upon banks, the flow of funds so that companies and industries that are important for its economic policy get sufficient funds. In this control of funds, the general public's interests are more or less ignored. The lack of concern with ordinary people's interest is represented by the nature of shareholders of Japanese companies. American shareholders are primarily interested in a company as a financial investment. The company is responsible for providing profits and dividends to them annually. In contrast, shareholders of Japanese companies are principally associated companies that are not primarily interested in annual profits and dividends. These companies are little concerned with small shareholders' interests.

A result of this transfer of wealth is that those immediately engaged in industry and government can live comfortably, while those outside them are taught to find happiness in hardship. The teaching has been done by Japanese religions as well as by education. While Japanese bars and cabarets are full of those in business and industry and in government on tax-allowable expense accounts,[31] ordinary people who have given their wealth to industry and government are also expected to give their health and welfare, and sometimes even their lives, as in the Minamata disease case. Thus, the real source of Japanese success in international competition is the attitude and socialization of the ordinary people.

In sum, Japan's economic success is explained in terms of effective coordination, motivation, and mobilization. Effective coordination is produced by groupism and hierarchical organization (based on authoritarian familism). Effective motivation is attributed to *seishin* education and to general insecurity. Insecurity generates energy for cooperation against external pressures. Instead of producing resentment and conflict, insecurity in Japanese underdogs is converted into cooperation through socialization to dependence and through a familistic relationship between superordinate and subordinate.

The mobilization of ideas (and techniques) was done through Japanese accommodationism. Japanese accepted ideas from more developed peoples freely in order to catch up with them. At the same time, they avoided social disintegration by keeping contradictory ideas (i.e., modern and traditional values) in harmony without making an effort to logically and ideologically integrate these ideas. The mobilization of capital was done through the government's control of people (exhorting them to save money and to be satisfied with their relative neglect by the government) and through the flow of funds to companies and industries according to government policies.

X

SUMMARY
AND
DISCUSSION

After describing suicides of young Japanese males, females, and writers, generalizations were made regarding suicidal motivation and self-destructive adjustment in terms of major value orientations of Japanese culture: nonrational tendencies toward an emphasis on faith and loyalty at the expense of reason (corollaries of monism), a stress on group goals at the sacrifice of establishing selfhood (groupism), the regulation of social interaction by familistic norms (authoritarian familism), and the attitude of compromising in the immediate situation (accommodationism).

Suicide motivation is considered to occur when a personality perceives a wide discrepancy between ego–ideal and self-conception. The discrepancy is produced by the disparity between goal and available means. Typically, the Japanese are quite ambitious. Because of the necessity to induce young people to strive for leadership positions in the effort to catch up with Western powers, the Japanese government has stressed success as a goal. Because of the emphasis on power and status differences in the traditionally authoritarian society and because of the misery accompanying failure among the remnants of the feudal condition, the goal of success (*shusse shugi*) became an obsession among the Japanese people.

The pressure for success is intensified by groupism (e.g., keen sensitivity to social cues) and familism (e.g., dependency upon parents in combination with parental pressure). When high aspiration is not attained, the frustrated person pressures his or her child to succeed. The tendency is epitomized by the *kyōiku mama* (education mother), who finds her primary meaning of life in pressuring her child to pass the entrance examination to a good university. Today, most Japanese mothers—particularly those in urban areas—appear to be *kyōiku mama*. Their pressure upon their children is strengthened by sex prejudice. The lack of opportunity for self-development for most Japanese women, their husbands' neglect of their needs, and social pressure for self-restraint combine to channel their hope and energy into their children's education and success. The maternal pressure is felt keenly by Japanese children because of their strong dependency upon their mothers. The maternal pressure often makes Japanese children hostile toward their mothers, who made them desperately dependent. The hostility produces guilt, because hostility against the object of dependence feels like rebellion against a goddess.

In contrast to their high aspirations, the Japanese often show personality traits that hamper them from attaining their goals. They often show dependence, ambivalence, passivity and resignation, ambiguity of their positions, feelings of despair, a sense of insecurity and inferiority, and a tendency to escape and avoid. Many Japanese are also characterized by a lack of both realism and imagination. As mentioned in chapter 4, Japanese youths generally have high objectives in life but are unable to give any details about them. Their strong dependency needs and their lack of realistic perception, of future orientation (e.g., scheduling), and of strong willpower (including strong impulse control) indicate a "weak ego." A weak ego is a natural product of the stifling of individuality by groupism and authoritarian familism and of the tendency toward accommodationism—that is, the tendency to adjust readily to the immediate situation for tension reduction.

Persons with weak egos are likely candidates for suicidal wishes. Suicide attempters have been found to be unenergetic and impulsive, leading depressed and lethargic lives. They are emotionally unstable and unsocial, and they lack the capability of reality testing. They are often immature in personality development. Thus, a weak ego may be considered as the most important factor in producing suicidal wishes in Japan. Although weak-ego persons may achieve a certain degree of success in a highly groupistic, familistic society, when they are placed in a frustrating situation they are vulnerable.

Dependence and the keen sensitivity to social pressures (due to groupism and familism) are necessary ingredients of altruistic suicides. The altruistically suicidal person shows an uncontrollable sense of obligation and an inclination toward abnegation, even to the point of masochism. Such a person not only has a strong sense of shame and guilt but also experiences mystical joy in self-sacrifice for a group goal. A weak-ego person is susceptible to fatalistic suicide in excessive social integration. He feels that "the future is blocked and passion is choked" (Durkheim, 1958). He experiences a sense of resentment, fear, and resignation, because he is not resourceful, flexible, or self-confident.

Weak ego also contributes to anomic suicide when social integration declines under rapidly changing social conditions. Under such conditions the weak-ego person, who lacks in effort and capability, may experience a strong sense of relative deprivation, greed, a feverish imagination, disillusionment, and jealousy. The more dependent a person is, the stronger the sense of disillusionment and jealousy he experiences.

Anomic suicide is characteristic of Japanese college students' suicides in Kyoto because of their susceptibility to such Western values as selfhood, rationality, and humanistic idealism. Despite their desire for modern and universal values, they are generally well socialized to the Nihonkyo worship of Japanese tradition. Their education, consisting mainly of memorization of fragmented bits of information at the expense of analytical, critical, and creative faculties, facilitates the retention of traditionalism. The greater the retention of traditional values, the more intense the conflict with the desired modern values. The resultant frustration is intensified in the person with a weak ego.

Suicidal motivation is converted to self-destructive behavior by the emphasis on self-restraint, a lack of social resources, a negative view of life, and accepting views of death and suicide, in addition to a personal tendency toward impulsiveness. An important element of Japanese accommodationism is impulsiveness, as shown by the comparison of Japanese and German university students in chapter 8 (table 42). Self-restraint, which prevents aggression from being directed toward external objects, is stressed in Japanese society, where the group is more important than the individual.

In a difficult situation, Japanese people tend to have a very constricted view of social resources (useful for tension reduction and problem solving). An authoritarian social structure prevents people from becoming independent and resourceful. Therefore, even when they feel sympathetic toward people in need, their own lack of confidence prevents them from offering help. The person in difficulty, however, projects his own lack of resourcefulness onto others and becomes pessimistic about possible assistance. Moreover, authoritarianism tends to make people insecure and pragmatic, concerned mostly with their own success and fame.

Despite the emphasis on groupism and familism, Japanese people—especially educated ones—may be highly egocentric, as shown by the comparison in chapter 8 of Japanese and German students with reference to their attitudes toward death. In the pursuit of success and fame, egocentric persons are inclined to use others, including friends and family members. This attitude hurts social relations. Intimacy is difficult to cultivate. The lack of intimacy makes a person more aggressive in his search for attention, further hurting his social relations and making him feel more lonely. The vicious cycle is formed easily in the person with a weak ego, resulting in mistrust of others and himself. Mistrust intensifies competitiveness. The "cut-throat competition among Japanese corporations because of fear of their own vulnerability"[1] applies to many Japanese individuals, too, although they usually hide their true feelings because of a fear of retaliation. They hide true feelings (*honne*), such as competitiveness, because the societal norm (*tatemae*) stresses group harmony. Japanese culture tends to produce mistrust and loneliness in persons who fail.

Such Buddhist teachings as "Life is sorrowful" and actual hardships in the regimented society produce not only pessimistic views of life but also accepting attitudes toward death and suicide. In addition, the neo-Confucian conception of honorable suicide, if it is committed for a group goal, promotes self-destruction. The readiness to regard suicide as an acceptable way to solve a problem is consummated in suicide because of Japanese mysticism. Monism does not clearly distinguish between human and nonhuman phenomena or between this world and an afterworld. Death may be perceived as a sort of travel and as natural as life is. (An example of this mystical acceptance of death was shown by Kawabata's suicide.) Japanese people in general believe that their souls or spirits stay as participants in their family affairs and become demigods who watch over their family members for their welfare. This belief gives a sense of continuity and lessens the fear of death.

Suicide as a way to solve problems or as an expression of the sense of responsibility is still favorably regarded by most Japanese people. Moreover, suicides, especially love-pact suicides and suicides for a group goal, are highly romanticized. Fatalistic and altruistic suicides are still dominant forms of suicide in Japan, although anomic suicides are increasing.

Thus, Japanese value orientations—monism, groupism, authoritarian familism, and accommodationism—tend not only to produce suicidal motivation but also to push the motivation to self-destructive behavior. These value orientations, however, are also major factors in Japan's success in economic competition. The success is explained in terms of coordination, motivation, and mobilization.

Japanese coordination is effective because of groupism and authoritarian familism. The common goal of Japanese behavior is "the survival and the maximum well-being of the tribe."[2] The self is mystically merged into society, hence the emotional faith and loyalty to the group, with reason regarded as an obstacle. Mysticism and emotionalism are essential ingredients of Nihonkyo (Nipponism), the primary religion in Japan. In Nihonkyo, Japanese society and tradition becomes the object of quasi-religious faith. Confucianism, Buddhism, and Christianity provide concepts for Nihonkyo to modify and integrate. Nihonkyo is said to be the strongest religion in the world,[3] because it permeates the Japanese mind so deeply that it is out of awareness. Through providing a common object of "religious" faith, Nihonkyo promotes cohesiveness.

Because of groupism, many Japanese regard their company as giving the major meaning to life. They are prepared to extend themselves for the company even to the point of sacrificing themselves and their families. Japanese unions regard their raison d'être to be that of contributing to the well-being of the company, because only the company's well-being guarantees workers' happiness. The group orientation of company executives contributes to effective coordination by making them refrain from being too selfish. Their primary responsibility is supposed to be to the group rather than to themselves. Japanese executives are often the first to decline pay raises or bonuses in time of recession. In general, Japanese leaders are expected to be exemplary figures of moral courage. Although the ideal is not always realized, it functions as a deterrent to selfishness.

Social interactions of Japanese workers are regulated by familism. Familism, an emphasis on family relations, is strong even in the

Japanese economy, the most modernized aspect of the culture. The emphasis on familistic relations is indicated by the worker's attitude of desiring a parental figure in his occupational superior. Eighty-four percent of Japanese subjects (in 1968), in contrast to 58 percent of persons of Japanese ancestry in Hawaii (in 1971), preferred to work with a chief who "sometimes demands extra work in spite of rules against it, but on the other hand, looks after the worker personally in matters not connected with work."[4] This particularistic type of chief (emphasizing personal connection) is contrasted with the "universalistic" chief, "who always sticks to work rules and never demands any unexpected work, but, on the other hand, never does anything for the worker in matters not connected with the work." The latter type of chief was preferred by 13 percent of Japanese, compared with 39 percent of persons of Japanese ancestry in Hawaii. If a comparable figure had been available for Americans of non-Japanese ancestry, the difference would have been much greater.

Institutionally, familism is represented by the requirement of a *mimoto hoshōnin* on job applications. The *mimoto hoshōnin* is a sponsor who guarantees that the applicant is reliable and morally upright. The sponsor commits himself to compensate any losses to the company incurred through an error made by the applicant, as the Japanese parent is responsible for the child. (Even today, a child's misbehavior occasionally causes his parent's suicide because of the parent's sense of responsibility to society.) According to a survey, 663 of 705 large Japanese companies studied required *mimoto hoshōnin* as a condition of employment in 1963.[5]

Familism also underlies various programs that companies provide to enhance the welfare of their employees. There are company houses, company bathhouses, flower-arrangement classes, workers' picnics, and summer or winter resorts—all analogous to displays of parental affection and concern. The more attractive these fringe benefits are, the more effective they are as social-control measures.

The authoritarian nature of Japanese familism is shown by its hierarchical structure. Hierarchy promotes the coordination of Japanese institutions and individuals, because their behavior is regulated by clearly specified norms in accordance with status, and this regulation eliminates unnecessary misunderstanding and friction. On the company level, Japanese companies are generally included in a large group centered on a parent company (*oya-kaisha*), which is a bank or a large industrial company. All companies in the larger group are different in power and status. The "child" companies (*ko-kaisha*) are tied to each other through specialization, interdependence, and shared common stocks, under the supervision of the parent company. The superordinate groups (*oya-kaisha*) are, in turn, coordinated under the direction of bureaucrats and business leaders. Such a hierarchical system facilitates not only coordination but also a long-range adjustment to changing situations.

On the individual level, Japanese workers are differentiated by power and status, correlated with different social expectations. Status difference is usually shown by different uniforms. A Japanese company has a highly centralized administration with autocratic decision making, although before a decision is made the decision maker attempts to pool other people's opinions. While the Japanese employer traditionally has *kenryoku* (legitimate power) to fire or punish his employees as he wishes, the employees have few *kenri* (rights), because *kenri* implies the requirement that the employee be evaluated in terms of objective criteria. *Kenri* prohibits the employer from dismissing the employee without going through proper procedures.[6] Even today, what is regarded by Westerners as the right to gainful employment is not considered a right, per se, to the Japanese mind. Japanese workers are inclined to say, *hatarakasete itadakimasu* ("I receive gratefully the favor of letting me work") rather than *hatarakimasu* ("I work"). A bonus, which usually amounts to about half of the worker's annual income, is considered a gift (*shōyo,* "award") from a benevolent employer rather than as rightfully earned income.

The Japanese hierarchy is determined not only by occupational status but by such personal status as sex and education. Women and subcontract firm workers, who are in general undereducated, are the first to be laid off during a recession. When they are not laid off, their payments are just high enough to enable them to survive if their employers cut costs to the bone.[7] The practice of underemployment contributes to Japan's low unemployment rate. Sex and educational prejudices make for cheap labor by women and subcontract firm workers.

The hierarchy contributes to effective coordination only when those in disadvantageous positions are satisfied. Japanese workers seem mostly well satisfied, largely due to effective socialization to the emphasis on "propriety" according to role expectations. As George A. DeVos says, the Japanese "learns to dedicate himself to the role prescribed for him by his culture, and finds it difficult to think of himself apart from it."[8] This process and state of mind is called "role narcissism" by DeVos. The Japanese have been taught that to claim one's rights is a selfish and evil act that disturbs "family" or "group" harmony. This is the major reason why the Western style of unionism has not developed in Japan. These underprivileged but satisfied workers provide flexibility and a competitive edge to the Japanese economy in international competition, and herein is the real key to Japanese economic success.

In addition to providing cheap labor, Japanese women contribute to effective coordination and economic success in another way. Unlike American homemakers, who seem to show greater dissatisfaction than their gainfully employed sisters, Japanese homemakers are well satisfied, as a result of role narcissism. Their satisfaction enables their husbands to devote themselves to work and their children to study without being troubled by family problems.

The Japanese workers, who are organized for a common goal by groupism and authoritarian familism, must be motivated to work hard. The motivation is achieved partly by the groupistic equation of business to war "for the survival and maximum well-being of the tribe." The motivation is reinforced by the revival of *seishin kyōiku* (spiritual education). Before World War II, all forms of Japanese education were *seishin kyōiku,* stressing devotion to the group, inclination toward psychological change (rather than problem solving), maturation through painful discipline, and self-mastery. Such education, based on authoritarian (patriarchal) familism and mystical thinking, promoted militarism.

The present-day *seishin kyōiku* also attempts to suppress the ego and direct suppressed energy against outsiders, by promoting the complex of loyalty, discipline, *esprit de corps,* and indomitable perseverance. Whether the present *seishin kyōiku* will lead the Japanese to chauvinism again is dependent upon the degree of authoritarian familism and mystical thinking which they retain.

Seishin kyōiku is very effective in Japan, because it capitalizes on the diffuse insecurity prevalent among Japanese people. Although some writers attribute Japanese success to worker security, people may not become "workaholics" without insecurity. The compulsive work among Japanese people is not only a product of their work ethic but is also a coping mechanism for diffuse insecurity. Diffuse insecurity is produced by Japanese familism, which makes for both strong dependency needs in the individual and an authoritarian social structure. Dependent persons are always insecure in a changing society, because there is no guarantee that the objects of their dependence will satisfy their needs.

Japanese social structure causes diffuse insecurity even in elite salaried men, who comprise only about 20 percent of the Japanese labor force and who enjoy many more privileges than do other workers. Their insecurity comes primarily from the lack of clearly stated objective criteria for promotion. Evaluations by superiors are subjective, influenced by personal and clique affiliations. Since they do not know where they stand in the eyes of their superiors, the only thing these workers can do to show their loyalty is by working hard and long.

Moreover, elite employees' insecurity comes from the severe competition that they have to undergo because of a limited number of higher positions. Executive positions in large companies are highly limited in number (in the eyes of employees) because future executives are predetermined largely by the prestige of the universities from which employees graduate. Each employee can compete for a higher position only within the predetermined range. The number of executive positions are further limited because of the *amakudari* (literally, "descent from heaven") of retiring government officials.

For nonexecutive career employees in large companies, expected pensions are small, and the retiree (at the usual age of fifty-five or sixty) often has responsibility for his son's education and daughter's wedding costs. The insecurity makes employees work hard to attain as high a position as possible.

Most Japanese workers work in small businesses, subcontract firms, or part-time jobs. Their insecurity is indicated by the finding of the Hakuhodo study (chapter 9) that 59 percent of the Japanese public are members of the "quasi-poor" (i.e., living "always at the edge of financial disaster") or of the "real poor" (who are constantly driven by unsatisfied needs). Their insecurity makes *sarakin* (salaried men's finance) loan-sharking a prosperous business. The insecurity is rooted in Japanese prejudices against females and undereducated people. Japan's economic success can be attributed to the effective socialization of these underprivileged people to accept their status and to work hard.

In addition to coordination and motivation, which were explained in terms of groupism and authoritarian familism, there is another factor in Japan's success—mobilization of techniques and monetary funds. The mobilization of techniques is attained through another characteristic of Japanese culture, that of accommodationism. Accommodationism, an attitude enabling one to compromise and to adjust to the immediate situation without ideological concerns, allows Japan to freely adapt techniques from more technologically advanced peoples.

A characteristic of Japanese accommodationism is the juxtaposition of contradictory ideas without any effort to logically integrate them. Japanese people accept technological ideas freely, but they modify nontechnological ideas to adjust to Japanese tradition. Some borrowed ideas, that are not in harmony with Japanese tradition but that cannot be rejected, are kept as *tatemae* (ideal "front," or words).

The mobilization of monetary funds is done by governmental control of the flow of funds between personal and industrial sectors. Japanese people have been taught to save for future security. They ordinarily save more than 20 percent of their disposable income, and they save even more at times of recession. Their savings are pooled to provide capital to industry. Japanese industry has been lent money at little or no real cost. Typically, Japanese companies operate on debt, often amounting to 70 or 80 percent of their funds.

In the control of the flow of funds, the general public's interests are largely disregarded. For example, individual depositors have received only a very low interest rate on their post-office or bank deposits. The government has used its influence to enable producers to take advantage of savers-consumers by raising prices beyond those that would result from a free market. Shareholders of Japanese companies are principally associated companies that are not primarily interested in annual profits and dividends, and the companies are little interested in small shareholders' profits, just as Japanese banks are not interested in small personal loans. Such attitudes toward the general public enable the companies to make long-range plans for international competition.

Coordination, motivation, and mobilization, which contribute to Japanese success, are effective only when people are cooperative. Japanese people's attitudes are formed by their value orientations—monistic emphasis on faith and loyalty, groupistic stress on common goals, authoritarian emphasis on "propriety" according to status, familistic regulation of social interaction, and the attitude to adjust to the immediate situation without ideological concerns. These orientations enable Japan to combine social cohesiveness with rapid industrialization.

The Japanese cohesiveness is rooted in moral and social homogeneity, dominated by tradition. Its justice is directed toward the subordination of the individual to the collective conscience. Durkheim calls this kind of cohesiveness "mechanical solidarity." Mechanical solidarity is acquired by people who think in the same way. It is in contrast to "organic solidarity," which is characterized by heterogeneity, individuality, and the awareness of the necessity of cooperation. Although the cohesiveness of mechanical solidarity, in combination with a strong achievement drive in individuals, has produced economic success in international competition, the mechanical solidarity has certain disadvantages.

First, since education in a mechanical-solidarity society approaches brainwashing, Japanese education tends to stifle independent thinking and creativity, which are needed for Japan as a leader of the world. Japan has to shift from a mechanical-solidarity goal to an organic one in which individuals and individual nations can develop their potentials in their own ways. After all, only educated individuals trained for self-expression, self-development, and self-reliance can function as agents of their own problem solving and as a check on the possible abuse of power by authorities, as in a true democracy. Only by producing organic solidarity can Japan become a full-fledged leader of the "free" world, to which Japan seems to aspire. If Japan can show the way toward organic solidarity without losing social integration, it would be providing a great contribution to the future of mankind.

Second, the general tendency to conform and the lack of genuine debate, as observed in university classes in Japan, forebode danger. Despite their professed desire for peace, conformers are easy objects of propaganda. The best insurance for peace is in the individuals who are unyielding to propaganda and who can stand up against authorities and group pressure because of their consciences or ideological convictions. The Japanese public's conformity and accommodationism were the primary causes of World War II.

Third, the cohesiveness with stress on groupism and hierarchy produces a difficulty in understanding universalistic (or suprasocietal) principles and values, which contribute to all peoples rather than to Japanese alone. For instance, Japanese people in general have difficulty in understanding the meaning of *ningen no songen* (dignity of man), despite the fact that it is declared as the essence of their new constitution. This difficulty is indicated by their deep sex, ethnic, and class prejudices.

Fourth, those victimized by sex, ethnic, and class prejudices are not given sufficient opportunity for self-development. They are frustrated and often distort their children's development. For example, the lack of opportunity for her self-development, in combination with her husband's neglect of her needs, results in the efforts of the typical Japanese mother to pressure her child to succeed. The pressure from the mother, upon whom Japanese children are highly dependent, seems to be a basic cause of both suicide and family violence by youths.

Fifth, too effective socialization toward self-restraint, whether for group goals or for one's own success, makes for a tendency toward emotional outbursts in a difficult situation. When this tendency is manipulated and aggressive energy is mobilized by shrewd leaders, there is the possibility of an emotional outburst on the national level, as happened prior to World War II.

Sixth, mechanical solidarity is attained by developing the authoritarian personality, whose characteristics are a keen sense of status difference, a strong desire for power, and obsequious submission to the stronger. Ironically, it is authoritarianism that made Japan democratic. Japanese people did whatever would make them appear to be a civilized, democratic people in the eyes of Westerners. Only when the Minamata disease was reported in the West did the Japanese government begin to correct the problem. Historically, Japanese innovations always came about through governmental order, under external pressures from stronger nations. However, when the Japanese people feel that they no longer have superior peoples to imitate, a condition they are approaching now, what will happen? With the decline of American prestige in the eyes of Japanese people, their traditionalism is returning strongly, as exemplified by the nationalistic rewriting of history.

Probably the weakness of Japanese cohesiveness, the source of their economic success, may be better understood with reference to an "ideal type" of democracy. World leadership in the "free" world requires the understanding of the principles underlying democracy:[9]

1. Liberal basis of organization, represented by constitutionalism (or rule of law) and republicanism (or government of popularly chosen representation of citizens).
2. The ethical responsibility of government to the people, and the "equality and brotherhood of man," as rooted in Hebrew-Christian tradition.
3. Humanistic individualism, as derived from Greek philosophy through Renaissance humanism, especially humanistic idealism.

The first principle has been accepted by the Japanese government as their official stance, although—as mentioned earlier—"the rule of law" has not really taken root yet in Japan because of the strong groupistic and familistic tradition. The principle of the equality and brotherhood of human beings has never really been accepted there. The principle was a recognizable element of Indian Buddhism, but when it was accepted by Japanese people it was modified to adjust to the Japanese culture, which is characterized by groupism and hierarchy. Therefore, Japanese people, who seem to consider themselves "status carriers" before human beings, have great difficulty in solving sex, educational, and ethnic prejudices.

The Japanese people will have even greater difficulty in satisfying the third requirement, that of humanistic idealism, especially its individualistic aspects. Humanistic idealism[10] stresses (a) the search for satisfaction and enrichment in secular matters, (b) the quest for new knowledge and understanding, and (c) individualistic self-expression, self-improvement, and self-reliance. Japanese people have been always humanistic in the first sense. Requirement (b) is not traditionally Japanese. Contemporary Japanese, however, show avid curiosity for new knowledge, especially in technology. Their curiosity is mostly concerned with "how to" rather than "why."

Japanese people face the toughest task with requirement (c). Instead of developing individual potentials, especially reasoning, humanism in Japan is typically interpreted as the acceptance of biological (especially sexual) needs. This conception is accepted readily by Japanese because it contributes to their primary value—that is, group harmony—as long as the needs are satisfied in accordance with status. However, the emphasis on self-expression and self-reliance is not conducive to group harmony, because these tend to be in conflict with monism, groupism, and authoritarian familism. Self-improvement in Japan means that an individual becomes selfless so that social expectations dominate his thinking. This is in contrast to the humanistic conception of developing human potential, especially reasoning, for one's own problem solving. Japanese problem solving relies on authorities' arbitration, and people are seen as recipients of the authorities' benevolence.

Despite these weaknesses, Japanese value orientations offer some suggestions for American people to consider. After all, such dichotomous concepts as nonrationality versus rationality and groupism versus individualism represent the two abstract extremes of human potential. The ideal personality combines them in equilibrium. For example:

1. Rationality is a requirement for modernization. However, "nonrational tendencies" are not always "premodern." On the other hand, "rationalism" often implies an overemphasis on the self-profit motive, endangering social integration. Scientists have "nonrational" faith in the validity of the scientific method. Although Japanese people tend to be overly sensitive to social cues, Japanese executives' alleged sensitivity to the feelings of their subordinates provides a good suggestion for a resolution of some of the labor-management problems in the United States.
2. The emphasis on group goals is particularly important for a capitalistic society, where people tend to be too self-profit–oriented. American selfishness is exemplified by the fact that General Motors doled

out·a huge amount of money in bonuses to its top executives in 1982. These bonuses were made possible by sacrificing American workers—first, by making workers agree to forgo their customary 3 percent annual raises for two years, and second by decreasing the number of jobs for American workers (through buying more cars and parts overseas to cut costs). Unrestrained selfishness is a seed of societal self-destruction. In a similar situation in Japan, most of a company's profits would be fed back into its operating funds for the purpose of expanding its market.

3. Democracy presupposes a breakdown of irrational authority (i.e., traditional authority maintained by negative sanctions, especially fear). However, the denial of irrational authority should not mean the denial of competent authority. Respect for competent and conscientious parents or teachers, as well as for any other authority figures, is a prerequisite for a stable society.

NOTES

I. INTRODUCTION

1. Ezra F. Vogel, *Japan as Number One: Lessons for America* (Cambridge: Harvard University Press, 1979).
2. Yukio Matsuyama, *Nihon Shindan* [Diagnosis of Japan] (Tokyo: Asahi Shimbun, 1977), p. 241.
3. Hiroshi Inamura, *Nihonjin no Kaigai Futekiō* [Inadaptability of the Japanese in foreign countries] (Nihon Hōsō Kyōkai Press, 1980).
4. *Shuukan Asahi,* 10 July 1980.
5. Alfred North Whitehead, *The Aim of Education* (New York: Mentor Books, 1949), p. 54.
6. Michael Kearney, *World View* (Novato, Calif.: Chandler & Sharp, 1984), p. 5.
7. F. R. Kluckhohn and F. L. Strodtbeck, *Variations in Value Orientations* (Westport, Conn.: Greenwood Press, 1976), p. 4.
8. Joan Robinson, *Freedom and Necessity* (New York: Pantheon Books, 1970), p. 122.

II. A PSYCHOCULTURAL VIEW OF SUICIDE

1. H. Hendin, "Suicide: Psychoanalytic Point of View," in *The Cry for Help,* ed. N. L. Farberow and E. S. Shneidman (New York: McGraw-Hill, 1961); idem, "The Psychodynamics of Suicide," *Journal of Nervous and Mental Disease* 136 (1963): 236.
2. S. Freud, "Mourning and Melancholia" (originally published in *Zeitschrift für Psychoanalyse,* Vol. IV, 1917), in *Standard Edition of the Complete Psychological Works* (London: Hogarth Press, 1953–1965), vol. 14.
3. K. A. Menninger, "Psychoanalytic Aspects of Suicide," *International Journal of Psychoanalysis,* 14 (1933): 376–390.

4. C. Jung, "The Soul and Death," trans. R. P. C. Hull, in *The Meaning of Death,* ed. Feifel (New York: McGraw-Hill, Blakiston Division, 1959).

5. Edwin S. Shneidman and N. L. Farberow, eds., *Clues to Suicide* (New York: McGraw-Hill, Blakiston Division, 1957).

6. Edwin S. Shneidman, *Voices of Death* (New York: Harper & Row, 1980), pp. 11–13.

7. Emile Durkheim, *Suicide* (first published in French in 1897), trans. John A. Spaulding and George Simpson (Glencoe, Ill.: Free Press, 1958), p. 212.

8. A. F. Henry and J. F. Short, *Suicide and Homicide* (New York: Free Press, 1954).

9. J. P. Gibbs and W. T. Martin, *Status Integration and Suicide* (Eugene: University of Oregon Press, 1964).

10. J. D. Douglas, *The Social Meanings of Suicide* (Princeton, N.J.: Princeton University Press, 1967).

11. R. W. Maris, *Social Forces in Urban Suicide* (Homewood, Ill.: Dorsey Press, 1969).

12. C. W. Mills, *Sociological Imagination* (London and New York: Oxford University Press, 1959), p. 6.

13. Jerry Jacobs, *Adolescent Suicide* (New York: Wiley Inter-Science, 1971), p. 28.

III. PATTERN OF JAPANESE SUICIDE ————————————————

1. Kenji Tamura et al., *Niigata-ken ni okeru Rojin no Jisatsu* [Old people's suicide in Niigata Prefecture], *Tōyō Daigaku Shakaigaku Kiyō,* nos. 11 and 12, 1975).

IV. SUICIDE OF YOUNG JAPANESE MALES ————————————

1. Jushiro Koshinaga, "Jisatsu to Isho" [Suicide and suicide notes], in *Nihon Hōigaku Zasshi* [Japanese forensic journal], 33, no. 5 (1979): 476.

2. Akira Kurihara, *Gendai Seinen-ron* [On contemporary youth] (Tokyo: Chikuma Shobo, 1981), p. 177.

3. Kenshiro Ohara, *Nihon no Jisatsu* [Suicide in Japan] (Tokyo: Seishin Shobo, 1965), p. 81.

4. Ibid., p. 82.

5. Ibid., p. 83.

6. William Caudill, "Around-the-Clock Patient Care in Japanese Psychiatric Hospitals: The Role of *Tsukisoi,*" *American Sociological Review* 26 (1961): 204–214.

7. Otoya Miyagi, *Nihonjin to wa Nanika* [Who are the Japanese?] (Tokyo: Asahi Shimbun-sha, 1972), p. 208.

8. K. Ohara and M. Iga, "Family Problems in Suicide Attempts of Japanese Youth," *Memorial Issue in Honor of Prof. Takehisa Kora* (Jikei University

School of Medicine, 1965), p. 401; K. Ohara and H. Mashino, "Jisatsu to Katei Kankyo" [Suicide and family environments], *Seishin-Igaku* Tokyo: Igaku-shoin 3, no. 9 (September 1961): 781.

9. Douglas G. Haring, *Personal Character and Cultural Milieu* (Syracuse, N.Y.: Syracuse University Press, 1956), p. 432.

10. Robert C. Christopher, *The Japanese Mind: The Goliath Explained* (New York: Linden Press/Simon & Schuster, 1983), p. 271.

11. Takeo Doi, "*Amae:* A Key Concept for Understanding Japanese Personality Structure," *Psychologia* 5, 1 (March 1962).

12. Chie Nakane, *Japanese Society* (Berkeley, Los Angeles, London: University of California Press, 1972), p. 27.

13. George M. Foster, "Peasant Society and the Image of Limited Good," *American Anthropologist* 67 (1965): 293–315.

14. George A. DeVos, "The Relation of Guilt toward Parents to Achievement and Arranged Marriage among the Japanese," *Psychiatry* 23, no. 3 (1960): 287–301.

15. Stuart Picken, *Nihonjin no Jisatsu* [Suicide of Japanese people] (Tokyo: Simul Press, 1979), p. 193.

16. Ibid., p. 194.

17. Ronald Dore, *The Diploma Disease* (Berkeley, Los Angeles, London: University of California Press, 1975), p. 50.

18. Helmut Morsbach, "*Gambare:* Socio-Psychological Aspects of Persistence in Japan" (undated MS), p. 7.

19. Ichiro Kawasaki, *Japan Unmasked* (Rutland, Vt.: Charles E. Tuttle Co., 1969).

20. NHK, "Gozonji-desuka" [Do you know?] 1 July 1979.

21. *Kashu Mainichi,* 27 September 1978.

22. Hisao Naka, "Young People's Suicide and Family," *Seinen-Mondai Kenkyu* [Study of youth problems], December 1962, p. 46.

23. Miki Kan, "Korean Problems," in Tetsuo Mabara et al., *Gendai Nihon no Shakai Mondai: Shihai to Sabetsu* [Social problems in modern Japan: control and prejudice] (Tokyo: Chobun-sha, 1967), pp. 51–91.

24. Saburo Ienaga, *The Pacific War* (New York: Pantheon Books, 1978), p. 84.

25. *Pacific Citizen,* 30 May 1980.

V. FEMALE SUICIDES

1. Kenshiro Ohara, *Nihon no Jisatsu* [Suicide in Japan] (Tokyo: Seishin Shobo, 1965), p. 81.

2. Hisao Naka, "Jyosei no Jisatsu" [Suicide of women], in M. Kosaka and N. Usui, *Nihonjin no Jisatsu* [Suicide of Japanese people] (Tokyo: Sōbun-sha, 1966), p. 78.

3. Robert C. Christopher, *The Japanese Mind: The Goliath Explained* (New York: Linden Press/Simon & Schuster, 1983), p. 271.

4. Robert J. Lifton, "Individual Patterns in Historical Change: Imagery of Japanese Youth," in N. J. Smelser and W. T. Smelser, ed., in *Personality and Social System* (New York: John Wiley & Sons, 1970), p. 561.

5. Akiko Kobayashi, "Gendai no Rikon" [Modern Divorce], *Jurist: Gendai no Josei* [Modern woman], June 1976, p. 218.

6. Naka, "Jyosei no Jisatsu," p. 81.

7. Nobuhiko Matsugi, *Seishun no Isho* [Suicide notes by adolescents] (Tokyo: Chikuma Shobo, 1974), p. 219.

8. Ibid., p. 220.

9. Tetsuo Mabara et al., *Gendai Nihon no Shakai Mondai: Shihai to Sabetsu* [Social problems in modern Japan: control and prejudice] (Tokyo: Cho-bun-sha, 1967), p. 18.

10. George DeVos and H. Wagatsuma, "Minority Status and Attitude toward Authority," in G. DeVos and H. Wagatsuma, *Japan's Invisible Race: Caste in Culture and Personality* (Berkeley and Los Angeles: University of California Press, 1966), p. 262.

VI. JAPANESE WRITERS' SUICIDES

1. Kenshiro Ohara, "Sakka to Jisatsu" [Writers and Suicide], *Kaishaku to Kanshō* [Interpretation and appreciation] 36, no. 15 (October 1971), p. 8.

2. Kenshiro Ohara, *Nihon no Jisatsu* [Suicide in Japan] (Tokyo: Seishin Shobo, 1965), pp. 202–205 (based on the list compiled by Jyoji Hirayama in "Nihon Bungaku ni Arawareta Jisatsu no Shosō" [Phases in suicides as appeared in Japanese literature]).

TAKEO ARISHIMA

3. Juliet Mitchell, "Women: The Longest Revolution" in *Family in Transition,* ed. A. A. Skolnick and J. H. Skolnick (Boston: Little, Brown & Co., 1971), p. 275.

4. Hiroshi Minami et al., "A Content Analysis of Postwar Japanese Popular Songs in Japanese Popular Culture," in *Studies in Mass Communication and Cultural Change,* ed. and trans. Hidetoshi Kato (Rutland, Vt.: Charles E. Tuttle, 1959), pp. 109–123.

RYUUNOSUKE AKUTAGAWA

5. According to the Reuter News Service, in the Siemens-Bickers case in 1914, high officers of the Japanese Navy were bribed with half a million yen to purchase warships from a German company. Another recipient of a bribe (amounting to more than 1 million yen), was the Mitsui Trading Co. Ultimately, none of the major suspects was severely punished. One of the minor persons involved hung himself. One of the major culprits (Wa Matsumoto) professed that he had received the money for the benefit

of the entire nation, because he wàs regarded as the next minister of the navy and needed secret funds.

6. In the Ōura case (1915), Kanetake Ōura, using his position as the minister of domestic affairs, meddled in a political campaign with extensive bribery. He gave money to desirable candidates and received bribes from many sources, including the army and the Mitsubishi Industrial Company. No high-ranking person involved in this case was punished.

7. In the Army Secret-Fund case (1926), General Giichi Tanaka, then minister of the army, and General Hanzo Yamanashi, vice minister of the army, pocketed a part of the army's secret funds for their private use. The public prosecutor of this case was found murdered. The matter was not pursued further after his death.

8. Seiichi Yoshida, "Kaisetsu" [Commentary], in *Complete Works of Akutagawa Ryuunosuke* (Tokyo: Shinchosha, 1969), p. 562.

9. Ibid., p. 535.

10. Ibid., p. 550.

11. Henri de Régnier (1864–1935). Poet and novelist. It is believed that the reference is to "Bonheurs perdus" [Lost happiness].

12. Philip Mainländer (or Philip Bate) (1841–1876). "Die Philosophie der Erlosung" [The philosophy of redemption]. Mainländer was a disciple of Arthur Schopenhauer and glorified suicide, which he committed at the age of thirty-five.

13. Heinrich von Kleist (1777–1811). German Romantic writer. Committed suicide with another man's wife.

14. Jean Racine (1639–1699). Regarded as the master of French tragedy in the so-called classical period.

15. Molière (Jean-Baptiste Poquelin) (1622–1673). French actor and dramatist.

16. N. Boileau–Despreaux (1636–1711). A French poet.

17. While having an affair with Akutagawa, Mrs. X also had sexual relations with a younger friend of his.

OSAMU DAZAI

18. In traditional Japan, a geisha had an owner, who was called her mother or father. Her freedom was bought, and her purchase usually meant the payment of all expenses incurred by the owner in rearing her from childhood (when she was bought from her biological parent) and educating her as a geisha, plus the future loss of income that the owner would suffer because of the loss of her service. Dazai's marriage to Hatsue probably meant that his family had to purchase her with this amount of money, which he, a twenty-two-year-old student, could not afford to spend. Saburo Nakamura estimates that 85 percent of geisha were prostitutes (i.e., selling sexual favors) in 1954 (*Nihon Baishun Shakaishi*) [Social history of Japanese prostitution] (Tokyo: Seiabo, 1959), p. 30.

19. Osamu Dazai, *Complete Works* (Tokyo: Shinchosha, 1969), p. 28.
20. Toshiki Shimazaki and Y. Fukunaga, "Dazai Osamu," in *Gendai no Esupuri: Sakka no Byōseki* [L'esprit d'aujourd'hui: Etiology of writers' illness], Otohiko Kaga, ed., July 1971, p. 200.
21. Dazai, *Complete Works,* p. 32.
22. David Riesman and E. T. Riesman, *Conversations in Japan* (New York: Basic Books, 1967), p. 113.
23. Dazai, *Complete Works,* p. 205.
24. Ibid., p. 333.
25. Tsukasa Terasono, "Dazai Osamu to Seisho" [Dazai Osamu and the Bible], in *Nihon Bungaku Kenkyū Shiryō Kankokai, Nihon Bungaku Kenkyū Shiryō Sōsho: Dazai Osamu* (Tokyo: Yuuseido, 1978), p. 160.

────────────── YUKIO MISHIMA

26. Gore Vidal, "Mr. Japan: Review of *Sun and Steel* by Yukio Mishima," *New York Times Book Review,* 17 June 1971, pp. 8–10.
27. E. G. Seidensticker, *Shuukan Gendai,* 12 December 1970, p. 88.
28. Mishima's works published in English:
    Kamen no Kokuhaku [Confessions of a mask] (1949)
    Ai no Kawaki [Thirst for love] (1950)
    Kinjiki [Forbidden colors] Parts I and II (1953)
    Manatsu no Shi [Death in midsummer] (1953)
    Shiozai [The sound of waves] (1954)
    Kinkakuji [The temple of the golden pavilion] (1956)
    Kindai Noh-gaku Shū [Five modern noh plays] (1956)
    Utage no Ato [After the banquet] (1960)
    Gogo no Eikō [The sailor who fell from grace with the sea] (1963)
    Sado Kōshaku Fujin [Madame de Sade] (1965)
    Haru no Yuki [Spring snow] (1966)
    Homba [Runaway horses] (1970)
    Akatsuki no Tera [The temple of dawn] (1970)
    Tennin Gosui [The decay of the angel] (1970)
29. Kenji Mizutsu, *Mishima Yukio no Higeki* [The tragedy of Yukio Mishima] (Tokyo: Toshi Shuppansho, 1971), p. 39.
30. Ibid., p. 118.
31. John Nathan, *Mishima: A Biography* (Boston: Little, Brown & Company, 1974), p. 23.
32. Ibid., p. 25.
33. Donald Keene, "Mishima," *New York Times Book Review,* 3 January 1971, p. 58.
34. Henry Scott-Stokes, *The Life and Death of Yukio Mishima* (New York: Farrar, Strauss, and Giroux, 1974), p. 167.
35. Akira Fukushima, "Mishima Yukio no Naiteki Seikatsu" [Inner life of

Mishima Yukio], *Sakka no Byōseki* [Pathography of writers], *Gendai no Esupuri,* July 1971, p. 258.

36. P. Shabicoff, "Mishima: A Man Torn between Two Worlds," *New York Times,* 26 November 1970.
37. Nathan, *Mishima: A Biography,* p. 196.
38. Ibid., p. 259.
39. Scott-Stokes, *The Life and Death of Yukio Mishima,* p. 166.
40. Gideon Sjoborg, "Folk and Feudal Societies," ed. J. L. Finkle and R. W. Gable, *Political Development and Social Change* (New York: John Wiley & Sons, 1966), pp. 45–53.
41. Ryotaro Shiba, *Nihonjin o Kangaeru* [Thinking about Japanese people] Tokyo: Bungei Shunju, 1978, p. 174.
42. Stuart Picken, *Nihonjin no Jisatsu* [Suicide of Japanese people] (Tokyo: Simul Press, 1979), p. 101.
43. Rodney Clark, *The Japanese Company* (New Haven and London: Yale University Press, 1979), p. 186.
44. Mizutsu, *Mishima Yukio no Higeki,* p. 44.
45. Ibid., p. 214.
46. Ibid., p. 167.
47. Ibid., p. 198.
48. Donald Keene, "To Die for His Own Fiction," *Mainichi Shimbun,* 26 November 1970, p. 7.
49. Hajime Nakamura, *Ways of Thinking of Eastern Peoples: India-China-Tibet-Japan* (Honolulu: East-West Center Press, 1964), pp. 531–576.
50. Yukio Mishima, "Todai o Dobutsuen ni Shiro" [Make a zoo out of Tokyo University], *Bungei Shunju,* January 1969, p. 257.
51. Mizutsu, *Mishima Yukio no Higeki,* p. 181.
52. Ibid., p. 70.
53. Shōhei Ooka, "Ikinokotta monoe no Shōgen" [Testimony for those who survive], *Bungei Shunju,* February 1971, p. 110.
54. Mizutsu, *Mishima Yukio no Higeki,* p. 110.
55. R. J. Lifton, "Youth in History: Individual Change in Postwar Japan," in *The Challenge of Youth,* ed. E. H. Erikson (New York: Doubleday Anchor Books, 1965), p. 272.

———————— YASUNARI KAWABATA

56. Tōkō Kon, "Honto no Jisatsu o Shita Otoko" [The man who committed real suicide], *Bungei Shunju,* June 1972, p. 349.
57. Shinichiro Nakamura, "Kyomu o Mitsumeru Bigaku" (Aesthetics gazing at vacuum), *Asahi Journal,* April 1972, p. 24.
58. *Bungei Shunju,* June 1972, p. 238.
59. Masanao Kurihara, *Kawabata Yasunari* (Tokyo: Chūo Kōron sha, 1982), p. 149.

60. E. G. Seidensticker, "Kawabata Yasunari to tomoni Hitotsu no Jidai wa Satta" [With Kawabata Yasunari, one period is past], *Chuō Kōron,* June 1976, p. 347.
61. Ken Hirano, "Bungei Jihyoka: Kawabata Yasunari" [Literary commentator: Yasunari Kawabata], *Sekai,* June 1972, p. 285.
62. Victor Frankl, *Man's Search for Meaning* (Boston: Beacon Press, 1962), p. 123.
63. Nakamura, p. 24.
64. Ruth Benedict, *The Chrysanthemum and the Sword* (Boston: Houghton Mifflin Co., 1946), p. 292.
65. Kon, "Honto no Jisatsu," p. 252.
66. Nakamura, "Kyomu o Mitsumeru Bigaku," p. 23.
67. Kon, "Honto no Jisatsu," p. 346.
68. *Bungei Shunju,* June 1972, p. 221.
69. Ibid., p. 223.

VII. Japanese Value Orientations —————————————————————

1. Jean Stoetzel, *Without the Chrysanthemum and the Sword* (New York: Columbia University Press, 1955), pp. 207, 214–217.
2. Robert C. Christopher, *The Japanese Mind: The Goliath Explained* (New York: Linden Press/Simon & Schuster, 1983), p. 271.
3. John Gillin, "National and Regional Cultural Values in the United States," *Social Forces* 34 (December 1955): 107–113.
4. Florence Kluckhohn and F. L. Strodtbeck, *Variations in Value Orientations* (New York: Row, Peterson & Co., 1976), p. 12.
5. Hajime Nakamura, *Ways of Thinking of Eastern Peoples:* India-China-Tibet-Japan (Honolulu: East-West Center Press, 1964), p. 350.
6. Ibid., p. 575.
7. James Hitchcock, "Comes the Cultural Revolution," *New York Times Magazine,* 27 July 1969, p. 4.
8. *Time: Japan,* 1 August 1983, p. 71.
9. *Kashu Mainichi,* 28 May 1981.
10. Takeyoshi Kawashima, *Nihonjin no Hō-Ishiki* [Legal consciousness of Japanese people] (Tokyo: Iwanami Shinsho, 1976), p. 44.
11. Jared Taylor, *Shadows of A Rising Sun* (New York: William Morrow & Co., 1983), p. 137.
12. Ichiro Hori, *Folk Religion in Japan* (Chicago: University of Chicago Press, 1974), p. 2.
13. *Kashu Mainichi,* 18 May 1982.
14. Geoffrey Murray, "Superstitions Hamper Equal Rights in Japan," *Christian Science Monitor,* 30 June 1980.
15. Nakamura, *Ways of Thinking,* p. 531 ff.

16. Kawashima, *Nihonjin*, p. 9.
17. Taylor, *Shadows*, p. 131.
18. Kawashima, *Nihonjin*, pp. 34–35.
19. C. K. Yang, "The Functional Relationship between Confucian Thought and Chinese Religion," in *Chinese Thought and Institutions*, ed. John K. Fairbank (Chicago and London: University of Chicago Press, 1967), p. 276.
20. Ryotaro Shiba, *Nihonjin o Kangaeru* [Thinking about Japanese people], (Tokyo: Bungei Shunju, 1978), p. 187.
21. William Theodore de Bary, *The Buddhist Tradition in India, China and Japan* (New York: Random House, Vintage Books, 1969), p. 9.
22. Ryotaro Shiba, "Nihon Bukkyō to Meishin Sangyō" [Japanese Buddhism and superstition industry], (*Bungei Shunju*, April 1982), p. 381.
23. Ibid.
24. de Bary, *Buddhist Tradition*, p. 332.
25. Ibid., p. 334.
26. Iichi Oguchi, *Nihon Shuukyō no Shakai-teki Seikaku* [Social character of Japanese religions] (Tokyo: Tokyo University Press, 1959), pp. 30, 107.
27. Ibid., p. 102.
28. Tokei Suuri Kenkyusho [Institute of Statistical Mathematics], *Nihonjin no Kokuminsei* [National character of Japanese people], no. 4 (Tokyo: Idemitsu Shoten, 1981), p. 59.
29. Isaiah BenDasan, *Nihonjin to Yudayajin* [The Japanese and the Jews] (Tokyo: Kadokawa Shoten, 1971), p. 115.
30. *Shuukan Gendai*, Dec. 12, 1970, p. 146; Henry Scott-Stokes, *The Life and Death of Yukio Mishima* (New York: Farrar, Strauss, and Giroux, 1974), p. 46.
31. Christopher, *The Japanese Mind*, p. 55.
32. R. J. Lifton, "Youth in History: Individual Change in Postwar Japan," in *The Challenge of Youth*, ed. E. H. Erikson (New York: Doubleday Anchor Books, 1965), p. 274.
33. Kawashima, *Nihonjin*, p. 142.
34. Ibid., p. 135.
35. Ibid., p. 183.
36. Minoru, Kida, *Nippon Buraku* (Tokyo: Iwanami Shinsho, 1970), pp. 29–31.
37. Ibid., p. 45.
38. Lewis Austin, "The Political Culture of Two Generations: Evolution and Divergence in Japanese and American Values," in *Japan: The Paradox of Progress*, ed. Lewis Austin (New Haven and London: Yale University Press, 1976), p. 237.
39. Minoru Masuda and T. H. Holmes, "The Social Readjustment Rating Scale: A Cross-Cultural Study of Japanese and Americans," *Journal of*

Psychosomatic Research, 11 (1967): 227–237.

40. Francis L. Hsu, *Iemoto: Heart of Japan* (New York: Halsted Press, 1975), p. 152.
41. Ruth Benedict, *The Chrysanthemum and the Sword* (Boston: Houghton Mifflin Co., 1946), p. 171.
42. Shichihei Yamamoto, *Nihon Shihon-shugi no Seishin* [Capitalistic spirit in Japan] (Tokyo: Kobunsha, 1979), p. 66.
43. Robert J. Lifton, "Protean Man," *Yale Alumni Review,* January 1969, pp. 14–21.
44. Lifton, "Individual Patterns in Historical Change: Imagery of Japanese Youth," in *Personality and Social System,* ed. N. J. Smelser and W. T. Smelser (New York: John Wiley & Sons, 1970), p. 558.
45. Ibid., p. 561.
46. Ibid., p. 558.
47. Jon Woronoff, *Japan: The Coming Economic Crisis* (Tokyo: Lotus Press, 1981), p. 267.
48. Heizo Toriyama, "Death and Personal Value Orientation: A Comparative Study between Japanese and German Cultures" (undated ms.).

VIII. JAPANESE CULTURE AND SELF-DESTRUCTIVE ADJUSTMENT ——

1. Douglas G. Haring, "Japanese National Character: Cultural Anthropology, Psychoanalysis and History," in *Personal Character and Cultural Milieu,* ed. Douglas G. Haring (Syracuse, N.Y.: Syracuse University Press, 1956), p. 432.
2. Otoya Miyagi, *Nihonjin to wa Nanika* [What is the Japanese?] (Tokyo: Asahi Shimbun-sha, 1972), p. 212.
3. Arthur L. Kobler and E. Stotland, *The End of Hope* (Glencoe, Ill.: Free Press, 1964), p. 50.
4. Robert Trumbull, "Japan Turns against the 'Gyangu,'" *New York Times Magazine,* 30 November 1958, p. 74; Kenshiro Ohara, *Nihon no Jisatsu* [Suicide in Japan] (Tokyo: Seishin Shobo, 1965), p. 267.
5. George Yoshinaga, "The Horse's Mouth," *Kashu Mainichi,* 25 September 1984.
6. Irwin Mahler, "What is Self-Concept in Japan?" *Psychologia* 3 (September 1976): pp. 127–133.
7. Mahler, "A Comparative Study of Locus of Control," *Psychologia* 3 (September 1974), pp. 135–139.
8. Heizo Toriyama, "Death and Personal Value Orientation," *Annual Report of Health Administration,* no. 8 (Kyoto Technical University, 1981), pp. 190–199.
9. Ryuusaku Tsunoda, W. T. de Bary, and D. Keene, *Sources of Japanese Tradition* (New York: Columbia University Press, 1958), p. 217.

10. Koji Sato, *Shi to Sei no Kiroku* [Record of death and life] (Tokyo: Kodansha, 1968), p. 124.
11. Ibid., pp. 74–75.
12. E. S. Shneidman, "Suicide and Death in Japan: A Personal Report," *VITA* (Official newsletter of the International Association for Suicide Prevention) 2, no. 1 (January 1966), p. 5.
13. R. J. Lifton, S. Kato, and M. R. Reich, *Six Lives: Six Deaths* (New Haven and London: Yale University Press, 1977), p. 7.
14. Ibid., p. 8.
15. *Kashu Mainichi,* 20 January 1981.
16. Lewis S. Feuer, *The Conflict of Generations* (New York: Basic Books, 1969), p. 211.
17. *Kashu Mainichi,* 26 and 29 June 1972.
18. Katsuichiro Kamei, *Sei to Shi no Tankyū* [Inquiry into life and death] (Tokyo: Daiwa Shobo, 1967), p. 143.
19. Hidetoshi Kato, "Jisatsu Sutairu no Hensen" [Change in suicide style], in *Gendai no Esupuri: Jisatsu,* ed. K. Ohara, January 1965, p. 228.
20. W. R. LaFleur, "Japan," in *Death and Eastern Thought,* ed. R. H. Holck (Nashville and New York: Abingdon Press, 1974), p. 212.
21. *Mainichi Shimbun,* 6 February 1980.
22. Aromu Mushiake, "Ninkyo Eiga wa Naze Sakaeru no ka" [Why do yakuza movies thrive?], *Bungei Shunju,* June 1970, p. 329.
23. *Kashu Mainichi,* 13 March 1983.
24. Donald Kirk, "Japan's Ritualistic Underworld Finds Status and Profit in an Alliance with the Far Right," *New York Times Magazine,* 12 December 1976, p. 91.
25. *Kashu Mainichi,* 13 July 1982.
26. Kirk, "Japan's Ritualistic Underworld," p. 61.
27. *Kashu Mainichi,* 13 July 1982.
28. *Christian Science Monitor,* 6 June 1974.
29. "Inside the Weeklies," *Japan Times,* 11 August 1975 and 6 July 1976.
30. Kirk, "Japan's Ritualistic Underworld," p. 61.
31. George Yoshinaga, "The Horse's Mouth," *Kashu Mainichi,* 25 October 1984.
32. Sam Jameson, "Japan's Bureaucrats Come Under Fire Over Good Life," *Los Angeles Times,* 9 December 1979.
33. Jon Woronoff, *Japan: The Coming Social Crisis* (Tokyo: Lotus Press, 1981), p. 213.
34. Hirotatsu Fujiwara, *Kanryō no Kōzō* [Structure of bureaucrats] (Tokyo: Kodansha, 1976), p. 106.
35. Marvin J. Wolf, *The Japanese Conspiracy* (New York: Empire Books, 1983), p. 211.
36. *Time,* 16 April 1973.

37. Woronoff, *Japan: The Coming Social Crisis,* p. 216.
38. Ibid., p. 203.
39. Fujiwara, *Kanryō no Kōzō,* p. 131.

IX. JAPANESE ECONOMIC SUCCESS

1. *Kashu Mainichi,* 1 February 1984.
2. Geoffrey Murray, "How Can U.S. and Japan Compete—and Still Play Fair?" *Christian Science Monitor,* 23 May 1983.
3. *Kashu Mainichi,* 17 June 1983 and 10 August 1983.
4. Rodney Clark, *The Japanese Company* (New Haven and London: Yale University Press, 1979), p. 51.
5. Robert E. Cole, *Japanese Blue Collar* (Berkeley, Los Angeles, London: University of California Press, 1973), p. 37.
6. Clark, *The Japanese Company,* p. 130.
7. Ibid., p. 64.
8. Robert Frager and T. P. Rohlen, "The Future of a Tradition: Japanese Spirit in the 1980s," in *Japan: The Paradox of Progress,* ed. Lewis Austin (New Haven and London: Yale University Press, 1976), p. 255.
9. Ibid.
10. Clark, *The Japanese Company,* p. 186.
11. "A Nation in Search of Itself," *Time,* 1 August 1983, p. 67; David K. Reynolds, *Naikan Psychotherapy: Meditation for Self-Development* (Chicago and London: University of Chicago Press, 1983).
12. Robert C. Christopher, *The Japanese Mind: The Goliath Explained* (New York: Linden Press/Simon & Schuster, 1983), p. 270.
13. Chie Nakane, *Japanese Society* (Berkeley, Los Angeles, London: University of California Press, 1972), p. 42.
14. Erik H. Erikson, *Childhood and Society* (New York: W. W. Norton & Company, 1963), p. 263.
15. Shunshin Chin and Shiba Ryotaro, "Nihonjin wa 'Rinsen Taisei' Minzoku" [Japanese are a "battle-ready" people], in *Nihonjin o Kangaeru* [Thinking about Japanese people], ed. Ryotaro Shiba (Tokyo: Bungei Shunju, 1978), p. 177.
16. David W. Plath, *Long Engagements: Maturity in Modern Japan* (Stanford, California: Stanford University Press, 1980), pp. 89–90.
17. Christopher, *The Japanese Mind,* p. 287.
18. Geoffrey Murray, "Burst Image that All Japanese Are Middle Class," *Kashu Mainichi,* 27 June 1984.
19. Jon Woronoff, *Japan: The Coming Economic Crisis* (Tokyo: Lotus Press, 1981), p. 265.
20. *Kashu Mainichi,* 6 July 1983.
21. Ibid., 16 August 1983.

22. Takashi Koyama, *Gendai Kazoku no Yakuwari Kōzō* [Role structure of contemporary families] [Tokyo: Baifukan, 1967), p. 49.
23. *Kashu Mainichi,* 11 May 1984.
24. Jack Seward, *The Japanese* (New York: William Morrow and Co., 1972), p. 131.
25. *Kashu Mainichi,* 25 April 1984.
26. Takeyoshi Kawashima, *Nihonjin no Hōishiki* [Legal consciousness of Japanese people] (Tokyo: Iwanami Shinsho, 1976), p. 3.
27. Kakuko Kobayashi, "Gendai no Rikon" [Contemporary Divorce], *Jurist,* no. 3 (June 1976), p. 216.
28. Christopher, *The Japanese Mind,* p. 314.
29. Naoki Kobayashi, *Gendai Kyōiku no Jyōken* [Requirements of contemporary education] (Tokyo: Yuhikaku Sensho, 1983), p. 203.
30. Clark, *The Japanese Company,* p. 229.
31. Ibid., p. 230.

X. SUMMARY AND DISCUSSION

1. Robert C. Christopher, *The Japanese Mind: The Goliath Explained* (New York: Linden Press/Simon & Schuster, 1983), p. 270.
2. Ibid., p. 55.
3. Isaiah BenDasan, *Nihonjin to Yudayajin* [The Japanese and the Jews] (Tokyo: Kadokawa Shoten, 1971), p. 115.
4. Tokei Suuri Kenkyusho [Institute of Statistical Mathematics], *Nihonjin no Kokuminsei* [National character of Japanese people] (Tokyo: Shiseido, 1974), Appendix, p. 51; idem, *Hawaii ni okeru Nikkeijin* [Persons of Japanese ancestry in Hawaii], 1973, p. 24.
5. Takeyoshi Kawashima, *Nihonjin no Hō-Ishiki* [Legal consciousness of Japanese people] (Tokyo: Iwanami Shinsho, 1976), p. 109.
6. Ibid., p. 32.
7. Christopher, *The Japanese Mind,* p. 287.
8. George A. DeVos, *Socialization for Achievement* (Berkeley, Los Angeles, London: University of California Press, 1973), p. 11.
9. Mark M. Hield, *A Free Society: An Evaluation of Contemporary Democracy* (New York: Philosophical Library, 1953), p. 269.
10. Ibid., pp. 202–203.

INDEX

Accommodationism, 117, 134–138, 186–187, 189, 191, 192, 195, 199–200, 201; and goal-means discrepancy, 139, 140; and impulsiveness, 193; prevents selfhood, 138

Action. See *Honne*

Age, as factor in suicide, 13–14, 15, 19, 20, 59. *See also* Students; Youth

Aggression: externally-directed, 14, 17, 22–23, 48–49, 140–141, 193 (*see also* Violence); internally-directed, 14, 17, 22–23 (*see also* Suicide); and restraint, 140–141, 193; of women, 48–49

Akita, 19

Akutagawa, Ryuunosuke, 70, 76–85; cynicism of, 78, 80; on death, 144; depression of, 81; family pressures on, 79; fears of, 78; homosexuality of, 78; intellectuals on, 80; lacks value orientation, 82; neurasthenia of, 81; pessimism of, 78; on self, 82; skepticism of, 78, 80; social conscience of, 77, 80; suicide of, 17, 79, 81, 82–85, 115; suicide note of, 82–84; on tradition, 82; on women, 81; writings of, 78, 80, 81, 82

Akutagawa Award, 86

Amae, 38, 96, 142

Amakudari, 166–167, 179, 199

Ambition/aspirations, ix, 114, 139, 178, 179, 191, 192

Ambivalence/ambiguity, 114, 140, 192

Ancestor worship, 119, 124, 126

Animism, 119–120

Anxiety: anticipatory, 108; of businessmen, 178–180; examination causes, 36; Kawabata's, 107, 108; Mishima's, 98; neurosis, 29, 31; of youth, 23–24, 25

Apology, 147, 151, 156, 158

Appearance, concern with, 60, 94, 135

Arishima, Takeo, 70–76; on Christianity, 118; on death, 75, 144; education of, 70–71; feminism of, 71; guilt of, 72; homosexuality of, 71; inferiority complex of, 72; on love, 75–76; romanticism of, 70; self-control of, 70, 71; sexual attitudes of, 71–72, 118; socialism of, 72, 73; suicide of, 17, 70, 71, 72, 74–75, 115, 147; writings of, 73

Army Secret-Fund Case, 77

Asahi shimbun, 163

Assassination, 99, 105
Asthenia, 25
Atonement, 105
Austin, Lewis, 130–131
Authoritarianism, 130, 200; in companies, 172, 173–174; and group identity, 178; and insecurity, 194; on power and status differences, 131, 139, 178, 202; in society, 178–179, 198. See also Familism, authoritarian; Personality, authoritarian

Banks, 181, 200
Beauty: in death, 111, 148; in suicide, 106
BenDasan, Isaiah, 126
Benedict, Ruth, ix, xiii, 135
Bonuses, 181, 197
Bowers, Faubian, 98
Bribery, 19, 77, 160, 161, 166, 167; in Lockheed scandal, 159, 163, 164
Buddhism, 121, 195; on death, 194; education influenced by, 184; on equality and brotherhood, 202; function of, 124; household shrine in, 148–149; Indian, 122–124; Japanese, 122–125, 126; and magic, 123; Nichiren, 124; and nonrationality, 125; as pessimistic, 194; v. Protestantism, 124–125; reason in, 124; and ritual, 123, 126; and salvation, 123, 147; Zen, 120–121, 124
Buraku, 130–131
Burakumin. See Outcastes
Bureaucracy, 77, 165, 166–168, 187–188
Burial, 123, 126
Business: as bureaucracy, 165, 166–167; discipline in, 176, 177, 178; discrimination in, 184 (see also Prejudice); -government ties, 162, 166–167, 179, 199; insecurity in, 199; interdependence in, 137, 172, 173; leaders trained in, 175–176; is

war, 99, 171, 172, 175, 176, 198; and yakuza, 162, 163–164, 165. See also Company; Employment; Workers
Businessmen, 185, 195, 199; anxiety of, 178–180
Butsudan, 148–149

California F Scale, 130
Capital, mobilization of, 188–190
Caste(s): love affairs between, 66–67; prejudice, 60, 63, 65–67; stratification, 65. See also Class; Outcastes
Census register, 66
Change (mujō), 145
Chikamatsu, Monzaemon, 61, 154, 155
Children: maladjustment of, 2; misdeed of causes suicide, 196; outmigration of, 19; overprotected, 43–44; and parents, 34–35, 184, 201; and stepparents, 34; suicide of, 18, 34, 129–130, 181. See also Students; Youth
China, 121–122, 179
Chores, 43–44
Christianity, 63, 124–125, 195; guilt in, 71; of intellectuals, 71, 77; as rebellion against feudalism, 108; on sex, 118; and suicide, 71
Christopher, Robert, 55, 115, 126
Chrysanthemum, ix, xiii, 110
Cities, suicide rates in, 19, 20–21
Clark, Rodney, 99, 176
Clark, W. S., 71
Class: consciousness, 60; prejudice, 201; stratification, 74
Cliquishness, 129, 168
Cohesiveness, 200–201, 202
Communism, 63, 77, 86, 90, 94, 108, 118
Community, 130–131
Company: as authoritarian, 172, 173–174; debt of, 189, 200; decision-

making in, 170, 173, 197; familism in, 172, 173–174, 184, 195–197; groupism in, 203–204; hierarchy in, 171, 172, 173–174; loyalty to, 171, 172, 176, 195. *See also* Business; Employment; Workers

Confidence, 140, 141, 142, 194

Conformism/conformity, xii, xiii, 1, 187, 188, 201

Confucianism, 195; Chinese, 121; Chu Hsi school of, 105; as ethics, 125–126; on filial peity, 121; on heaven, 104–105; on leadership, 173; on manual labor, 60; on non-rationality, 125; on propriety, 185. *See also* Neo-Confucianism

Constitution of 1947, 52, 55

Constraint, 8

Constriction, 6

Contract, 135–136

Contradictions, non-integration of, 57, 186, 190, 200

Cooperation, 179, 183–185

Coordination: familism and group-ism promote, 195; hierarchy pro-motes, 196; for success, 171–174, 189, 195, 197–198, 200

Corruption, 19, 166–167. *See also* Bribery

Cross-country studies: of suicide motives, 23, 24, 25; of suicide rates, 14, 16, 17, 18; of wage discrimi-nation, 57

Czechoslovakia, 14

Dazai, Osamu, 70, 85–92, 108; on aristocracy, 88–89; attempts sui-cide, 87; avoidance of, 90; as com-munist, 86, 90; on death, 144; dependency of, 87, 88, 90; drug use by, 86; fatalism of, 91; frustration of, 90; inferiority complex of, 88, 89, 90; militarism of, 89; mistrust of, 88, 90, 91; narcissism of, 87, 88, 90; nihilism of, 91–92; opposes tra-ditionalism, 85; personality traits of, 86–87; on postwar Japan, 90–91; realism lacking in, 87, 90; sense of sin of, 89, 90; students on, 85; sui-cide of, 17, 92, 115; on *tatemae* v. *honne,* 85; writings of, 87–89, 91, 92

Death: attitudes toward, 105, 144–149, 193; as beautiful, 111, 148; as biological termination, 145; Bud-dhism on, 194; communication after, 89; consequences of, 145, 146–147; as cosmic change, 145; as creative, 147; as emancipation, 147; as ethical, 147; and familism, 148; family membership after, 148–149, 194; fear of, 145; Germans on, 145; of hero, 94; honorable, 158; and immortality, 149; in literature, 148; as natural, 147–148; Neo-Con-fucianism on, 158; as only way out, 12, 141; wish (wish to die), 14, 16, 22–24, 29, 144–145; writers on, 75, 95, 105, 111, 144. *See also* Suicide

Debate, lacking, 164

Deming, E. E., 170

Democracy, xiii, 77, 109, 131, 164; ideal, 202–203

Dependency, 198; Dazai's, 87, 88, 90; insecurity causes, 184; as suicide factor, 26–27, 87, 88, 193; of women, 184; of youth on parents, 26, 139–140, 149, 192, 201

Depression, 25, 29, 81

Despair, 22–23, 48, 93, 110, 192

DeVos, George A., 197

Discrimination, wage, 57, 59, 60, 170. *See also* Prejudice

Distribution system, 169, 170

Divorce, 1, 58, 133, 187

Dogen, 124

Doi, Takeo, 142

Douglas, Jack, 8

Drug use, 86, 148

Durkheim, Emile, 193, 200; on suicide, 7–8, 9–12, 113, 151, 152–153

Edo Period, 151
Education/schooling, 164; Buddhism influences, 184; cliquism in, 168; competition for, 37–38; as financial burden, 42; government controls, 115, 140, 187, 188; group goals in, 184; independent thinking stifled by, 201; laws on, 187; level of, 44; memorization as basis of, xiii, 39, 42, 115, 142, 175, 176, 184, 188, 193; parental pressure in, 36, 43–44, 184, 192; prejudice in, 6–7, 66, 197, 199, 202; public v. private 183; samurai spirit in, 140; for socialization, 184; for social status, 37–38; spiritual, 174; status hierarchy in, 39–40, 41–42; as stressful, 36–37, 42, 45; for success, 174–177; as suicide factor, 36, 44 (*see also* Examination, hell); in Tokyo, 183
Ego: ideal v. self-concept, 11, 93, 94, 97, 98, 100, 107, 108, 110, 114, 115; weak, 26, 115, 140, 186, 192–193, 194
Egocentrism, 27, 145, 194
Emotionalism, 2, 102, 139, 195; and self-restraint, 201–202; and suicide, 2, 5, 6
Empathy, 141–142, 143–144
Emperor, 100, 105, 122
Employment: hours in, 171, 172; lifetime, 179, 180; part-time, 180, 184, 185, 199; prejudice in, 56, 57, 169–170; rights in, 197; security/insecurity in, 179, 199; separate living required by, 43, 183; sponsorship in, 196; status differences in, 197; subcontract, 169–170, 180, 184, 185, 199; and suicide, 20, 159–160, 161, 165–166; transfers in, 43, 183; under-, 197; of women, 26, 56–57, 59, 60–61, 181–182

Enlightenment, 122, 123
Entertainment industry, 59, 60–61, 183–184
Escapism, 115, 140, 192
Eta. See Outcastes
Ethics, 125–126; death as, 147
Ethnic prejudice, 22, 45–47, 65–68, 115, 201, 202
Ethnocentrism, 1, 127, 128
Examination, 192; anxiety over, 36; criticized, 188; hell, 22, 36–44, 177; one-shot principle in, 38–39
Extortion, 145, 162

Failure, 178, 192; causes guilt, 42, 45; as suicide motive, 45, 154, 155
Familism, 117, 126, 200; authoritarian, 129–134, 139, 140, 172, 173–174, 184, 191, 195–197; in companies, 172, 173–174, 184, 195–197; and coordination, 195; and death, 148; and goal-means discrepancy, 139, 140; and groupism, 129, 130; hierarchy in, 196–197; individualism stifled by, 192; insecurity as result of, 198; as pervasive, 133; for social control/integration, 129, 131; for success, 189, 192; and suicide, 129–130, 193; of workers, 195–196, 198
Family: continuity, 148–149; membership after death, 148–149, 194; pressure, 22, 32–35, 51, 79; root- (*iemoto*), 133–134; structure, 130–131; suicide, 129–130, 181 (*see also* Parent-child suicide)
Fatalism, 91, 110, 155–156
Feudalism, 63, 151, 155; Mishima on, 98, 99–100, 101; rebellion against, 108; remnants of, xiii, 38, 55–56, 85, 98, 115, 185, 192
Feuer, Lewis S., 156
Filial piety, 121, 124
Financial problems: in education, 42; of outcastes, 66; savings prevents,

138; as suicide factor, 13, 22, 34, 44–45, 59–62; of women, 59–61, 181–182; of workers, 179, 180–181, 199

Four Noble Truths, 122–123

Frager, Robert, 174–175

Frankl, Victor, 108

Fringe benefits, 170, 185, 199

Frustration, 25, 90, 100, 105, 108, 110; as suicide motive, 8

Fujimura, Misao, 157

Fukumoto, Mariko, 67–68

Funerals, 123, 126

Future orientation, 102, 117, 134–135, 137, 138

Gangsters, 77. See also *Yakuza*

Geisha, 86. *See also* Entertainment industry

Germans, 127, 145

Gibbs, Jack, 8

Gift-giving, 166, 167, 168

Gillin, John, 116

Goal-means discrepancy, 26, 116, 191; and accommodationism, 139–140; and familism, 139–140; as suicide motive, 9, 114, 115

Gods, 119

Goto, A., 159

Government: bureaucracy in, 165, 166–167, 187–188; -business ties, 166–167, 179, 199; as central, 166; as corrupt, 167; education controlled by, 115, 140, 187, 188; financial policy of, 174, 181, 200; industrial policy of, 137, 170, 174, 189, 190; on welfare, 143; and *yakuza,* 162–163, 164, 165, 168

Group: identification, 158, 172, 178, 195; loyalty, 177; responsibility to, 151; self-sacrifice for, 158

Groupism, 117, 126–129, 137, 200; and altruistic suicide, 193; in companies, 203–204; coordination promoted by, 195; and education, 184;

and familism, 129, 130; and goal-means discrepancy, 139, 140; individualism stifled by, 192; rural, 129; selflessness stressed in, 143–144, 191, 192; for success, 172, 173, 189, 192; and worker motivation, 198. *See also* Familism

Guilt, 72, 95–96, 131; in Christianity, 71; at failure, 42, 45; and hostility, 192; and parental expectations, 38; as suicide factor, 9, 45, 155, 193; Western v. Japanese, 155

Hagakure, 120

Hakuhodo Life Style Research Institute, 180, 199

Haring, Douglass, 155

Hatano, Akiko, 72, 74–75

Hawaii, Japanese in, 55, 131, 196

Hayashi, Hiraku, 180

Health: mental, 26, 27–31, 32; as suicide factor, 26, 27–31, 32, 51, 107–108, 111, 115

Heaven, 104–105

Heian literature, 109, 110, 111

Helplessness/hopelessness, 149, 154

Henry, A. T., 8

Hidemi, Oda, 165

Hierarchy: in companies, 171, 172, 173–174; coordination promoted by, 196; in familism, 196–197; of society, 178–179; of universities, 39–40, 41–42

Hino, Ashihei, 17

Hiraoka, Kimitake. See Mishima, Yukio

Hitotsubashi University, 174

Hokkaido University, 71

Homicide: child (*see* Parent-child suicide); for loyalty, 105

Homogeneity, 200

Homosexuality, 71, 78, 97–98, 100, 101

Honne. See *Tatemae-honne* disparity

Honor, 135

Hostility, 192
Hyperintention, 108

IBM scandal, 164
Ideal, 118–119
Idealism, humanistic, 203
Iemoto system, 133–134
Ikuta, Shungetsu, 17
Illness. *See* Health
Immortality, 148, 149
Impulsiveness, 49, 51, 138, 193
Inakamono complex, 88
Inamura, Hiroshi, 2
Inari, 119
Income levels, 19, 44, 184–185
India, Buddhism in, 122–124
Individualism, 154; stifled, 20–21, 177, 192
Industry. *See* Business; Company
Inferiority complex, 27, 29, 63–64, 72, 88, 89, 90, 94–95, 96, 192
Infidelity, 51, 52, 54, 58
Inimicality, 5–6
Insecurity, 114, 178–182, 189, 192; and authoritarianism, 194; of businessmen, 199; dependency caused by, 184; and empathy, 143–144; familism produces, 198; financial, 59–61, 138, 179, 180–182, 199; of intellectuals, 77; and *seishin,* 198; social structure causes, 199; of women, 59–61, 181–182; of workers, 179, 180–181, 199; of youth, 140
Integration: of contradictions, 57, 186, 190, 200; familism for, 129, 131; lack of, 11, 57, 86, 190, 200; social, 7–8, 20–21, 117, 129, 131, 177; as suicide factor, 7, 8, 11, 20–21
Intellectuals: on Akutagawa, 80; alienated, 106; insecurity of, 77; nihilism of, 104; suicide among, 71 (*see also* Writers)

Intimacy, lacking, 179, 194
Introspection, 177
Intuition, 120–121
Ishihara, Shintaro, 106
Ishikawa, Michiko, 86

Jacobs, Jerry, 8–9
Japan Broadcasting Corporation, 43
Japan Times, 13
Jōshi. See Love-pact suicide
Jumping, suicide by, 157, 158, 159
Junshi, 75, 151

Kachiki, 26, 27
Kagoshima, 19
Kamakura-Sengoku period, 151
Katō, Michio, 17
Kawabata, Yasunari, 70, 106–113; anxiety of, 107, 108; as chrysanthemum, 110; on death, 111, 144; ego-ideal/self-concept disparity for, 107, 108, 110; fatalism of, 110; health of, 107–108, 111; on loneliness, 110, 111; Nobel Prize for, 106; pessimism of, 110–111; as rebel, 108–109, 110; on sensuality, 106, 108–109; sleeping pills used by, 148; social attachments lacking for, 110–111, 112–113; suicide of, 17, 106–107, 113, 115, 194; as traditionalist, 109–110; writings of, 106, 108, 110, 111, 112, 113
Kawakami, Bisan, 17
Kawashima, Takeyoshi, 127, 186
Keene, Donald, 96, 100
Keidanren, 174
Kida, Minoru, 130
Kill. *See* Wish
Kinship, 133. *See also* Family
Kitamura, Tōkoku, 17
Kobayashi, Hideo, 101
Kobe, 20, 21
Kōchi, 19
Kodama, Yoshio, 163

Kokusai Denshyin Denwa Kōsha, 159, 160, 167
Kon, Tōkō, 111
Koreans in Japan, 46–47, 60
Kōzō-oshoku. See Corruption
Kuukai, 123
Kyoto, 20, 21
Kyoto Ceramic (Kyocera), 171, 172
Kyoto University, 26, 40, 41, 42

Labor: costs, 169–170, 197–198; force (see Workers); and management, 170–171; manual, 60
Language, 95, 121
Law/legal system, 118–119, 129, 186–187. See also Litigation
Levinson's IPC Control Scale, 142–143
Lifton, Robert J., 136–137, 148, 149
Limited good, image of, 38
Literature: Heian, 109, 110, 111; love and death in, 148; suicide in, 61, 69–70, 151, 154, 155
Litigation, 127–129, 187
Loans, 131–132, 180–181, 199
Lockheed bribery scandal, 159, 163, 164
Loneliness, 97, 110, 111
Love: affairs, 51–52, 53, 66–67; inter-caste, 66–67; in literature, 148, 154; v. obligation, 147, 154, 155; -pact suicide (jōshi), 61, 71, 74–75, 93, 101, 154, 158, 195; parents disapprove of, 149; as suicide factor, 51–52, 53, 67, 157; and tragedy, 76
Loyalty, 99, 191; to company, 171, 172, 176, 195; to group, 177; suicide for, 105; of workers, 172, 199. See also Seishin

McCracken, Paul, 169
Magic, 123
Mahler, Irwin, 142
Mainländer, Philip, 82, 83

Makino, Shinichi, 17
Maladjustment, 2, 3, 5–6
Maris, Ronald, 8
Marital problems, 51, 52, 58–59. See also Infidelity
Marubeni Corporation, 164
Marxism. See Communism
Masakatsu, Morita, 98
Masochism, 193
Matsugi, Nobuhiko, 60
Matsuyama, Yukio, 1
Means. See Goal-means discrepancy
Mechanical solidarity, 200–201, 202
Meditation, 175, 177
Meiji Period, 74, 151, 154
Men: death wish of, 14, 16, 22–24, 29, 48, 145; eldest son's role of, 71; middle-aged, 13; and nature, 116, 117; personality traits of, 25; suicide by, 13, 17, 22–47, 48, 59; suicide notes of, 22, 23. See also Writers; Youth
Merchant culture, 100–101
Middle Way, 122, 123
Militarism, 89, 98–99, 109, 110, 122
Mills, C. W., 8
Mimoto hoshōnin, 196
Minamata disease, 144, 189, 202
Ministry of Welfare, 20, 51
Minobe, Ryokichi, 107
Mishima, Yukio, 70, 89, 92–106, 108, 109; amae of, 96; as anti-Communist, 94; anxiety of, 98; on aristocracy, 88; on death, 94, 105, 144; despair of, 93, 101; ego-ideal/self-concept disparity of, 93, 94, 97, 98, 100; elitism of, 99, emotionalism of, 102; on emperor, 100; feminine identity of, 95; on feudalism, 98, 99–100, 101; frustration of, 100, 105; guilt of, 95–96; homosexuality of, 97–98, 100, 101; on ideology, 102–103, 104; inferiority complex of, 94–95, 96; limited experience of,

100, 101; on loneliness, 97; on militarism, 98–99; narcissism of, 94, 96, 97, 98, 100, 101; nihilism of, 103–104, 105; obscurantism of, 102; pessimism of, 103; private army of, 96, 98, 103, 105; on samurai code, 105–106; status-consciousness of, 95; suicide of, 17, 93, 96, 101, 105–106, 115, 126, 156; as sword, 93, 110; on tradition, 99, 100, 105; Vidal on, 93; on women, 99–100; writings of, 92–93, 94, 95, 96–97, 98, 99, 101, 102, 103–104
Mistrust, 88, 90, 91, 194
Mitsubishi, 164
Miyagi, Otoya, 141
Mobilization, 186–190, 195, 199–200
Monism, 117–126, 191, 194, 195, 200; and goal-means discrepancy, 139, 140
Morimoto, Atsukichi, 71
Mortuary tablets, 149
Mother: -child bond, 184, 201; dependency on, 201; education, 184, 201; pressure by, 201. *See also* Parent
Motivation, 174–185, 189, 195, 198–199, 200
Motives, for suicide, 5, 6, 12, 19, 33, 81, 85, 159–160; Caucasian v. Japanese, 23; converted to action, 9, 101, 103, 193; cross-country studies of, 23, 24, 25; despair as, 22–23, 48, 93, 110; ego-ideal/self-concept gap as, 93, 94, 97, 98, 114, 115, 191; ethnic prejudice as, 22, 45–47, 65–68; examination hell as, 22, 36–44; failure as, 45, 154, 155; family problems as, 22, 32–35, 51, 79; financial problems as, 13, 22, 34, 44–45, 59–62; frustration as, 8; goal-means discrepancy as, 9, 114, 115; guilt as, 9, 45, 155, 193; health as, 26, 27–31, 32, 51, 107–108, 111, 115; helplessness as, 149, 154; love as, 51–52, 53, 67, 157; loyalty as,

105; marital problems as, 51, 52, 54, 58; out-migration as, 19; philosophical, 156–157; revenge as, 51, 154; role conflict as, 59, 63–65; sense of responsibility as, 13, 149, 151, 154, 195; shame as, 130, 193; wish to kill as, 48–49
Mujō, 145
Mysticism, 102, 148, 194, 195

Naien relationship, 58–59
Naka, Hisao, 51–52, 59
Nakamura, Hajime, 120
Nakamura, Shinichiro, 111
Nakane, Chie, 178
Narabayashi, Dr. Sho, 43
Naramoto, Tatsuya, 63
Narcissism, 27; Dazai's, 87, 88, 90; Mishima's, 94, 96, 97, 98, 100, 101, 105; role, 197, 198
Nathan, John, 98
National Police Agency, 14
Naturalism, 80, 108
Nature, 116, 117–118
Negation, 140, 148
Negotiation, 135–136
Nenko joretsu, 172
Neo-Confucianism, 158, 194
Neurasthenia, 29, 31, 81
Neuroses, xii, 29, 31
Newsweek, 144
Nihilism, 91–92, 103–104, 105, 108
Nihonkyo worship, 126, 193, 195
Niigata, 19
Nikkeiren, 185
Nobel Prize, 42, 97, 106, 107
Noble Eightfold Path, 122, 123
Nonrationality/nonrational tendencies, 102, 120–125, 139, 140, 191, 203; and religions, 125; and suicide, 101, 103
Nursing, 26, 59–60

Obligation, 149, 154, 155
Obscurantism, 102

Obscurity, 120, 121
Occupation of Japan: democracy imposed by, 109; on labor-management relations, 170–171; suicide rates during, 44, 45, 59, 61, 62
Okamoto, Kōzō, 156
Oligarchy, 173–174
Ooka, Shohei, 103
Organic solidarity, 200, 201
Orphans, 112
Osaka, 19, 20, 21, 129
Oshio, Heihachiro, 104
Ōura, Kanetake, 77
Outcastes, 60, 63, 65–68
Oyabun, 120, 142
Oyako shinjū. See Parent-child suicide

Pantheism, 85
Parent: absence/presence of, 32, 35; approval of, 51, 52, 149; -child relationship, 34–35, 184, 196, 201; -child suicide, 18, 34, 129–130, 181; dependency on, 26, 139–140, 149, 192, 201; expectations of, 38; pressure by, 36, 43–44, 139–140, 178, 179, 184, 192, 201; -role person, 120, 142; step-, 34; suicide by, 196
Particularism, 105, 172, 196
Passivity, 114, 140, 192
Past orientation, 134
Peers School, 71, 95
Pensions, 179, 199
Persistence, 42, 175
Personal connections, 166–167
Personality/personality traits, 136–137; and attempted suicide, 192; authoritarian, 202; hysterical, 51; as suicide factor, 5, 22–31, 48–51, 86–88; valued, 116, 117; of women, 48–51; of youth, 22–31, 48–51, 114–115, 140
Perturbation, 6
Pessimism, 78, 103, 110–111, 194
Plath, David W., 179
Polytheism, 119

Poverty, 180, 199
Power, 131, 139, 178, 202
Pregnancy, 51, 52
Prejudice: caste, 60, 63, 65–67; class, 201; in employment, 56, 57, 169–170, 184, 197; in education, 6–7, 40–42, 66, 197, 199, 202; ethnic, 22, 45–47, 65–68, 115, 201, 202; against women, xiii, 43, 52, 55–65, 115, 169–170, 181–182, 192, 197, 199, 201, 202; women accept, 182
Present orientation, 135–137
Prices, 170, 189, 200
Priests, 147
Problem solving, xiii, 142, 177, 184
Promotions, 173, 179, 199
Propriety, 185, 197, 200
Prostitution, 118
Protestantism, 124–125. *See also* Christianity
Protzman, Charles, 170

Quality control, 170

Rationality/rationalism, 121–122, 203. *See also* Nonrationality/nonrational tendencies
Realism: lack of, 87, 90, 192; situational, 135
Reason/reasoning, 120–121, 124
Régnier, Henri de, 82
Religion, 121–126, 164. *See also* Buddhism; Confucianism; Christianity; Nihonkyo; Shintoism
Remonstrance, suicide for, 105, 147, 151, 158
Resentment, 160–161
Resignation, 192
Resources, 9, 194; lack of, 193; negatively perceived, 140, 141–144
Responsibility, 9; to group, 151; and suicide, 13, 149, 151, 154, 195
Restorationism, 137
Restraint, 140–141, 193, 201–202
Retirement benefits, 179, 185

Revenge, 51, 154
Rohlen, T. P., 174–175
Role: conflict, 59, 63–65, 115; expectations, 197; narcissism, 197, 198
Romanticism, 156; Arishima's, 70; of suicide, 154, 155, 156–158, 195
Rōnin, 40, 41, 42
Rorschach test, 25
Rozenzweig P-F study, 25
Running away from home, 35
Rural-urban suicide rates, 19, 20, 21

Salvation, 123, 147
Samurai, 65, 99, 100, 101, 120; on appearance, 60; businessman, 178, 180, 185, 199; in education, 140; Mishima's suicide and, 105–106; yakuza based on, 164, 165
Sarakin, 180–181, 199
Sarasohn, Homer, 170
Satomi, Ton, 77
Savings, 135, 138, 179, 188, 200
Scandals, 167; IBM, 164; Lockheed, 159, 163, 164; suicide after, 18–19, 77, 159, 165–166
Scapegoat suicide, 18, 77, 159–160, 161, 165–166, 168
Schizophrenia, 29
Science, 117–118
Scott-Stokes, Henry, 96
Seidensticker, E. G., 93
Seishin, 174–177, 178, 198
Self/selfhood, 82, 126, 138; groupism denies, 191, 192
Self-awareness, 71
Self-concept, 142–143; v. ego-ideal, 11, 93, 94, 97, 98, 100, 107, 108, 110, 114, 115
Self-confidence, 140, 141, 142, 194
Self-control, 70, 71
Self-Defense Forces, 93, 175
Self-destructive behavior, 12, 110, 139–168, 191, 193, 195. See also Suicide
Self-development, 177

Self-disembowelment (seppuku), 93, 101, 158
Selflessness, 151; in groupism, 143–144, 191, 192
Self-mastery, 177
Self-negation, 140, 148
Self-restraint, 14, 17, 140–141, 193, 201–202
Self-sacrifice, 147, 149, 151, 155–156, 165–166, 193. See also Suicide, altruistic
Self-sufficiency, 112, 175
Sensualism school, 106, 108
Seppuku, 93, 101, 158
Sewayaku, 130
Sexual desires, 71–72, 118
Shakyamuni, 123
Shamanism, 126
Shame, 9, 130, 131–132, 193
Shareholders, 189, 200
Shiga, Naoya, 77, 101
Shimane Prefecture, 129
Shimoda, S., 158–159
Shingon Mikkyō, 123
Shinkei suijaku, 29, 31, 81
Shinoda, Masahiro, 106
Shinran, 123, 124
Shintoism, 60, 119, 124, 125, 126
Shirakaba Group, 72, 80
Shneidman, Edwin, 5–6, 148
Short, J. F., 8
Siemens-Bickers case, 77
Sin, sense of, 89, 90
Sincerity (makoto), 126–127
Skepticism, 78, 80
Sleeping pills, 81, 148
Smith, W. Eugene, 144
Social attachments, 110–111, 112–113
Social conscience, 77, 80
Socialization, 189; education for, 184; self-restraint in, 140–141; and success, 199
Society/social structure, 45; anxiety-producing, 178–179; authoritarian, 178–179, 198; education and, 37–

38; and goal-means disparity, 114, 115–116; insecurity in, 199; stratified, 65, 74, 178–179; as suicide factor, 6–7, 18–19, 114

Sōkaiya, 163–164

Status differences, xiii, 39, 60, 65, 74, 95, 184, 192; and authoritarianism, 131, 139, 178, 202; consciousness of, 95; in education, 40–42; education marks, 37–38; of workers, 197

Stepparents, 34

Stoetzel, Jean, 114, 140

Students, 85; don't work, 42, 43, 44; suicide of, 14, 26–31, 32, 114, 154, 193; worries of, 36–37 (*see also* Examination)

Success, ix, 1, 3, 99, 139, 169–190; as compulsive, 178; cooperation for, 183–185; coordination in, 171–174, 189, 195, 197–198, 200; education for, 174–177; emotionalism and, 2; familism for, 189, 192; and future orientation, 135, 137; as goal, 191–192; groupism for, 172–173, 189, 192; and mechanical solidarity, 200–201; and mobilization, 186–190, 195, 199–200; and motivation, 172, 174–185, 189, 195, 198–199, 200; socialization for, 199; and value orientation, 5, 195

Sugiyama, Akio, 6–7

Suicide: age as factor in, 13–14, 15, 19, 20, 59 (*see also* Students; Youth); altruistic, 8, 9–11, 14, 20, 61, 115, 151, 154, 158, 159–160, 193, 195; anomic, 8, 11, 21, 59, 114, 115, 154, 193, 195; as apology, 147, 151, 156, 158; after assassination, 99, 105; for atonement, 105; attempted, 26, 27, 29, 35, 51, 86, 87, 192; attitudes toward, 105–106, 149–158, 193, 194–195; contemplated, 26, 28, 29; dependency as factor of, 26–27, 87, 88, 193; developmental study of, 8–9; double (*shinjū*), 72, 86; Durk-

heim on, 7–8, 9–12, 113, 151, 152–153; ego and, 26, 93, 94, 97, 98, 100, 114, 115, 140, 191, 192–193; egoistic, 8, 11, 113, 115, 154; of elderly, 19; and emotionalism, 2, 5, 6; employment/unemployment as factor of, 20, 159–160, 161, 165–166; familism and, 129–130, 193; family, 129–130, 181; fatalistic, 11–12, 14, 20, 21, 59, 114, 115, 151, 154, 155, 193, 195; and fear of being killed, 161, 162; ideological, 93; imitative, 157–159; *junshi,* 75, 151; justified, 149; in literature, 61, 69–70, 151, 154, 155; love-pact, 61, 71, 74–75, 93, 101, 154, 158, 195; male, 13, 17, 22–47, 48, 59; methods of, 61, 63, 81, 83, 84, 93, 101, 106, 157, 158, 159; motives for (*see* Motives, for suicide); nonrationality and, 101, 103; in Occupation, 44, 45, 59, 61, 62; as only way out, 12; parent-child, 18, 34, 129–130, 181; and personality traits, 5, 22–31, 48–51, 86–88; psychocultural view of, 5–12; psychological studies of, 5, 6, 8; rates of, 13–14, 16, 17, 18, 19, 20–21, 44, 45, 59, 61, 62, 115; rational, 115; as remonstrance, 105, 147, 151, 158; restitutional, 105; rural v. urban, 19, 20–21; after scandals, 18–19, 77, 159, 165–166; scapegoat, 18, 77, 159–160, 161, 165–166, 168; self-sacrificial, 147, 149, 151, 155–156, 165–166, 193; of slaves, 11; society as factor of, 6–7, 18–19, 114; of students, 14, 22, 26–31, 32, 114, 154, 177, 193; of women, 13, 16, 17, 18, 36, 44, 48–68; of writers, 13, 17, 69–113, 115, 126, 147, 156, 194; writers on, 69–70, 82–84, 91, 151, 154, 155; youth, 13, 20, 22–47

Suicide notes, x, 6–7, 39, 41, 45, 51, 58, 61, 64–65, 67–68, 156–157, 159; Akutagawa's, 82–84; Fujimara's,

157; resentment in, 160–161; Tamura's, 47; Yasuda's, 160–161; youth's, 22, 23
Superordinate/subordinate relationships, 130, 173, 178, 179, 184, 189, 196
Sword, xiii, 93, 110

Taisho Period, 76–77
Takano, Etsuko, 63
Tamura, Masaaki, 47
Tanaka, Eikō, 17
Tanaka, Kakuei, 163
Tanishō, 147
Tanizaki, Junichiro, 121
Tanshin funin, 183
Tatemae, 200; -*honne* disparity, 19, 82, 85, 135, 168, 194
Taylor, Jared, 119
Tennessee Self-Concept Scale, 142
Thurstone test, 25, 51
Time, 135, 138
Time orientation, 102, 116–117, 134–137, 138
Tōkei Suuri Kenkyusho, 127
Tokugawa Period, 65, 74, 101, 140
Tokyo, 19, 20, 21, 183
Tokyo University, 40, 41, 42, 174
Toriyama, Heizo, 138, 145
Tradition/traditionalism, 117; 134–135, 193, 202; acceptance of, 126; Akutagawa on, 82; Dazai opposes, 85; Kawabata on, 109–110; Mishima on, 99, 100, 105; revival of, 115; as suicide factor, 20–21. *See also* Accommodationism; Familism; Groupism; Monism
Transfers, 43, 183
Transformationism, 137
Tsukamoto, Fumi, 79

Uchimura, Kanzo, 71
Unemployment, 44. *See also* Employment
Unions, 172, 195

United States: democracy in, 164; on future, 117; labor costs in, 169; man-nature relationship in, 117; social integration in, 117; on valued personality type, 116, 117; value orientations of, 4. *See also* Occupation of Japan
Universalism, 105, 196
Universities, 39–40, 41–42

Value orientations, 9, 82, 114–138, 140, 191, 203–204; Japanese v. Western, 4, 116; and self-destructive behavior, 195; and success, 5, 195; as suicide factor, 5, 7. *See also* Accommodationism; Familism; Groupism; Monism
Vidal, Gore, 93
Violence, 2, 14, 201
Visiting, custom of, 107
Vogel, Ezra F., 1

Wage, discrimination in, 57, 59, 60, 170
Waley, Arthur, 121
Walker, Rev. Sir Alan, 118
Wang-Yang-min, 104, 105
War, business is, 99, 171, 172, 175, 176, 198
Weber, Max, 125
Welfare, 143
Whitehead, Alfred North, 3, 122
Wish: to die, 14, 16, 22–24, 29, 48, 144–145; to be killed, 22, 23, 48–49; to kill, 22, 23
Wolf, Marvin, 166
Women, 81, 99–100; attempt suicide, 51; dependency of, 184; employment of, 26, 44, 56, 57, 59, 60–61, 169–170, 181–182; ethnic prejudice against, 65–68; externally-directed aggression of, 48–49; financial insecurity of, 59–61, 181–182; own property, 182; personality traits of, 48–51, 183; prejudice against, xiii,

43, 52, 55–65, 115, 169–170, 181–182, 192, 197, 199, 201, 202; role conflict of, 63–64, 115; and role narcissism, 198; separate living quarters of, 183; status/role of, 43, 51, 56, 57–58, 60, 70, 182–183, 198, 201; suicide by, 13, 14, 15, 16, 17, 18, 36, 44, 48–68, 114, 115; wages of, 57, 59, 60, 61, 170

Word. See *Tatemae*

Workers; ethic of, 198; familism of, 195–196, 198; financial insecurity of, 179, 180–181, 199; hours of, 171, 172; housing for, 180, 183; intimacy among, 179; loyalty of, 172, 199; motivation of, 198; part-time, 180, 184, 185, 199; status difference among, 197; subcontract, 169–170, 180, 184, 185, 197, 199. *See also* Company; Employment

Yakuza, 162–163, 164–165, 168, 179

Yamagata, 19

Yamagata, Masaaki, 147–148

Yamaguchi, 159, 167

Yamamoto, Shichihei, 135–136

Yamaoka, Sohachi, 112

Yasuda, T., 160–161, 165–166, 167

Youth: ambition of, 114; anxiety of, 23–24, 25; dependency of, 26, 139–140, 149, 192, 201; insecurity of, 140; maladjustment of, 2, 3; personality traits of, 22–31, 48–51, 114–115, 140, 192; suicide among, 13, 20, 22–47; suicide notes of, 22, 23; violence among, 2, 14; wish to die of, 14, 16, 22–24, 29, 48, 145

Zaikaijin, 174

Zen, 120–121, 124

Designer: Kitty Maryatt
Compositor: Janet Sheila Brown
Printer: Vail-Ballou Press
Binder: Vail-Ballou Press
Text: 10/12 Bembo
Display: Codex